I0761568

Bull Moose on the Stump

Bull Moose on the Stump

The 1912 Campaign Speeches of Theodore Roosevelt

EDITED BY
LEWIS L. GOULD

University Press of Kansas

Published by the University Press of Kansas (Lawrence, Kansas 66045), which was organized by the Kansas Board of Regents and is operated and funded by Emporia State University, Fort Hays State University, Kansas State University, Pittsburg State University, the University of Kansas, and Wichita State University

Library of Congress Cataloging-in-Publication Data

Roosevelt, Theodore, 1858–1919.
Bull Moose on the stump : the 1912 campaign speeches of Theodore Roosevelt / [compiled by] Lewis L. Gould.
p. cm.
ISBN 978-0-7006-1606-0 (cloth : alk. paper)
1. Roosevelt, Theodore, 1858–1919—Political and social views—Sources. 2. Presidents—United States—Election—1912—Sources. 3. Progressive Party (1912)—Sources. 4. Progressivism (United States politics)—Sources. 5. United States—Politics and government—1909–1913—Sources. 6. Speeches, addresses, etc., American.
I. Gould, Lewis L. II. Title.
E765.R66 2008
973.91'1092—dc22
2008024158

British Library Cataloguing-in-Publication Data is available.

Printed in the United States of America

10 9 8 7 6 5 4 3 2 1

The paper used in this publication is recycled and contains 30 percent postconsumer waste. It is acid free and meets the minimum requirements of the American National Standard for Permanence of Paper for Printed Library Materials Z39.48-1992.

Contents

Editor's Preface

The inspiration for this volume stemmed from research on a book about the 1912 presidential election. When I was writing *Four Hats in the Ring: The 1912 Election and the Birth of Modern American Politics,* I wanted to consult the speeches of Theodore Roosevelt during his fall campaign as the Progressive Party presidential candidate. It was not difficult to locate four important speeches in *The Works of Theodore Roosevelt,* published during the mid-1920s. The excellent study of John Milton Cooper, *The Warrior and the Priest,* took me to two other published accounts of Roosevelt's speeches in the *Outlook* magazine for fall 1912. As far as I could tell, that was the extent of Roosevelt speeches on which historians had based their major conclusions about what he had said on the stump.

Since the campaign speeches of Woodrow Wilson had been available for more than half a century and were also printed in Arthur S. Link's edition of *The Papers of Woodrow Wilson,* it struck me that the balance of information between Wilson and Roosevelt was somewhat skewed. Why was Roosevelt not better represented in terms of available speeches, and did contemporary newspapers or Roosevelt's own manuscripts contain more of his campaign addresses? The work of an important Roosevelt scholar, Kathleen Dalton, indicated that some of the candidate's speeches were in his papers at the Library of Congress.

Looking in the microfilm edition of the Roosevelt Papers brought some progress. There were typescripts of Roosevelt's speeches during the early days of his campaign in August. Speeches in Providence, Rhode Island, Boston, Massachusetts, and especially St. Johnsbury, Vermont, revealed much about the initial phase of his national campaign. However, the information in the Roosevelt Papers was spotty. After the August speeches, there was an important address to the Levee Convention in Memphis, Tennessee, in late September, but nothing for the period from early September through the date of the attempt on Roosevelt's life on 14 October.

The next step was to look at contemporary newspapers to see whether they carried the text of Roosevelt's remarks. This strategy proved successful at once. For example, the *Des Moines Register and Leader* carried a stenographic report of Roosevelt's 4 September address to the Iowa Progressive State Convention. Similarly, the San Francisco *Examiner* had a fuller text of what Roosevelt said in that city on 14 September than did the speech text in

Roosevelt's published *Works.* I decided a thorough examination of what the newspapers contained about Roosevelt's campaign addresses might warrant a book.

Thanks to the Internet and the proliferation of newspapers in online form, the task was easier than it would have been even a decade ago. The *New York Times,* the *Washington Post,* the Boston *Globe,* and the *Chicago Tribune,* with their indexes to news accounts, were very helpful in finding out what Roosevelt had said. Yet regional papers proved to be the most vital. Newspapers in Oregon, North Dakota, Minnesota, Louisiana, Georgia, and Missouri filled important gaps in coverage of Roosevelt's candidacy.

The resulting research produced thirty-seven of Roosevelt's speeches or statements delivered between 16 August and 3 November. For reasons of space and to keep the volume within reasonable limits, I have not included every single speech for which I have text. Like any candidate, Roosevelt gave a set speech to many different audiences. Thus, to avoid repetition, I have included two speeches from the same day in North Dakota: the full text of one at Grand Forks and an excerpt from another at Fargo. Similarly, the Roosevelt papers contained two typescripts for appearances in Boston on 17 August, early in the campaign. A stenographic account in the Boston *Globe* seemed to provide a better record of Roosevelt's addresses, so I opted to include that for his day in Massachusetts. On the whole, however, I believe these thirty-seven documents provide a much more complete and nuanced portrait of Roosevelt as a presidential candidate than has previously existed.

The title of the book comes from the famous statement in Chicago in June 1912 that he felt like a bull moose. Cartoonists soon made the bull moose a symbol of his campaign. Roosevelt's energy and commitment to social justice echo through the addresses he made across the country from August into early November. They reflect a significant American political leader in his most radical phase, when he and his newly formed third party challenged partisan orthodoxy in a very special campaign.

The importance of these speeches for the confrontation between Wilson and Roosevelt in autumn 1912 is clear. Until now, historians have had an almost complete record of Wilson's words and only a partial account of what Roosevelt said about trusts, tariffs, and social justice. This volume makes it possible to study this campaign more thoroughly than ever before. The encounter between the New Freedom and the New Nationalism appears in much sharper focus when Roosevelt's contributions are included in detail. The history of the 1912 campaign and its impact on American liberalism is richer when Roosevelt's speeches are seen in the context of the events of that significant election.

Many people helped make this project a reality. I am indebted for relevant information to Pamela Arceneaux of the Historic New Orleans Collection, Scott Daniels of the Oregon Historical Society, Peter Nelson of Amherst College, and William Offhaus of the University at Buffalo. Professor Bret Weber of the University of North Dakota helped me obtain a copy of Roosevelt's speech at Grand Forks. John Pope of the New Orleans *Times-Picayune* enabled me to find a copy of Roosevelt's speech in that city. Joella Werlin of Portland, Oregon, secured a copy of speeches from Roosevelt's time there. Jason dePreaux of Austin, Texas, delivered timely research assistance as well. Stacy Cordery saved me from many slips.

Wallace F. Dailey of the Theodore Roosevelt Collection at Harvard University was very generous with information and assistance from his rich knowledge of Roosevelt and his writings.

John M. Cooper answered many queries, read the introduction to my profit, and encouraged the development of the book. John Morton Blum was enthusiastic about the idea of a book of Roosevelt's 1912 speeches and took time to read the entire manuscript for editorial errors and for questions of substance. He has inspired generations of Roosevelt students with his kindness and thoughtful criticism, and I am delighted to be one of the beneficiaries of his scholarly wisdom. Fred Woodward and his team at the University Press of Kansas provided support and thoughtfulness from the moment they heard about the possibility of this book. Karen Gould listened to endless discussions about the difficulties of editing the Roosevelt speeches and never failed to sustain my efforts. Any errors in transcription and the notes are mine alone and should not be ascribed to Roosevelt.

Lewis L. Gould
Austin, Texas
January 2008

Introduction: The Bull Moose on the Stump

One of the most dramatic periods in the colorful political life of Theodore Roosevelt came between August and November 1912. As the presidential candidate of the Progressive Party, Roosevelt took to the hustings in mid-August 1912 in New England to sell his third-party run to a skeptical nation. After Labor Day, he embarked on the first of two projected cross-country campaign swings. In September he reached the West Coast and then headed back east through the Southwest and South. Resting briefly in early October, he then set out on another series of speeches in the Middle West. On 14 October, he was shot in Milwaukee, Wisconsin, and narrowly escaped death. After recuperating for two weeks, he finished out the campaign with a series of speeches in New York City just before the election.

The 1912 campaign has become justly famous for the political confrontation between Roosevelt and the Democratic candidate for president, Woodrow Wilson. Ever since the pioneering work of Arthur S. Link during the 1940s, historians have seen this contest as a struggle between Roosevelt's philosophy of the New Nationalism and Wilson's counterproposals of the New Freedom.

Wilson's part in this crucial dialogue has been well chronicled. During the 1950s, John Wells Davidson edited *A Crossroads of Freedom* (1956), which collected Wilson's campaign speeches based on the stenographic records of Charles Swem. An accomplished shorthand transcriber, Swem took down what Wilson said, and this gave Davidson and later scholars an accurate text for the candidate's remarks.[1]

1. John Wells Davidson, ed., *A Crossroads of Freedom: The 1912 Campaign Speeches of Woodrow Wilson* (New Haven, Conn.: Yale University Press, 1956).

The Wilson speeches received careful treatment two decades later when Link reached fall 1912 in his mammoth project, *The Papers of Woodrow Wilson.* The twenty-fifth volume of that series covered August 1912 through the end of the year. Link and his colleagues provided a thorough and reliable account of what Wilson said, the people to whom he referred, and the allusions and comments he offered on the campaign. Thus, by 1980 it was possible to fully interpret how Wilson performed as a presidential candidate in his public speeches.[2]

For Roosevelt, most of his campaign speeches were forgotten or ignored. Only a few were in print. Because his campaign ended in defeat, there was less immediate incentive to bring together his speeches in some coherent form. The Progressive Party leaders, including Roosevelt, had enough problems holding their new organization together. Nonetheless, in 1913, a single publication assembled some of the Progressive leader's public addresses from the previous year. The editor of *Bankers Magazine,* Elmer Haskell Youngman, approached Roosevelt about collecting in one volume the speeches the candidate had made in the primary campaign against William Howard Taft and the general election race. The result was a small book called *Progressive Principles,* which appeared at the end of 1913.[3]

Youngman's volume contained the complete text of Roosevelt's "Confession of Faith" to the Progressive National Convention on 6 August and the speech he gave at Milwaukee, Wisconsin, on 14 October after he was shot. There were excerpts from other fall campaign addresses, but these were not identified by place or date. For example, on 14 September in San Francisco, Roosevelt answered a Wilson speech from five days earlier. In the address Roosevelt attacked his rival's statement that "the history of liberty is the history of the limitation of government power, not the increase of it." Youngman titles the excerpt from Roosevelt's speech "Limitation of Governmental Power" and does not supply the date or any context. The same approach occurs for other important Roosevelt addresses during the fall campaign.[4]

Youngman's volume did not achieve wide circulation and is now available only in research libraries or on eBay and other Web sites at a handsome

2. Arthur S. Link, et al., eds., *The Papers of Woodrow Wilson, Volume 25—1912* (Princeton, N.J.: Princeton University Press, 1978).

3. Youngman to Roosevelt, 8 March 1913, 29 March 1913, Youngman to Frank H. Harper, 27 August 1913, 30 September 1913, Theodore Roosevelt Papers, Manuscript Division, Library of Congress, describe Youngman's role in compiling the book. Elmer H. Youngman, ed., *Progressive Principles of Theodore Roosevelt: Selections from Addresses Made During the Presidential Campaign of 1912* (New York: Progressive National Service, 1913). Theodore Roosevelt, *The New Nationalism* (New York: The Outlook Co., 1910), of course, contains only speeches from that year.

4. Youngman, *Progressive Principles,* pp. 208–219.

price. A copy on eBay was listed during summer 2007 at $710. As a guide to what Roosevelt said during the 1912 campaign, Youngman is an important historical source but far from satisfactory from an editorial perspective.

The next attempt to provide information about Roosevelt's 1912 campaign speeches came when Hermann Hagedorn edited Roosevelt's *Works* during the mid-1920s. For the volume *Social Justice and Popular Rule,* Hagedorn settled on copies of four speeches—San Francisco (14 September), Milwaukee (14 October), New York (30 October), and Oyster Bay (2 November). The texts of the first two were taken from *Progressive Principles* and the last two were based on reports in the *New York Times.* Portions of two other Roosevelt speeches were published in the *Outlook* during the fall campaign. Historical evaluations of what Roosevelt said as a presidential candidate have rested on these texts in his *Works* and the two *Outlook* articles.[5]

Yet these are far from the only records of Roosevelt's speeches in August, September, and October 1912. The Roosevelt Papers at the Library of Congress contain the texts of eight other speeches. The contemporary newspapers published stenographic reports of some of the speeches and extended excerpts of others, providing text for more than thirty speeches, not just four or five. The upshot is that Roosevelt's performance as a candidate and the nature of his political appeal during the autumn of 1912 have yet to be fully evaluated on the basis of what he actually told his audiences. That is the purpose of this book.

By the time he prepared to launch his presidential campaign, Roosevelt had already had a turbulent political year. When 1912 began, he was nearing a challenge to the renomination of William Howard Taft as the Republican candidate for president. By February Roosevelt's hat was "in the ring" and all-out combat against his former political ally was under way. Despite winning several big primaries during the spring, Roosevelt came to the national convention in Chicago without a majority of the delegates. The Republican National Committee, which the Taft forces controlled, seated 235 disputed delegates and ensured Taft's selection. Angry at what he believed to be the theft of delegates who were rightfully his, Roosevelt bolted from the convention and organized a third party.

After Roosevelt's departure, the Democrats chose Woodrow Wilson as their standard-bearer for the fall race. As a progressive, Wilson undercut some of Roosevelt's appeal. Nonetheless, the former president pushed

5. *Social Justice and Popular Rule: The Works of Theodore Roosevelt* (New York: Charles Scribner's Sons, 1926), 17:306–314 (San Francisco), 320–330 (Milwaukee), 334–340 (Madison Square Garden), 341–348 (Oyster Bay). The two *Outlook* articles are "The Taft-Wilson Trust Programme," *Outlook* 102 (21 September 1912): 105–107, and "The Minimum Wage," *Outlook* 102 (28 September 1912): 159–160.

ahead with what became the Progressive Party. He and his supporters met in Chicago in early August. The delegates selected California Governor Hiram Johnson as Roosevelt's running mate. With Taft likely to have a minimal role as an active campaigner and Socialist Eugene V. Debs not seen as a credible challenger, the race came down to most observers to a battle between Roosevelt and Wilson.

Following his nomination at the Progressive National Convention in early August, Roosevelt and his advisers decided that he must make a national campaign across the country to sell his new third party. They planned two extensive tours. The first, in September, would move across the Middle West, go through the Rocky Mountain states to the Pacific Coast, and then return through the Southwest and South. A second campaign swing, in October, would focus on the Middle West and end up with a series of speeches in the Northeast and Middle Atlantic. Because of the attempt on his life, Roosevelt did not get a chance to complete the second part of the campaign schedule.

During August, while planning for his main speaking tours went forward, Roosevelt opened his campaign in New England, first with a speech in Providence, Rhode Island, on 16 August, and then with appearances in Boston the following day. Later in the month, he spoke in Vermont and Connecticut before leaving for the Middle West. The reasons for beginning in New England, where Roosevelt was not at his most popular, probably related to the election calendar. The elections in Maine and Vermont came in early September, and the Progressives hoped to show electoral strength against the Republicans. Roosevelt aimed to stir up enthusiasm and demonstrate that his third-party race was genuine and viable.

Following his New England tour, Roosevelt turned to the main business of the campaign. From 3 September through the end of the month, he and his associates boarded their two railroad cars for the cross-country trek. The campaign had two private cars, the *Mayflower,* in which Roosevelt worked, and the *Sunbeam,* which held the reporters covering the candidate. These were attached to regular trains for the most part, though on occasion the cars became a special train. In addition to reporters, Roosevelt had a motion-picture camera operator with him to record events for the Progressives. He also brought along his own doctor, Scurry W. Terrell, to treat his throat daily.[6]

6. Oscar King Davis, *Released for Publication: Some Inside Political History of Theodore Roosevelt and His Times, 1898–1918* (Boston: Houghton Mifflin, 1925), pp. 352–358, discusses the arrangements for Roosevelt's campaign trips.

The itinerary of the journey was somewhat improvised given how late the campaign trip began and the lack of a fixed schedule. The Roosevelt train moved from place to place, often in response to urgent pleas from Progressive state committees that "the Colonel" must make an appearance in that state or this city. Roosevelt himself sometimes yielded to these entreaties and thus complicated the lives of those who scheduled his train and his meetings.

In this initial phase, the campaign did not have a means of following Wilson's speeches, other than what appeared in the daily newspapers. That resulted in some repetition of Roosevelt's basic speech and failure to respond as quickly as possible to his rival. By the time the candidate embarked on his second tour, his aides had assembled much more thorough material on Wilson. Despite these problems, Roosevelt maintained a steady fire on Wilson throughout the second half of September.

In preparing his speeches, Roosevelt dictated drafts of several orations that evolved into his standard message for the voters. From experience, he knew that reporters would transmit his words to their papers with greater accuracy if they enjoyed a prepared text. Wilson, on the other hand, did not believe he could be effective with a speech written in advance.

Roosevelt changed the text of his stump message as the campaign evolved and he spoke about local issues as well. Reporters with him appreciated that Roosevelt would alert them when he was going to insert new material, such as an attack on Wilson, into his usual remarks. Reporters became familiar with the catchphrases he employed. To Civil War veterans, he would remark, "You who wear the button," a reference to the Grand Army of the Republic lapel button that still dotted the crowds that came to see Roosevelt. When children assembled on the railroad track, Roosevelt warned them of the danger of the train backing up suddenly. Besides, he added, "We can't afford to lose any little Bull Mooses, you know."[7] Few of these signals to reporters were included in the published accounts of the candidate's speeches.

Like any candidate, Roosevelt did indulge in a recitation of the same basic speech over and over. To have said something fresh each day at each stop would have been impossible. Yet it is striking how often Roosevelt did say something substantive about a particular issue, such as the tariff or the trusts, within the same overall framework. His speech at St. Johnsbury, Vermont, is notable for its recounting of the individuals who shaped Roo-

7. Charles Willis Thompson, *Presidents I've Known and Two Near Presidents* (Indianapolis: Bobbs Merrill, 1929), pp. 143–144.

sevelt's reform ideas. The address at San Francisco responding to Wilson's comments about government power also incisively restates Roosevelt's thinking. The speech to the Levee Convention in Memphis, Tennessee, sets forth some of the issues that culminated a generation later in the Tennessee Valley Authority. These examples do not exhaust Roosevelt's originality in 1912. He advocated using public schools as polling places and for political discussions. He spoke out about prison reform, agricultural marketing innovations, and soil conservation. His 1912 campaign proposed reforms that would not come to pass until the New Deal and beyond.

The idea that Roosevelt and Wilson debated the New Nationalism and the New Freedom during 1912 has become so fixed in scholarly literature that the other issues they addressed have received less attention. The tariff question was a constant source of disagreement between the two men. Wilson took the conventional low-tariff Democratic position, on which most members of his party were united. Roosevelt, for his part, had to balance the sentiment for lower duties among Progressives with the traditional Republican devotion to high protective tariff rates. To that end, he recommended a tariff commission, which in theory would set rates based on dispassionate, nonpartisan inquiry. Throughout the campaign Roosevelt never sounded entirely comfortable with the tariff.

One related aspect that recurred in Roosevelt's campaign in 1912 was the issue of Canadian reciprocity. In 1910 Taft had negotiated an agreement with Canada for mutual tariff reductions. The arrangement, which was not a treaty but concurrent legislation in both countries, looked to lower duties on goods imported across the border. The deal was very unpopular with farmers in northern states. After initially approving the Taft program, Roosevelt changed his mind as the depth of opposition to it among progressive Republicans emerged during 1911 and into 1912. The issue was tricky for Roosevelt because of his political shift, but he used it extensively as he campaigned in Vermont, North Dakota, and other border states.

There were several other recurring themes throughout Roosevelt's appearances. Not all of them worked to his benefit. He had to spend a significant amount of time dealing with the question of campaign contributions from the 1904 presidential election. His enemies raised that troubling matter in August 1912 when the unlikely pairing of conservative senator Boies Penrose of Pennsylvania and the progressive Republican Robert M. La Follette teamed up to have the Senate inquire into fund-raising in 1904 and 1908. The charge was that Roosevelt had accepted corporate money, particularly from Standard Oil, in his race for the White House. A Standard Oil executive, John D. Archbold, was Roosevelt's primary accuser. The controversy that developed diverted attention from Roosevelt's message and throughout September forced him to devote significant blocks of key speeches to rebutting his critics.

The campaign fund matter fed into Wilson's charge that Roosevelt's position on the trusts put him at the mercy of corporate power. Roosevelt's friend and financial backer, George W. Perkins, a one-time partner of J. P. Morgan, also became a target of criticism from the Democrats and within the Progressive campaign itself. A similar attack went toward the Republican boss of Pittsburgh, William Flinn, a strong Roosevelt supporter whose political muscle accounted for the Progressives' carrying Pennsylvania against both Wilson and Taft. Roosevelt had to spend a good deal of time explaining why his alliance with a corporate magnate and a political boss did not undercut his Progressive principles.

From the outset of his tours, Roosevelt battled the perception that the Progressive Party was nothing more than a vehicle for his presidential ambitions. He argued throughout the fall that he and his fellow Progressives meant to make their third party a lasting force on the American political scene. He repeated that if the Progressive Party was simply a "one-man" cause, he would not be part of it. He spoke out for Progressive candidates on the state level and sought to distinguish his appeal from both Wilson's and Taft's. That the partisan alignments retained a strong hold on his audiences everywhere is evident from the responses Roosevelt's pleas evoked.

In his speeches attacking Wilson, Roosevelt often quoted from his opponent's speeches and writings. His handling of his rival's words was not always careful. A close examination of what Wilson said in the campaign reveals that Roosevelt massaged these quotations to serve his polemical purposes. Whether these manipulations were the fault of those who researched Wilson's utterances for Roosevelt or were the actions of the candidate himself is now very difficult to determine with any precision. The mishandling of Wilson's words does suggest that Roosevelt's conduct as a candidate needs additional careful analysis as scholars revisit his performance in the 1912 primaries and general election.

In the end, of course, Roosevelt did not succeed in his improbable third-party venture. He accomplished the defeat of Taft but Wilson held on to the core Democratic vote. That enabled the Democratic candidate to achieve an electoral landslide in November 1912. Wilson won 435 electoral votes to Roosevelt's 88 and Taft's 8. Roosevelt placed second in the popular vote with 4,119,507 Americans supporting the Progressive cause. On the national and state levels, the Progressives did not do as well as Roosevelt. They elected seventeen members of the House, but no senators and no governors. Two years later, Progressives lost ground in the 1914 congressional elections and the party imploded in 1916, with many of its members crossing over to support Wilson for reelection.

Despite his political failure in 1912, Roosevelt had set out ideas for the nation's political agenda that had lasting influence. He spoke out for a minimum wage for women, protection for child labor, agricultural marketing programs, and a broader role for the federal government in regulating corporations. In 1916, Wilson co-opted some of these ideas to gain reelection. Other proposals from Theodore Roosevelt would not emerge until the New Deal in the 1930s. In that sense, Roosevelt's campaign in 1912 deserves closer study for what it reveals about both the politics of the Progressive era and the course of reform during the twentieth century.

Editorial Note

Tracking Theodore Roosevelt's speeches during the 1912 presidential campaign presents a very different problem from the one Arthur S. Link and his colleagues faced in dealing with the addresses Woodrow Wilson delivered. Wilson had the services of Charles Swem, a stenographer, to take down what he said. Although Swem's presence did not mean that every speech was recorded precisely, the stenographer provided a basic framework for establishing what Wilson had said on most occasions.

In Roosevelt's case, however, no such record was provided. An editor therefore depends on newspaper accounts in most instances to determine what Roosevelt uttered as he traveled around the country. In 1912, however, the major metropolitan newspapers—the *New York Times,* the *New York Tribune,* the *Washington Post,* and the *Los Angeles Times*—opposed Roosevelt's candidacy. As a result, they had little interest in providing a full account of his remarks. The *New York Times* did supply, on occasion, the full text of what Roosevelt said or, in other instances, extensive excerpts, but its coverage was far from complete. The *Chicago Tribune,* on the other hand, was pro-Roosevelt. The newspaper tracked his movements but did not print his speeches regularly.

Smaller newspapers, however, did endeavor to give their readers the full text of Roosevelt's speeches in their city. In the Middle West, for example, the *Des Moines Register and Leader* and the *Grand Forks Herald* ran what Roosevelt had said in a complete text, as did the Portland *Oregonian* and the San Francisco *Examiner* on the West Coast. In the South, newspapers in New

Orleans, Atlanta, and Columbus, Georgia, provided either the full text or extensive news reports with ample quotations.

The Roosevelt speeches printed in this volume are taken in most instances from those contemporary newspaper accounts of his appearances in various cities during his campaign tours. The Theodore Roosevelt Papers at the Library of Congress have manuscript drafts of speeches he gave in New England during August and early September, a speech he delivered in St. Louis, and the address to the Levee Convention in Memphis at the end of the same month. I have tried in each instance to use the newspaper version of the speech as the closest possible approximation of what Roosevelt said at the time.

It would have been welcome to have had parallel texts to use to more precisely determine what Roosevelt said. In most instances, there was only one complete version. I have reproduced the text exactly as it appeared at the time. I have retained the paragraphing, punctuation, capitalization (or not) in the originals. In speeches where the stenographer or reporter clearly made an error, I have corrected the mistakes when possible and indicated those changes. Roosevelt dictated all his drafts, and his secretary's errors carried over into the newspapers' reports.

I have supplied annotations to identify individuals Roosevelt mentioned and to provide context for his references to contemporary events. I have also sought to include sufficient background data for readers unfamiliar with the unfolding drama of American politics in 1912 that will explain Roosevelt's allusions and asides as he moved across the country.

The task of reconstructing what Roosevelt said as the Progressive Party candidate for president has proved interesting and has illuminated a chapter in his life that has not received the full attention it merits.

I

Starting Out in New England

Theodore Roosevelt launched his presidential campaign in Providence, Rhode Island, on 16 August 1912. He prepared a lengthy address that set out the reasons he was running and the programs he supported. His text included references to the seventeenth-century thinker on international law, Hugo Grotius, as well as the writings of Senator Cushman K. Davis of Minnesota, who had died twelve years earlier. When it came time to speak at Infantry Hall in Providence, however, Roosevelt abbreviated his remarks and focused on some issues about the tariff and banking that he had not outlined in his text. The crowds were enthusiastic and friendly, and Republicans worried that Roosevelt's defection might throw the state into the Democratic column. The candidate spoke twice, once at Infantry Hall and again at the local opera house. The New York Times *printed an account of what Roosevelt had said in its news columns the following day.*[1]

Portions of a Speech at Providence, Rhode Island, 16 August 1912

I take particular pleasure in making my first speech as nominee of the Progressive Party here in Rhode Island. You have suffered, as in my own State of New York we have suffered from boss rule in the most extreme form of development. The Progressive movement is aimed at the rotten machines, the rotten boss systems of both parties. Only by supporting the Progressive Party can you strike any effective blow against boss rule and machine and ring politics in the United States.

There is nothing whatever to choose between the two old parties in this

1. "Roosevelt Crowds Worry Republicans," *New York Times,* 17 August 1912.

"That Awful Moment when the man ahead of you tells exactly the same thing you were going to say." Roosevelt battled the perception during the 1912 campaign that Woodrow Wilson's reform credentials made him the better choice for president. (Cartoon from the New York Times, *reproduced in* Current Literature *53 [August 1912]: 125)*

respect. At this moment the domination of Tammany in New York, of the Taggart machine in Indiana, the Sullivan machine in Illinois, within the Democratic Party, is as unquestioned as the domination of the Barnes-Guggenheim-Penrose machines within the Republican Party.[2] Nothing whatever of permanent value is to be gained by exchanging one set of bosses for the other, one set of machines for the other. The success of the Democratic National ticket means enthroning in power one set of bosses; the success of the Republican National ticket means enthroning in power the other set of bosses. The effort at this time to replace one set of bosses by voting for the candidate of the other set of bosses is from its very nature bound to result in mere futility.

In their essence the Democratic and the Republican machines are alike. Both are controlled by the like powerful beneficiaries of privilege: privi-

2. Roosevelt attacked the bosses in both parties during his speeches. The Democrats to whom he referred were Thomas Taggart (1856–1929), the most influential Indiana Democrat, and Roger C. Sullivan, who played a similar role in Illinois. Both men had been instrumental in the nomination of Woodrow Wilson at the Baltimore Convention in late June 1912. The Republicans he mentioned were William A. Barnes, Jr. (1866–1930), a New York conservative who had kept his state's delegation in line for William Howard Taft at Chicago; Boies Penrose (1860–1921), a Republican senator from Pennsylvania and a notorious reactionary; and Simon F. Guggenheim (1867–1941), a Colorado senator from 1907 to 1913.

leged political and privileged financial. To try to punish one set of defenders of political and industrial privilege by occasionally voting for the nominees of the other set is to play into the hands of both. Nothing pleases the bosses of the two parties more than the action of the nominal independent who shows his independence purely by raising to power first one party and then the other.

We Progressives stand against both. We take as our motto Emerson's phrase, "The best political economy is the care and culture of men."[3] We are interested in property; we will defend the rights of property; but we put man above what man has made. We feel that the rights of humanity ordinarily coincide with the rights of property, but if there is a conflict between them then our allegiance is due to human rights first.

There is a peculiar need of leadership for this fight here in New England. New England took the lead in the great contest which resulted in the founding of this Government in the days of Washington. It took the lead in the great contest which resulted in perpetuating this Government in the days of Lincoln. Surely it ought not to be content merely to follow in this great third contest for the rights of the plain people.

It has been a matter of concern to me to see how many of those here in New England who should be leaders in the new movement turn cold-heartedly from it. I believe that half of the opposition to our cause in New England is due to sheer plain ignorance, half of the remainder to hard-shelled prejudice, and the other half of the remainder to craven fear of what is new.

One of our great troubles, here in New England as elsewhere, is that the representatives of privilege in finance and politics control most of the newspapers so that the ordinary man finds the channels of information choked. I do not so much mind the editorial columns being against us; but it is a matter for real regret that the news columns are closed to us.

There is good reason why many men should bitterly oppose the Progressive Party. Every political jobber, every crooked business man, every beneficiary of privilege, and every paid employe of such beneficiary—all these are naturally against us. But I hold that every self-respecting ordinary citizen should be for us. I challenge as our right the support of all the men from the humbler walks of life, and of all really sincere, upright, and far-sighted men, no matter of what walk of life.

We are making our fight for the plain people, for their right to rule, and for their duty to secure for themselves and for others social and industrial

3. Ralph Waldo Emerson wrote, "The best political economy is care and culture of men."

justice. The men for whom we are making the fight are not politicians, and are not men of great wealth. They are busily engaged in their daily toil; they do not appear as speakers at public meetings; they do not take prominent parts in political canvasses; and they cannot contribute large sums of money for the furtherance of the campaign on their behalf. But I believe that their feelings are all the more intense and their sympathy the more keen just because of the fact that hitherto they have never been stirred as now they are stirred.

Hitherto, as a standpatter, a reactionary Congressman from Kansas, with involuntary truthfulness put it, these plain people have been regarded by politicians as only entitled to pay the price of admission and sit on the bleachers and watch the politicians play the game for their own benefit.[4] Under this Congressman's view, the plain people have nothing to do except to pay the expenses of the contest which the rulers wage for their own benefit. The Progressive doctrine, on the contrary, is that the plain people of America are not after this to sit on the bleachers and look on at [as] the politicians play the game, that the plain people are to be their own masters and masters over all their public servants.

We do not for a moment pretend that what we advocate will bring about the millennium. Unless the average man has the right stuff in him he can neither be master of himself nor avoid falling under the dominion of those men who should be his servants. We understand thoroughly that after everything that can be done by law has been done it will yet remain true that the fundamental factor in determining any individual's success must be that individual's own character.

But we also insist that we can do more for furthering happiness and prosperity in this dearly beloved land of ours by introducing the right type of law, by insisting on the right kind of administration of the law, alike by the executive officer and the Judge, and, finally, by arousing the public conscience so that it will refuse longer to tolerate iniquity either in the world of politics or in the world of business.

We intend to work for prosperity, but we wish to see prosperity cast around.[5] We stand for a protective tariff, but we wish to see the benefits of

4. The congressman was Philip Pitt Campbell (1862–1941), who had written a letter to Roosevelt earlier in the year. See Philip P. Campbell to Chester I. Long, 21 March 1912, Chester I. Long Papers, Kansas State Historical Society, Topeka, where Campbell said, "My reference to the umpire and the bleachers seems to have struck a weak spot." In the voting in Kansas, the Roosevelt forces had defeated the Republicans in the state's primary to get their presidential electors on the ballot.

5. The reporter may have misheard Roosevelt, who probably said "passed around" after former senator Albert J. Beveridge (1862–1927) of Indiana gave the keynote address at the Progressive Convention in Chicago, titled "Pass Prosperity Around."

the protective tariff get into the pay envelope of the wageworker. Instead of decreasing, we wish to increase the amount of the prize money that is rightfully due those who work hard in industry; but we stand for a more equitable division of the prize money. Moreover, our movement is not only for economic but for ethical betterment. We hold that no man can be permanently benefited unless we make it easier for him to get for himself and his wife and his children a proper share of what is necessary for their bodies. But we insist no less upon the need of each man taking thought for his soul as well as for his body.

We do not accept the view that greed and selfishness are the only factors to be considered in government. We intend to work for the economic betterment of the average citizen. We intend to insist upon the average man having a greater share than now of the good things which by his labor are produced. But we intend also to work for a broader and kindlier charity of relationship as between man and man.

We are opposed to the sordid views of those who base morality, and, therefore, law, only on fear and greed, and who have twisted a just regard for property rights into the creation of a noxious fetichism which would make of privilege masquerading as property an idol before which the rights of men, women, and children are to be sacrificed without remorse. We stand for real popular government, for the overthrow of the dictation of the boss and the crooked financier, the dictation which has corrupted the political management and the economic policy of this Republic, and which treats with sneering derision every attempt to place our Government on a basis of human equity.

The Progressive platform has really faced the real issues of to-day. It has done this as regards the trusts, as regards the rights of labor, as regards the tariff. I do not see how the people of New England can for one moment support either the Republican or the Democratic tariff platform.

Remember that when I use the word Republican now I do not refer to the rank and file of the Republican Party, but to the bosses, the Barneses, the Penroses, and Guggenheims, who have usurped the control of the machinery of the party, who have betrayed the rank and file of the party, who have twisted it into direct and fundamental opposition to the principles for which Abraham Lincoln stood, and who have made the party of financial and political privilege.

The Republican proposal is a tariff for privilege in industry. The Democratic proposal is a tariff for the destruction of industry. The Progressive proposal is a tariff in the interest of labor in industry.

At the time the Payne-Aldrich bill was put through Congress it was currently reported not only in the newspapers but by private men who ought to know that the cotton schedule, for instance, was written by a then private citizen of Rhode Island, now a senator from your State, Mr. Lippitt, and Mr. Lippitt was credited with making the statement that Mr. Aldrich had been "good to him." The Republican purpose is to have future tariffs written by the Mr. Lippitts of the party, or else by the party leaders who are "good" to the Mr. Lippitts.[6]

The Democratic proposal is to hurt the Mr. Lippitts by hurting everybody, big and little, connected with the industries which have built up States like the New England States. Our proposal is not merely to reform schedules of the tariff, but to reform the methods and purposes of tariff making. We propose to reduce the various schedules as to which the duty is undoubtedly too high. We propose to deal with the tariff, schedule by schedule, in accordance with the reports of a non-partisan commission of experts who shall make their reports not on the theory of being "good" to anybody, but with the theory of doing justice primarily to the American wageworker and the American consumer.

Acting after getting full information from such a commission we will give to the Mr. Lippitts their rights; we will do them full justice, but instead of permitting them to make the tariff to suit themselves we shall carefully investigate how their business is carried on. We shall get the judgment of those able to say what the needs of the workmen employed by the Mr. Lippitts are, and able to say whether enough of the tariff gets into the pay envelopes of the workman; the judgment of those able to say, after full investigation, whether the consumer, the average citizen who buys Mr. Lippitt's products, also gets fair treatment.

In other words we shall do full justice to the Lippitts industry, but we shall also do justice to the workmen employed by the Lippitts, and we shall see that no protection is afforded to the Lippitts unless a full proportion of the benefit gets past the front office into the pay envelopes of the workingmen; and finally we shall see that the general consumer has his rights fully protected.

6. Henry Frederick Lippitt (1856–1933) succeeded Nelson Aldrich (1841–1915) in the Senate as a Republican and served from 1911 to 1917. The Payne-Aldrich Tariff of 1909 had produced a split in the party between protectionists and midwestern progressives who wanted lower rates on some products. Roosevelt was in Africa when the bill was passed, and he did not denounce it when he returned. In Rhode Island and elsewhere he was careful not to alienate high-tariff Republicans with attacks on the policy of protection itself.

If the Democratic platform were carried out in good faith your factories would have to close altogether, for their proposal is to prevent the Mr. Lippitts from prospering by the simple process of preventing every one from prospering.[7]

The Republican proposal is only to give prosperity to the Mr. Lippitts and then to let it trickle down according as they may condescend to permit such trickling.

Our proposal is to keep the factories open, to see that the Mr. Lippitts receive full justice, but to see also that they do justice as well as get it, that they do justice to the wageworkers whom they employ, and to the customers whom they serve, and make their own profits only as an incident of thus rendering service to the advantage of the public as a whole.

One of our National problems calling for immediate solution is that of our banking and currency system. It has been demonstrated beyond any question that the present system is unscientific and ineffective, and that if we are to enjoy a full measure of prosperity we must adopt a modern and proper system necessary to our needs, a system that will be on a basis at least as stable as the financial systems of France, England, and Germany.

The suffering and loss occasioned by our present defective system of credits and reserves has in time past been very great and very general, and we cannot be confident that panics so widespread as to affect one and all will not recur unless we change our present banking laws. The country should have as good a system as any in the world, one that affords protection to all legitimate interests, one that insures proper and reasonable accommodation at reasonable rates to all who may be entitled to it, whether they be laborers, farmers, manufacturers, or merchants, in any and all parts of the country; one which will at least retard and minimize, if not fully prevent, inflation and speculation and thus insure a proper use of the funds of the people of our country.

We must have a currency that will meet the requirements of the whole country. It must have elasticity. It must be absolutely beyond question in character, ranking with the best in the world. The issue of currency should be a government function, and, therefore, the currency issue should, every dollar, be as good as gold, and this it can only be if issued against assets so good that the general business sense of the community will unhesitatingly accept them as being as good as gold.

7. The Democrats and Woodrow Wilson favored lower tariff rates, and the party platform even indicated that the protective tariff was itself unconstitutional. Roosevelt would return to that point often in his campaign speeches.

Above and even more important than these requirements, any system adopted must be beyond the control of the great Wall Street and other similar interests. The Monetary Commission which has recently reported to Congress has collected an immense amount of valuable information, especially on the foreign banking systems. This should be more generally disseminated among the whole people for their information. Some of the recommendations of the commission are excellent. I strongly object to certain features of their plan, because in my judgment they do not sufficiently safeguard the public against the danger of control by special or speculative interests in Wall Street.[8]

Any plan adopted must keep the control absolutely in the hands of the Government; only in this way can we prevent the growth in this country of the most dangerous of all trusts, the Money Trust. Even at present there are disturbing symptoms of the appearance of such a trust; the Aldrich proposal as far as concerns the proposed methods of control, would tend to increase the danger of the growth of such a trust. Our proposal is absolutely to prevent it by keeping the control in the hands of the Government.

New York Times, 17 August 1912.

Roosevelt delivered several speeches in the Boston area on 17 August during a busy day of campaigning. The prepared texts for these remarks are in the Roosevelt Papers at the Library of Congress. The account of what Roosevelt said on the Boston Common, however, as printed in the Boston Daily Globe, *gives the flavor of Roosevelt's actual appearance and interaction with his audience better than any of the other addresses printed in this volume. It may have been that the* Globe, *which was not friendly to Roosevelt, stressed the negative in its account. Nonetheless, as a version of Roosevelt in action it warrants inclusion at this point in the record of the Progressive campaign. The headings of the sections are those of the* Globe *story.*

8. The Aldrich-Vreeland Act of 1908 had created the National Monetary Commission to study the nation's banking laws in the wake of the Panic of 1907. The commission submitted its proposal early in 1912. Much work remained to be done, however, before the passage of the Federal Reserve Act under Woodrow Wilson in late 1913.

A Speech on Boston Common as Reported in the Boston Globe, *17 August 1912*

My friends, it is a very great pleasure to be here in Boston, in Massachusetts this evening, and to thank you for coming out to meet me. As I was driving here I began to complain and told them they oughtn't to have brought me as nobody would turn out. (Laughter and cheers). But it looks as if there were a good many Bull Moose. (A voice: "There will be a good many in November.")

And now, friends, I feel that I have peculiar right to come here, to come here to Massachusetts to make my appeal for the Progressive party because Massachusetts has in every great contest in the past always taken a position of leadership, and we have a right friends to look to you for leadership now, and I wish to open this campaign now by coming here in New England for I feel that it has been misrepresented by its public men of recent years (applause) and I appeal from the politicians to the people.

Friends, our movement is in its essence an absolutely simple movement and its proposals are definite. We proceed upon the assumption that the American people are fit to rule themselves at least (A voice: "Good boy, Teddy, we are with you."). And that only by them thus ruling themselves would it be possible to get real social and economic justice in this country. (A voice: "Is the hat still in the ring?") The hat is in the ring sure. And, friends, if any man thinks that a boss can rule him better than he can rule himself, then he doesn't belong with us. (Applause). He ought to go with one of the old parties, for that is his place. (A voice: "You're honest, Teddy.")

Principles Born of Experience

I'll talk clearly enough to you. If he feels that he himself is out to do his part in the great work of self-government, then we ask his support, then we feel that we have a right to expect him to be with us. And, friends, we are asking, we wish for popular rule as a means of getting fairer play, getting a square deal (applause) for all the people.

And now, friends, the principles which I champion I have not come to as a result of mere study in a library. I have come to them because I have lived and toiled with men, because I have worked with my fellows, because I know how they live and how they feel, what are their needs and how they look at life. I have seen life at a good many points.

Now, friends, you will read in the papers that we got along perfectly well with our old Representative system but we don't. I have tried that out in the primaries. If we hadn't had primaries I wouldn't have gotten one delegate from Massachusetts (Applause). Not one! And you know that as well as I do. You know I wouldn't have had any show. We did not go down into Connecticut and Rhode Island because there was no primary law in those States, and I knew I couldn't get any response from the politicians.

It would have been a waste of my time to go there. But now I am going there for now we come to an election and I can turn to the people themselves and ask for their support and ask them to stand by the cause which I am championing. (A voice: "You'll get it too!"). Yes, we'll get it. (Applause).

This is People's Fight

And I'll tell you why we will get it, friends. Because it is your fight. [Word faded in original] And because you are honest I have to be honest, yes. Because it is your fight. (Applause) Because you are honest, I try to be honest, yes. Because it's your fight. Now as I said in the primaries last year I said, "Now if the people beat me it is all right, I have nothing to say, but if the people are for me and the politicians beat me out of victory I'll have a good deal to say." (Applause) And I am saying it now. I'm saying it now.

We are asking that you govern yourselves. That doesn't mean that you won't sometimes make mistakes. We will when we govern ourselves make mistakes sometimes, but, after all we will make them ourselves. (Applause).

And we have got to make them. I don't want anyone else to make them for me. We make a mistake, we won't make it twice, and if the politician makes it for us Heaven only knows how often he'll make it. (Applause)

And, friends, our proposals are perfectly definite and concrete. We believe emphatically in bringing prosperity. We do not intend to pull any man down, but we want the prosperity passed around. We want to give a fair show to every man who has the right stuff in him.

And, friends, I am not promising you the millennium. It is a good way off and no law that we will make will give to any man success if he doesn't have in him the qualities which will command success. (Applause). If he is [word illegible] drunken, lazy, we can't make any law that will make him succeed. We all know that practically.

(Applause: "What makes him that way?")

Warns against Two Kinds of Men

You understand, friends, that any honest question I am glad to answer, and I am glad to have you put questions like that, because they help me to put, to make my point clear. Now, we know if a man by his innate character is shiftless and worthless then we are not going to be able to help him, but when, through no fault of his own, he is pressed down by unfair conditions, then we can right those conditions and give him a chance (Applause). Now, isn't that fair and common sense? (Voices: "That's right, that's right.")

Now, again, I don't for a moment say that we can right all those wrongs at once. There are two people against whom I will always warn you. In the first place, there is the individual who won't try to right anything because he says: Well, I guess things will get along well enough; they always have. I have no use for him. There is any amount of injustice and wrong, any amount of things that aren't as they ought to be, which we can cure, and we are not excused if we don't try to cure them.

On the other hand, I would warn against any man who promises the impossible, who says that he will get, by anything he does, everything all straight at once, bring the thing into good shape immediately. It can't be done, but I will tell you what can be done. There are a couple of hundred steps at least that we have got to take before we can get things satisfactory.

You can't try to take the 200th step before you have taken the first hundred, it is too big a stretch: you don't get there. But we can take the first, one, two, three, five, ten steps, and when we have taken those we will have gotten ourselves into better shape to face the remainder of the ascent. Do you see what I mean. You see what I mean.

Stand on the Tariff

Now, take such a matter as the tariff for instance. I believe in a protective tariff, but I don't believe in a protective tariff the benefits of which all stop in the front office. (Cheers and applause). I wish to see a proper share of those benefits get into the pay envelope. (A voice: "How are you going to do it?") How am I going to do it? In this way. You give me a show and I am just going to answer you.

Now here is how I am going to do it. Take the commission, the Tariff Commission, and make it their business to look into the conditions of life in every protected industry. The protection is supposed to be put on for the benefit of the wage worker.[9]

Take the report of those men who have studied the subject, who see what is actually done, and if they find that the man at the head has made an enormous amount of money and that the man lower down is paid insufficient wages, living under improper conditions, then say to this man: "These conditions are unsatisfactory. If in a given time—six months or a year whatever it is—the conditions are not satisfactory, if the wage rate is not satisfactory and proper, if the conditions of life among your laboring people are not proper, then we recommend that the tariff be taken off entirely from your product." (Applause)

Now that is a perfectly definite and feasible proposition and I want right here to say that is just the kind of a question I want put to me. I am not making any proposals which I don't think can be put into immediate effect—well, I say "immediate" of course I might mean a few months—but proposals—not proposals which I do not think can be put into effect, and there is no proposal I have to make that I am afraid to be questioned about. I want to have any question such as that put to me, as long as it is put in good faith.

"How About the Canal?"

Now you ask what my proposal is, that we shall say that the protective tariff on any given industry, I don't care what it is be put on with the idea that it shall benefit the workingmen employed in that industry.

If the benefit doesn't come to him, if it stops utterly somewhere else, then there is no warrant in keeping the tariff on, and the tariff goes off. (Applause). Now, friends, don't you think that would be a good deal of a step. (A voice: "How about the Panama Canal?")

About the Panama Canal? All right, I'll tell you about the Panama Canal. I am perfectly delighted to tell you about, because I had a good deal to do with it. Now, when I became President and the Panama Canal was under discussion, that was one of those cases where they declared that I acted unconstitutionally.

9. The idea of a nonpartisan tariff commission to set rates apart from political considerations had been popular for several years before the 1912 election. The platform of the Progressive Party endorsed the idea.

So now I will tell you just what I did. (A voice: You put it through.) I did, I put it through. (A voice: And you are going back to open it up.) I hope so. (Applause). And, after all, if I had to choose, I would rather have dug it than see it opened. (Laughter and applause)

Now, when I became President I found that negotiations about digging the Panama Canal were going on in Washington as they had been going on for over 50 years. The Spaniards had crossed the Isthmus four centuries before and had then said it would be "so nice" to dig a canal, and there had been four centuries of conversation on the subject.[10] (Laughter)

Just Took Canal Zone

And I thought the time had come to translate it into action. I did my level best to get Colombia to behave so that I could treat her well, and after a while I was forced to the conclusion that Colombia intended to hold up Uncle Sam and I don't like to have Uncle Sam held up (applause and laughter) and I then had two courses of action open to me.

If I had wanted to avoid trouble—I never hunt trouble, but I don't avoid it if it comes my way (applause) I could have done one of two things. If I had wished to avoid trouble I would have made a masterly report to Congress and Congress would have held a series of able debates on the masterly report and we would have had half a century of mere conversation. (Applause and laughter) And the canal would be 50 years off now.

Instead of doing that I took the zone and started the canal. (Applause). And I allowed Congress, instead of debating the canal, which would have been a misfortune, to debate me (laughter), which didn't make any difference to anybody, and least of all to me. (Laughter) And in consequence of that we came to a fair working compromise.

We got the Canal and Congress got the debate. (Laughter). And the debate about me is still going fitfully on, and I think it won't close until long after I am dead (laughter) and the canal will be finished in another year! (Applause and cheers).

10. The literature on Roosevelt and the creation of the Panama Canal is enormous. For a brief discussion, see Lewis L. Gould, *The Presidency of Theodore Roosevelt* (Lawrence: University Press of Kansas, 1991), pp. 91–98.

Went after Rations in Cuba

Now, friends, I have answered that question, and just let me illustrate by an incident of my experience the way I have tried to act in that and in all similar matters when I was President of the United States, and I want you to understand that I don't take back anything or apologize for anything I did. (Applause). I stand on it. (A voice: You don't have to.) No, I don't have to. (Applause). I stand on it, and you know what you will get if you get me. (Laughter).

Now, in the Spanish war I was colonel of a regiment known as the Rough Riders (Applause). It wasn't a very big war but it was all the war there was. (Laughter), and after the first night there was a break in the cracker line and we got short of food. We had nothing at all but salt pork and hard tack, and I sent in one or two requisitions for more food, and I guess they sent them to Washington. I never heard of them afterward. (Laughter)

So I made up my mind that I would go after it myself and I took about 40 of my men and marched them to a port Siboney where I heard provisions had been landed. When I got there there were many things being landed and everything was higgledy-piggledy over the beach.

Pretty soon I found a commissary officer and he asked me what I wanted, and I asked him what he had got (laughter) because I wanted it all (Laughter.) Well, he told me to look them over, and pretty soon I discovered a number of sacks of beans, about 1100 pounds—I forgot the exact number, but about 1100 pounds (a voice: Boston baked beans?). They weren't baked, but to judge from the way they tasted, they must have come from Boston (laughter) they were A1. (A voice: You don't mean that.) A1? Sure. (Applause)

Got the Beans All the Same

I found there were 1100 pounds of beans, so I went up to the commissary officer and put in requisition for 1100 pounds of beans. That was all I discovered! And he took a book of regulations and showed me regulation 7, division 3, section B, or whatever it was, showing that beans were only used for the officers' mess. I told him that my officers and men ate alike. Well, he said he was sorry, very sorry, and I told him I was more sorry.

Then he said he couldn't give me the beans, so I went back and thought about it a little while, then I came back with another requisition and my request for 1100 pounds of beans for the officers' mess. (Laughter). Then he looked at me and he said, "Your officers can't eat 1100 pounds of beans," and I answered him, "You don't know what appetites they have." (Laughter.) So then he thought he would have to refer the requisition to Washington. (Laughter). I said, "That's all right, if you will give me the beans." (Laughter). And he said he was afraid that they would take it out of my salary, and I told him I thought so too (applause and laughter), and they did—but I got the beans.

Never Mollycoddle

I remember telling this anecdote once in the presence of a perfectly good, straightlaced Army officer, and he said it was against the regulations; that it was unconstitutional. I said I knew it was against the regulations in letter, but it could not be in spirit.

The regulations were made for a time of peace, when officers and men alike had all they could eat, and it was all fair to have a difference in the mess. At a time of war my men did not have enough to eat, and you can guarantee that in my regiment if there was anybody who did not have enough to eat nobody did, and it was my duty to keep that regiment in first-class fighting trim.[11]

Mind you, I never mollycoddle. If any man shirked his work or shirked his fighting I cinched him. I wanted them to do their work and do it manfully, and I took care of them if they did their work. And that is the only way you can get anything out of a man in war or anywhere else. I do not want any man ever to spare me work or to spare anyone else who is fit to work, but I want every man to be treated fairly if he does his work. Do you see what I mean? That is the way I handle them.

Uncle Sam Got His Beans

Now, I feel that I should have contempt for myself, colonel of my regiment, if I had not seen that my regiment got their fair share of whatever

11. Roosevelt did not relate this precise anecdote in his memoir about his military service in Cuba, but he did refer to buying food for his men. See Theodore Roosevelt, *The Rough Riders: The Works of Theodore Roosevelt* (New York: Charles Scribner's Sons, 1926), 11: 71, 126.

was going; I would not have felt I was competent for my job. Well, now, when I was President of the United States it was the same way: when Uncle Sam needed 1100 pounds of beans I got them for him.

Now, friends, the propositions that I put before you are perfectly simple. I ask you to go with us because we and we alone are honestly endeavoring to promise nothing that we cannot perform, and at the same time devise measures which shall really meet the genuine economic evils and injustices of today.

It is essential that the people shall rule themselves and you will not get economic justice because now you depend upon men who are not responsible to you. In practice I know what our Government amounts to. It amounts to, and always did, a Government by the bosses for the special interests.

It has been so in my State, in Pennsylvania, in every State that I know, this is not a matter of theory with me. I am not asking you to read books about representative governments. I am asking you to learn from your own actual experience and the experience of our people. If we do not keep the Government in such shape that you can rule yourselves you can guarantee that some one else will rule and will rule you in his interest and not in yours. (A voice: "How about Perkins?")

Position of Perkins

How about Perkins.[12] I will tell you about him: As I say if you will ask me an honest question that I can answer I will do so. I am going to answer one question. I can answer only one at a time. You cannot ask me a question I will not answer so long as the question is an honest one and asked for an honest purpose.

Mr. Perkins is a rich man. He came into this movement not at my request at all, on his own initiative. I have known him some 14 years. After he came in, after he had been in two or three weeks, I felt the same curiosity that that man back there, who put the question did, and I put the same question to Perkins himself. I said, "Mr. Perkins, I want to ask you a question and I hope you won't call it offensive because I do not mean it to be."

12. George Walbridge Perkins (1862–1920) was a former partner of financier J. P. Morgan who had become Roosevelt's closest adviser on economic matters within the Progressive Party. Because of his corporate connections, Perkins had become a target of both the Democrats and the Republicans. He also aroused opposition among Progressives who feared his influence on Roosevelt and his desire to dominate the presidential campaign.

He said, "Ask it." I said, "why are you supporting me?" He flushed for a moment and he said, "I do not know but that I ought to feel offended." I said, "No, you ought not; I asked that in perfect sincerity and I want to know why you are supporting me." He said, "My reason is I have children: I have all the money I want, and my children are well provided for and I have come to believe in recent years that the country won't be a good place for any of our children to live in when those children grow to the age that we are, unless by some method substantial justice is obtained for all our people, unless business and the Government are brought into proper relations, unless the relation of capitalist and wage-earner put on a better basis than they now are."

"I wish to take part in the movement that will bring about those better conditions, and I believe you are the only public man who is in good faith trying to bring about these conditions; and I am supporting you because I wish this land to be a good land for my children to live in, for the children of my friends to live in when they grow to my age, and it won't be a good land for them to live in unless such principles as those you advocate are put into real, living, working effect in this country." (Cheers and applause.)

Flinn and Perkins in Open

(A voice: How about Flinn?)[13] You can see that the questions that are most serious I am answering just as rapidly as I can. I wanted to say what I was going to say about Mr. Perkins. I have told you literally what Mr. Perkins said to me. Curiously enough it was almost exactly what, not long afterward, Mr. Flinn of Pennsylvania said to me, the difference being that Mr. Flinn made the remark to me without my asking him the question.

But as to Mr. Perkins, I asked the question. I have immensely appreciated the support of Mr. Perkins and Mr. Flinn, it has been very valuable, and I immensely appreciate it. Besides, it was given in the open, the support has come in the open. There is nothing invisible about this movement. (Applause) You know the full details of all that goes on [in] this movement.

That Mr. Flinn and Mr. Perkins both heartily approve of the platform we adopted at Chicago, of my speech made before the Chicago conven-

13. William Flinn, a political boss of the Republican machine in Pittsburgh, was a Roosevelt supporter in 1912 who had gone with the Progressives. His loyalty to Roosevelt would help win Pennsylvania for the Progressives, but his background somewhat belied the reform claims of the third party.

tion. Mr. Flinn in Pennsylvania had secured the combination in Pennsylvania of practically the same platform for the State of Pennsylvania, a platform which aimed to give genuine control to the people themselves, giving them the primaries, giving a complete referendum and recall, giving every man the controlling power absolutely of their own public service and securing to them economic justice.

Story of Mr. Flinn

I will tell you this story about Mr. Flinn. There was one instance that did not get in in connection with Mr. Perkins. I said to Mr. Perkins: "I am thoroughly appreciative of this. Before you support me I want you to understand that I intend to work for complete and effective regulation of all the big industrial concerns, including the Steel Corporation, and that I intend to work to secure in our continuous industries, and that includes steel, a six-day week; that is one day off in the steel works, and a three shift day."

And Mr. Perkins: "I will support it. I understand that is your principle and it has got to come."

Now, Mr. Flinn knows what I am standing for; I am working for the Workmen's Compensation Act. He said, "I believe in it." He said, "One of my foremen came to me and said a stone in the pit broke the leg of a man. I asked how did it happen?" Said the foreman, "It was a stone that was displaced rolled and broke the man's leg." Flinn said, "If it had been a bucket what would you have done?" The foreman said, "we would have mended the bucket." "Then," he replied, "mend the man."

"Watch Me in the Future"

If Mr. Flinn and Mr. Perkins had supported this movement without asking a thing, with the assurance personally given to me that they have nothing of any kind or sort to ask, they are doing all they can financially and otherwise to help me start this movement for social and economic justice, I know that they are honestly and in good faith entitled to the respect of every good citizen for their work. That is absolutely my attitude toward them.

But look here. You can watch me in the future. If ever I do anything for Mr. Perkins or Mr. Flinn that is in the least particle of the way anything I ought not to do, then I am to be condemned and they are to be condemned; but unless that happens it is to their credit that they should support a movement like this, and it is a small mind which shows a small character to object to honest men who are supporting a movement for the common good. (Cheers and applause.)

(A voice: How about the Socialists? Another voice: How about Wilson?)

Attitude as to Socialism

You ask about the Socialists. Of course that is a question altogether too big to answer at this time. What I can say is this: in our platform we have grappled with certain of the evils with which the Socialists have striven to grasp. The difference is that we are grappling with those evils in a practical way that will cure them, and the Socialists are chasing will-o'-the wisps. That is the difference. That is the first difference between us and them.

And on the other hand you will read in the papers tomorrow that men say, the editorials say, that I am a Socialist or that I am an anarchist. Now, friends, you have listened to me tonight. I am preaching neither anarchy nor socialism; I am preaching the curative to socialism and the antidote to anarchy.

I am preaching and trying to practice the policy of a square deal to every man and woman in this republic. There isn't a symptom in either of the old parties in purpose to really grapple with the evil conditions of the present day. Both of the old parties shirk it and confine themselves in their platforms to beating over again the straw that has been threshed to little pieces.

In the platforms of the political parties of the last 30 years the only platform which honestly attempts to grapple with the real and leading issues of today is ours, we have put them into speeches, and you can get as many copies as you want, you can see exactly what I have said in those speeches, and we have told you what we believe, and we have given you a number of specific remedies which we intend to try to introduce.

Will Carry Out Promises

Neither the old Democratic nor the old Republican party makes any effort to deal with this question. The machines of both parties are corrupt and boss-ridden and have no power to turn and face the vital issues of the present day. We have turned to face them, we have resolutely faced ourselves toward solving the grave social problems that confront us and are solving them in the interest of the average man and average woman.

We do not promise you the millennium. We do say that if you choose to put into power either of the old parties you will make no progress at all toward any solution; you will keep this country in the same condition of simmering unrest that it is now without giving any outlet for betterment.

If you support us, if you stand with us, that is, if you stand with yourselves for all we are trying to do is to give you, yourselves a chance to rule for yourselves and to get some solution in these matters. If you support us we won't solve all the problems, but we will solve some of them and we will advance a measurable distance toward solving the others. We have promised nothing we can't perform.

We will keep every promise we have made, and we have for the first time in the political history of this country seen a great party resolutely set its face toward the future in an effort to deal with the tremendous problems caused by the growth of our modern civilization.

Only Hope in New Party

Now, friends, I have told you as far as I could in a brief time what our purpose is. (A voice: How about woman suffrage?)

Now, gentlemen, you see you would like to keep me here all night to answer your questions. I have now answered all the most important ones and if you will go to the Progressive headquarters you will see in the speech I made at Chicago a full discussion of the cost of living issues. You will find, you friend over there—you will find a discussion of the colored question. It contains my speech and my letter on the subject. (A voice: That is all right, Teddy.)[14]

I think I am and, in short, friends, I feel that the only party that offers any chance of solving these great problems is the Progressive party. We have taken up the task where others have faltered. But a few years ago, friends down there, I hoped that men would do that task who I regret to

14. The issue of African Americans in the Progressive Party was another controversy that dogged Roosevelt. He had come out against black participation in the third party in the South at the national convention in August. He had explained his reasoning in his speech at the convention but the printed version in *Social Justice and Popular Rule*, 17, omitted that subject. The party published a separate pamphlet on the issue. The letter to which Roosevelt referred was probably Roosevelt to Julian La Rose Harris, 1 August 1912, in Elting E. Morison, et al., eds., *The Letters of Theodore Roosevelt* (Cambridge, Mass.: Harvard University Press, 1954), 7:585–590, in which Roosevelt made the case for excluding blacks from the party.

say have since shown themselves powerless even to undertake it. The time demands the fearless and resolute and common sense effort to meet the great issues impending. (A voice: How about Wilson?)

I have spoken to you friends of the old Republican and old Democratic parties. I have gone over that once and perfectly clearly. If you think you can get anything good, anything of hope out of the old Democratic boss-controlled, machine-ridden Democratic party, then I admire your optimism, but I pity your judgment. (Cheers and applause).

So, friends, we put our case before you. We feel that the old parties are no longer fit to grapple with the living issues of the day. We feel that neither has any serious purpose of trying to grapple with them. We have set ourselves with all of courage, of honesty and sincerity that we possess to dealing with those issues. We have put before you what we intend to do.

Every promise that we make we can keep and we will keep, and we ask the American people to be true to themselves. We ask you of Boston, you of Massachusetts be true to yourselves and to stand with us who stand, and we alone stand, for the genuine right of the people to rule and for their duty so to rule as to bring social and industrial justice throughout this great land of ours. Good night. (Wild applause.)

Globe, 18 August 1912; there is a draft version of this address in the Roosevelt Papers at the Library of Congress.

Following his brief New England swing, Roosevelt returned to his home in Oyster Bay, New York, to plan for another brief foray to Vermont and Connecticut at the end of the month before he embarked on his western tour. On 22 August he made a short trip to Wilkes-Barre, Pennsylvania, to honor his friend, Roman Catholic priest Father John J. Curran, who was celebrating his jubilee as a clergyman.[15] *During his visit to the Pennsylvania city, Roosevelt addressed a controversy about his conduct in the 1904 election that had just surfaced. William Randolph Hearst, the newspaper publisher, had charged Boies Penrose, the Republican senator from Pennsylvania, with taking bribes from Standard Oil. In response, Penrose claimed that he had raised money from the oil giant for Roosevelt's campaign in 1904. There was talk of a Senate investigation, and the issue would soon become a major preoccupation of Roosevelt. In brief remarks in Wilkes-Barre, he spoke out about Penrose and the allegations.*

15. Father John J. Curran (1859–1936) was a figure in the settlement of the 1902 anthracite coal strike when he got to know Roosevelt.

A Speech in Wilkes-Barre, Pennsylvania, 22 August 1912

Father Curran made a speech in which he praised his friend Mr. Roosevelt to the highest. Father Curran, in an indirect way, made the first allusion to the candidacy of Mr. Roosevelt. Father Curran said: "I brought a President of the United States here for the first time; I have brought an ex-President here again tonight, and I pray that I may be instrumental in bringing another President here."

After Colonel Roosevelt had paid a tribute to Father Curran, he said:

"And now a word about honesty. We can't have reform unless we have honesty in both business and politics. By a natural sequence of thought I now come to Senator Penrose of Pennsylvania.

Recently certain definite and specific charges were made against Senator Penrose. I personally knew nothing of them, and had not even looked into the charge until Mr. Penrose succeeded in riveting my attention upon them. Yesterday he got up in the senate to deny those charges and brought in hearsay charges against me.[16]

I call your attention to an analogue to Senator Penrose among the inferior forms of animal life—the cuttlefish. When the cuttlefish is attacked by an enemy which it lacks the courage to oppose, it squirts ink and tries to escape, trusting that the enemy will attack the ink instead of the cuttlefish. I now propose to clear away the ink and attack the cuttlefish.

The statement of Mr. Penrose was that he had heard that by my direction $100,000 was asked for from the Standard Oil Company for my campaign and contributed, and that further sum was asked for. Mr. Penrose gave this evidence on hearsay. It is a thoroughly base and contemptible thing for Mr. Penrose to repeat such evidence on hearsay."

Col. Roosevelt then referred to the letters which he gave out last night, which he sent to George B. Cortelyou, chairman of the Republican national committee in 1904, directing that no campaign contribution be received from the Standard Oil Company.

"Any man who reads these letters," he continued, "is bound, if he is an honest man, to state that I acted in absolute good faith and that if any contribution was made by the Standard Oil Company it was without my knowledge and in spite of my absolute prohibition.

The proof of the pudding is in the eating. Every trust controlled news paper in the land is doing everything in its power to beat me. Do you think

16. Penrose made the charges in a speech to the Senate. See U.S. Congress, *Congressional Record*, 62nd Cong., 2d Sess., 1912, 11466–11468.

A Republican senator from Pennsylvania, Boies Penrose launched the congressional investigation into campaign finances that dogged Roosevelt throughout the campaign season in 1912. (Library of Congress)

that these trust papers would be trying to beat me if I had been satisfactory to the Standard Oil Company and that crowd? They are against me because no one trust, not one individual, was able to use or influence me while I was president. That's why they hate me.

So much for the ink. Now for the cuttle-fish. Mr. Penrose states that he received $25,000 for use in Pennsylvania and that he used it to help me in my election. By running I helped Mr. Penrose. He didn't help me. If he doubts that I ask him to compare his experiences in 1904, when he was helping me and in 1912, when he went it alone. It was Penrose hanging on to Roosevelt in 1904, and the ticket went through with 500,000 majority. It was Penrose without Roosevelt in 1912, and he got just about six or eight delegates—I forget the number now.

Men of Pennsylvania, it is your fight and not mine. If you like Mr. Penrose, keep him. But I earnestly hope you will adopt the principle of popular election of United States senators. Let Mr. Penrose come squarely before the people, as I have done, and if he wins out, well and good. I should feel like the Scotch minister, who after reading from the Bible that the Lord loved David, said, 'There's no accounting for tastes!'"[17]

Wilkes-Barre *Times Leader,* 23 August 1912.

17. Penrose ran for reelection in 1914 after direct election of senators had been adopted, and he defeated both Gifford Pinchot for the Progressives and A. Mitchell Palmer for the Democrats. At that time, Roosevelt wrote of the general Republican success Penrose represented that "the dog has returned to its vomit." Roosevelt to William Allen White, 7 November 1914, in Elting E. Morison, et al., eds., *The Letters of Theodore Roosevelt* (Cambridge, Mass.: Harvard University Press, 1954), 8:839.

2

The Second New England Tour

On 28 August, Roosevelt left to make speeches in Vermont, a state that would be electing its governor and other officials early in September. With its proximity to the Canadian border, where farmers disliked President William Howard Taft's reciprocity agreement, Vermont seemed to offer an opportunity for Roosevelt to demonstrate his appeal in the Northeast. He made a series of addresses. The most important of these occurred at Burlington and St. Johnsbury on 29–30 August. He then went to Connecticut, where he gave another significant speech at Hartford on 2 September. In his remarks, Roosevelt spoke about farming issues and examined the roots of his personal commitment to progressive reform.

A Speech at Burlington, Vermont, 29 August 1912

Here in Vermont I feel that we have a peculiar right to appeal on behalf of the Progressive party. You men and women of Vermont represent the very type of American citizen to whom we must trust when we strive to make this Government really a Government by the people themselves in the interest of all the people and not of any one class of the people.

From the days of Ethan Allen to the present time the people of Vermont have sustained the same character for rugged independence and for the possession of a strong individual initiative combined with the ability to cooperate one with another.[1] These are the very qualities that we are endeavoring to make more widespread in this Republic of ours and to develop as basis [basic] in our Government.

1. Ethan Allen (1738–1789) was a legendary figure in Vermont history for his capture of Fort Ticonderoga in 1775 with his Green Mountain Boys.

The National Progressive platform, like your own Progressive platform here in Vermont, represents radically a new departure when compared with any of the political platforms of the last 40 years. But the principles that our platform contains are not new. They are fundamentally the principles of Lincoln, the principles of Washington.

What is new is that we Progressives are trying in good faith to apply these principles to the actual and vital needs of the present day instead of confining ourselves to praising our forefathers for having applied them to the needs of their day.

In 1860 it was of no use merely to profess allegiance to the principles of 1776, what was necessary then was to apply those principles to the current year.

So we in our turn must not confine ourselves to praising the men of Lincoln's time for the way they met issues that were living then, but are dead now. We must take the principles of Abraham Lincoln and apply them to the issues of the present day. The National Progressive convention at Chicago thus applied the principles of 1776 and 1860 to the issues of 1912.

Both of the old parties, on the contrary, have confined themselves to thrashing over again the old straw. There is not one particle of hope for social or economic reform contained in the triumph of either the Democratic or Republican policies.

Each is boss-ridden and privilege controlled. Neither dares to face the real issues of today. Each proposes sham remedies and tries to distract attention of the people from their real needs by the empty sound and fury with which they quarrel over false issues. The two old parties have utterly lost touch with the facts of modern economic life, and they serve no other purpose than that of screens, each for its own sinister alliance of crooked politicians and crooked financiers who rule and pillage with impunity.

It is no wonder that where this is the case the average man grows to regard politics as a game between two sets of sharpers at the expense of a muddle-headed public. Instead of a representative Government, ours has become an unrepresentative Government, and the popular will is continually frustrated by the politicians misrepresented in the Legislature, set at naught by the courts and trampled on by the forces of privilege.

Neither of the old parties shows even the least faint promise of breaking up this condition of affairs. The triumph of either would perpetuate it. The leaders of neither show even an understanding of what the problem means. There is nothing in either the Republican or the Democratic platform which so much as hints at even an understanding of what issues are really vital to our people.

The Progressive platform, on the contrary, boldly grapples with these issues. Remember that loyalty to a name often means the most dreadful disloyalty to the principle for which that name once stood. In 1860 loyalty to the parties of Jefferson, Jackson and Henry Clay could find expression only by repudiating the parties that still bore the names of those great men and joining the new Republican party.

So in our day we can be loyal to the Republicanism of Lincoln by scornfully tossing aside the Republicanism that dances in fetters of corruption under the whips of Penrose, Barnes and Guggenheim. The Progressive Party is the only party of today which in any shape or way represents the Republican party of Lincoln's time, and in reality is a continuation of Lincoln's party.

Now here in Vermont remember that your State campaign is hitched with the National campaign. This is so in the first place because our opponents, representing both the old machines, are doing everything they can to elect their respective candidates here with the avowed purpose of thereby influencing the effect in other States. It is so in the next place because our Progressive platform deals with great reforms which must be largely accomplished through State action no less than through National action.

No man has a right to call himself a progressive at all if he is supporting either of the old parties, whether in the Nation or in the several States. Neither of these old parties has shown the slightest understanding of the need for social and economic reform. Whoever supports either of them here in Vermont, whether in the National election or the State election, is turning his back on the future and is setting his eyes to the past.

Nor can any candidate claim to be really a Progressive candidate unless he repudiates the National platforms of both the old parties and supports us and our platform. Our candidate for governor in Vermont, Mr. Metzger, is a man who is with us and is a leader among us because he possesses the vision clearly to see both the evils that afflict us and the need for grappling with those evils, and because he possesses also the high purpose and intelligent ability necessary if those evils are to be met and abated.[2]

If you elect him and make your State Government progressive you will put Vermont in the lead of the new movement. If you fail to do so you will not stop the movement, but you will put Vermont in the position of being dragged on by it instead of heading it.

2. Reverend Fraser Metzger (1872–1954) was the Bull Moose candidate in Vermont. He was defeated and later served as dean of men at Rutgers University from 1925 to 1944.

We shall win this fight. And my plea to you is that Vermont, the Green Mountain State, which has always stood aright in every great movement of the past, shall take the lead in standing right in this great moment of the present.

I make an especial appeal to the farmers of Vermont. Our platform alone of the three platforms shows an intelligent purpose to deal fundamentally with the causes that are at work to harm American agriculture and to diminish the full value of life in the open country.

We are ready to grapple with the immediate evils susceptible of remedy and with the deeper-rooted ones which need long and careful work in the way both of examination and of action on examination. The problem is of vital importance. No war could damage this Nation to the extent that it would be damaged by even a small degree of soil exhaustion, and a large degree of exhaustion would work ruin such as no arts of peace could avert.

We are for the immediate repeal of the Reciprocity Treaty.[3] Many of us originally supported that treaty. I did myself, under the impression that it was honestly entered into for the benefit of all our people and to favor the reciprocal good relations between Canada and the United States.[4]

A full examination has convinced us that the treaty was improper, that it would not do what it purported to do, and that it would seriously damage our farmers without bringing any adequate compensation to any other body of our fellow citizens.

It remains on the statute books in such form that if at any time Canada chose to accept it, it would become law. The Progressive proposal is to repeal it, and once for all to put an end to all possible damage which it would bring to our people.

We are for the immediate recreation of the Country Life Commission, the abandonment of which has represented a thoroughly retrograde step by our Government. Many different forces must be used for the betterment of economic and social conditions in the open country. The farmer

3. The reciprocity agreement with Canada, which was not technically a treaty, had been adopted by Congress in the summer of 1911 through legislation. When Canada rejected the agreement in September 1911, that action still left the American law on the books. Seeking repeal of the law was one means of dramatizing the issue for farmers still unhappy about what the Taft administration had done.

4. Roosevelt had originally supported the Canadian reciprocity agreement in a letter to Taft. That document had been used against him during the Republican primary campaign. See Roosevelt to Taft, 12 January 1911, in Elting E. Morison, et al., eds., *The Letters of Theodore Roosevelt* (Cambridge, Mass.: Harvard University Press, 1954), 7:206. See also Richard C. Baker, *The Tariff Under Roosevelt and Taft* (Hastings, Neb.: Democrat Printing Co., 1941), pp. 163–164, 174–176.

must himself, of course, take the lead in the movement, but it is the duty of all the rest of us and of our Government agents to aid him in his work.[5]

The problem affects all of us, for one main reason because the high cost of living is the failure to get the most possible out of our soil, and especially the failure to use the best business methods in marketing the products of the soil. Altogether too much is absorbed by the middleman. Not only can the farm's productiveness be increased, but by wise cooperation the products of the farm can be brought with much less intervention by middlemen than at present directly to the consumer. The result would be that while the farmer would get more for his product the consumer would pay less.

If the Democratic platform on the tariff is sincere the first step that the Democratic party would take if it came to power would be to pass a tariff law which would work the utmost possible damage to the farmer, and yet which would, I firmly believe, do practically nothing whatever for the consumer.

In reality, the tariff changes proposed by the Democratic party, while they would cause utter ruin both to our agricultural and industrial community, would have almost no effect in helping the producer.

Our proposal, on the contrary, is to help the farmer and at the same time to lower the prices of the products to the men who actually consume them. We intend to work for the betterment of conditions of production on our farms, so that the farm shall be made both more fruitful and at the same time more valuable in the future as well as the present.

We also intend to work for better business handling by the farmer of his products. Finally, through many different agencies—through the country Y.M.C.A.'s, through the churches, through farmers' institutes, through fitting the country school to the needs of country life, through favoring the movements for good roads and helping out still further along the lines of Rural Free Delivery, we intend to better social conditions for the men and women who live and bring up their children in the open country.

We in America have much to do in the way of teaching ourselves. At last we are waking up and I wish to bear testimony for the way in which certain nonfarmers' organizations, such as the Spokane Chamber of Commerce and the Illinois Bankers' Association, have helped in this way, recog-

5. Roosevelt took a special interest in the problems of rural America and he was especially proud of the Country Life Commission, which he had established in 1908. When he sent the report of the commission to Congress in early 1909, lawmakers refused to appropriate the money to print it. Taft did not continue the work of the commission, an act that irritated Roosevelt.

nizing that the interests of all of us are bound up with the welfare of the man who tills the soil.

It was the Spokane Chamber of Commerce which published the Country Life Commission's report when Congress refused to do so, and the Illinois Bankers' Association, under the lead of the president, B. F. Harris, is now urging in Congress the need of enacting a law which will extend to the North and West the benefit of the field demonstration plan.[6]

The plan is to send qualified demonstrators right to the farmer on his farm to work it with him and show him right there on the average farm how to better results. In the South there have been nearly 200 such demonstrators at work and in seven years the results have been literally marvelous.

It is an ominous and serious thing that here in the United States the average yield of our two greatest cereals, corn and wheat, is less than it was 40 years ago. In other words, we permit an altogether improper percentage of what may be called dormant unemployed soil fertility on our farms—any banker who in his business permitted so large a percent of it to consist of dormant, unearning cash reserve would certainly go to the wall.

Our wheat crop in this country, for instance, averages less than 14 bushels an acre, whereas our best farmers here, and the average farmer in many countries in Europe—on land that has been farmed for a thousand years—will average from 26 to 40 bushels. Now every farmer knows that a 80 bushel average corn crop will make more net profit in one year than a 50 bushel average in four years. Well, one bushel per acre increase on all improved agricultural land in the United States would mean that there would be 12,500 extra trains of cars needed each year to transport it. Mind you, this increase could be obtained while at the time increasing the permanent value of the land, as the experience of Germany, France and Denmark has shown.

This experience has also shown that cooperative banking, marketing and purchasing organizations in the country can be developed to a marvelous degree, to the profit of the producers. Certain of our States, I am happy to say, have already begun to prove experimentally what can be done in cooperative handling and marketing of farm products, as well as in fire insurance, telephone and even banking organizations—these organizations being cooperative, with service rather than profit as the prime object.

6. B. F. Harris was a Chicago banker with an interest in rural questions. See his essay, "Improvement of Country Life—Policies the Progressive Party Would Put into Practice," in George Henry Payne, *The Birth of the New Party or Progressive Democracy* (n.p.: H. E. Rennels, 1912), pp. 174–191.

While the cost of living has risen all over the world, it has risen more rapidly here in America than almost anywhere else, and the prime cause, I believe, is to be found in the failure to do what should be done for and by the people who live on the soil. If we choose, I am sure that we can so handle the problem that the farmer will have more profit on the very products that cost the consumer less money.

We cannot employ all European methods here, but we can learn by them, so as to do away with waste and inefficiency in our methods, so as to get more out of the soil, to conserve the value of the soil, and to secure a better organization among farmers, alike in selling their products and in purchasing their requirements. We do not promise the impossible; we do not promise the millennium, but we do promise intelligent and genuine work to accomplish what can be accomplished; and neither of the old parties so much as understand the need of such work. Vermont is one of these States to which, because of our attitude in this matter, we should be peculiarly able to appeal.

Every party should be judged by the character and spirit of its representatives who take the lead in actual party management, by the character of its platform and by the way in which, taken as a whole, its deeds and words make good its professions.

Now I wish to ask your very cordial consideration to the record of the man whom the Progressives have put up for Vice President, Gov. Hiram Johnson of California.[7] It happens that this year of the six party nominees for President or Vice President, four are or have been governors of their respective States. Mr. Wilson is Governor of New Jersey, Mr. Marshall of Indiana, I was Governor of New York, and Mr Johnson is Governor of California.[8]

For a generation California has been controlled in merciless fashion as few other States have been controlled by the representatives of special privilege and the politicians in alliance with them. When Mr. Johnson took office as Governor he had before him a herculean task if he was to make good the promise of the Progressives.

Well he accomplished the task, and he absolutely made good the promises. Under his leadership California has established a system of direct primaries, including Presidential primaries; it has adopted the system of electing United States Senators by popular vote; it has applied the initiative, the

7. Hiram Johnson (1866–1945) was governor of California and the vice-presidential candidate of the Progressive Party.

8. Thomas Riley Marshall (1854–1925) was governor of Indiana and the running mate of Woodrow Wilson.

referendum and the recall in thoroughgoing fashion, it has provided for the nonpartisan election of judges, it has provided for the shortening of the ballot; it has provided for county and city home rule, it has provided for the revision of criminal procedure, it has taken the first steps in securing the proper method of treatment for first offenders against the law, it has established a Conservation Commission with ample jurisdiction, it has given full power for the regulation of all public utilities, it has passed a first class Employers' Liability act; it has secured the adoption of woman suffrage, it has regulated the working hours of women and minors, it has abolished race track gambling; it has passed a Full Crew bill and a Pay Check bill, prohibiting the payment of wages in nonnegotiable form.

No other Governor of any State since the close of the Civil War has, during his term as Governor, achieved such a mass of effective work for the people as Gov. Johnson has achieved. He represents the type of man who ought to be nominated for Vice President, but to whom it means a real sacrifice to accept the nomination.

He accepted our nomination because he regarded it as a call of the highest duty. He is not only fit at this moment to be President; he is fit at this moment to be a great President.

Boston *Daily Globe,* 30 August 1912.

A Speech at St. Johnsbury, Vermont, 30 August 1912

The Progressive platform is the first platform since the close of the Civil War which has fearlessly, fully, and intelligently faced the needs of our people, which has promised everything that ought to be promised, and which has promised nothing that cannot be and ought not to be fulfilled. I call your attention especially to what our platform says about business and trusts. In the National Government two methods of dealing with big business have so far been tried; one that of regulation through the Interstate Commerce Commission, the other that of destruction by means of the Antitrust Law. The first has been eminently successful, the second has broken down. The Progressive platform faces this fact. It states that the test of true prosperity must be the benefits conferred thereby on all citizens, not the benefits confined to individuals or classes, and that the test of corporate efficiency must be the ability better to serve the public. The platform demands efficient and thorough-going National regulation of all these

Roosevelt campaigned throughout 1912. He spoke from many platforms and his admirers provided him with suitable floral tributes on those occasions. (Theodore Roosevelt Collection, Harvard College Library)

great industrial concerns doing an interstate business. The law is to be made definite so that honest men will not be under continual threat of law proceedings. However, the Anti-Trust Law is to be kept on the statute books, and instead of the enforcement against the big trusts being as now merely farcical, it is to be the duty of the commission to aid in seeing that every trust guilty of bad conduct shall be really and not merely nominally dissolved, and the men guilty of the misconduct punished.

This programme is the only programme that offers the slightest chance of real accomplishment. We propose to give the honest business man certainty as to what the law is and is not, so that he will no longer be nervously unable to tell whether he has made himself subject to its penalties. We propose to create an administrative commission which shall superintend big business in thoroughgoing fashion, and stop every species of wrongdoing precisely as the best class of public utilities commission now does in States and municipalities, precisely as the Interstate Commerce Commission will again do when we get rid of the mischievous Commerce Court, the creation of which represented a long step backwards, of benefit only to the trusts themselves.[9] The Anti-Trust Law by itself can never in any shape or way solve the problem of dealing with the trusts. As at present enforced, and still more as it would be enforced if the recommendations of the Stanley Committee were enacted into law, it is and would remain a mere policy of make-believe strangle, a policy nominally against the interests of the huge swollen trusts but really in their favor, and a menace only to honest business men with businesses of moderate size.[10] It is curious to see how closely the old parties stand together in this matter, and how eagerly the representatives of the big trusts and of their tools and allies in the Government would rally to the help of either as against the Progressives. The recent action of Mr. Penrose and Mr. Archbold is a striking illustration of the chances with which the Standard Oil Trust and its creatures in politics see that their real foes, the foes whom they hate and dread, are to be found only in the Progressive party, and against these foes they will do everything in their power in the interest of either or both of the old parties, with the old, corrupt, machine organizations.[11]

The promises of the Democratic and Republican platforms can be tested by the performance of the representatives of the two parties at the present time; for instance by the Administration's acceptance as satisfactory of the results in the suit against the Standard Oil and Tobacco Trusts and by the Stanley Committee's report on the proper method of dealing with these trusts. The only actual result of the suits against the Oil and Tobacco Trusts was greatly to increase the value of the holdings of the big financiers who were nominally supposed to be punished, while small competitors were put in a worse position than before, and the cost of living was raised to the public generally, as the products were increased in price. The recommendations of the Stanley Committee do not deserve to be treated seriously. If adopted they would probably accomplish nothing whatever, being mere sound and fury; but if they did accomplish anything

9. Taft had persuaded Congress to create the Commerce Court in 1910 and regarded it as one of the achievements of his administration.

10. The Stanley Committee was the panel that Augustus Owsley Stanley (1867–1958), a Kentucky Democrat, chaired in the House to investigate the U.S. Steel Company. Roosevelt had testified before the committee in 1911 and had little regard for the recommendations Stanley and his colleagues advanced to deal with the trust issue.

11. John D. Archbold (1848–1916), a Standard Oil Company executive, and Boies Penrose had charged that Roosevelt accepted corporate contributions from Standard Oil in his race for the White House in 1904. Roosevelt had sought to testify before the Senate committee looking into the allegations in August, but the members had left Washington to frustrate Roosevelt. He would not get a chance to make his case in public until early October. He had sent a lengthy letter to the chair of the committee, Senator Moses Clapp of Minnesota, denying the charges. The controversy ran throughout September as Roosevelt returned to it again and again in his appearances.

whatever it would be a partial paralysis of production, which would inevitably raise the cost of living. If successful they would merely represent a blow at abundance, a method of securing scarcity; and scarcity means high prices. As for the recommendation of the Stanley Committee that the size of a corporation be limited, its worth can be tested by what the Department of Justice secured when the splitting up of the Standard Oil Corporation into some thirty companies was accomplished by the decree of the lower court. The actual effect of this decree shows with absolute clearness what would be the effect of the Stanley Committee recommendations if they were ever tried in practice. Nominally the corporations would remain small; really they would all be together in the same big combination. Nothing would have been gained in the way of controlling the trusts, and much would have been lost from the standpoint of the consumer.[12]

After the decree against the Standard Oil and Tobacco Trusts, Wall Street was for a moment alarmed and showed symptoms of coming toward the plan of governmental control and regulation which I had so long been advocating. Even the big crooked trusts thought it would be better to submit, however reluctantly, to such control than to be destroyed. But in a very few weeks it was seen that the decree against them was pure sham and mockery. The trusts at once turned in with enthusiasm to uphold the Department of Justice in its advocacy of the Anti-Trust Law and the Stanley report has been, quite rightly, a subject of mere derision with all trust magnates. The attitude of that portion of the metropolitan press controlled by Wall Street in favor of the old Democratic and Republican party organizations and against the Progressives shows conclusively how well they understand this fact. The words of the Republican and Democratic platforms and the utterances of the candidates who stand on them are at the moment to be tested by the performances respectively of the Department of Justice under Mr. Wickersham and of the Stanley Committee and the attitude of the Wall Street press and especially of those great corporation papers which most faithfully represent the big Trusts, showing how entirely satisfied Wall Street is with the conduct of those managing the Republicans and Democratic politics and how eagerly it will champion either party or both parties, against the Progressives and the Progressive candidate.[13]

12. James C. German, Jr., "The Taft Administration and the Sherman Antitrust Act," *Mid-America* 54 (July 1972): 172–186, provides good background information for these events.

13. George W. Wickersham (1858–1936) was Taft's attorney general. His approach to the Sherman Antitrust Act is analyzed in James Clifford German, Jr., "Taft's Attorney General: George W. Wickersham" (PhD diss., New York University, 1969), 107–200.

The Democratic and Republican platforms uphold the Anti-Trust law as in itself a sufficient panacea, and the one is backed by the action of the Department of Justice and the other by the action of the Stanley Committee of the House of Representatives.[14] The big trusts cordially approve of both platforms; and they approve of the Department of Justice and of the Stanley Committee. They draw no sharp line between the Democratic and the Republican platforms in this matter; they draw no sharp line between the action of the Department of Justice at present and the action proposed by the Stanley Committee. They are entirely satisfied with both the Democratic and the Republican platforms. They are entirely satisfied with the Stanley Committee and with the present Department of Justice. Some of them are supporting the Republican candidate; more of them are supporting the Democratic candidate; for every big financial magnate connected with a crooked trust knows that neither the Democrats nor the Republicans menace him or his interests in the slightest degree, and that they have nothing to fear except from the Progressive Party. The action of these people is well set out in the remarks of Mr. Corey, ex-president of the Steel Trust, in his recent announcement that he intends to support the Democratic Party and their candidate.[15] He and his friends are entirely right in this position. But every honest and farsighted business man, great or small, who wishes to put business on a really satisfactory condition, who believes in the policy of openness, of frankness and fair play with the people of the United States, should stand with us. We propose that there shall be real and effective control over big business organizations, a control which will secure the public in its rights, which will secure fair treatment for the wage-workers, the small competitors and the consumers alike. But we also intend to do absolute justice to the business man himself just so long as he himself does justice, and makes his profit by rendering service to the public while at the same time acting fairly by his employees and his less powerful rivals.

Now, friends, I wish that you would for yourselves carefully and fairly compare the several actions and promises of the Progressive, the Republican and the Democratic parties in this matter. You will find in the first place that we are sincere and that our opponents are obviously insincere. You will find in the next place that we understand what the problem is and that our opponents either do not understand it or deliberately refuse to un-

14. Republican National Committee, *Republican Campaign Text-Book 1912* (Philadelphia: Press of Dunlap Printing Co., 1912), pp. 272–273, 279, gives the language of both platforms.

15. William Ellis Corey (1866–1934) was the president of U.S. Steel.

derstand it. Our opponents' denunciation of the trusts is mere sound and fury. They have no proposals to make for really controlling them; all that they propose, both of them alike, Republicans and Democrats alike, is to continue the policy of make-believe strangle, to continue a policy which leaves the great lawbreaking trusts at liberty to defy the law not only with impunity but with profit, as has just been shown in the case of the Standard Oil and the Tobacco trusts, and yet which keeps every honest business man of moderate means in a condition of perpetual uneasiness lest he has unwittingly violated the law.

Of all the planks of the Progressive platform, and they are all of them good, the two which most go to my heart are the one which deals with the social and industrial justice and the one on country life.[16] Not only the present Republican and Democratic platforms fail in any way to deal with these matters as our platform deals with them, but no platform previous to ours has ever even shown an intelligent understanding of what social and industrial justice was. Our proposals are definite and concrete, and they are absolutely practical. We treat our whole platform as a covenant with the people binding upon ourselves and upon our candidates in State and in Nation. We pledge ourselves to legislation looking to the prevention of industrial accidents and occupational diseases. We intend to deal with the problems of involuntary unemployment and of overwork. We intend to secure compensation for men or women who are killed or crippled in industry; to prohibit sweated labor; to secure a minimum wage standard for working women, and a living wage in all industrial occupations. We pledge ourselves to secure one day's rest in seven for all wageworkers, and an eight-hour day in continuous twenty-four hour industries, the prohibition of night work and the establishment of the eight-hour day for women. We pledge ourselves to the abolition of the convict contract labor system, and the application of prisoners' earning to the support of their dependent families. We recognize in all matters such as these women are as vitally concerned as men. We recognize that there cannot be identity of function, but that there should be equality of right, between men and women, and we are therefore for equal suffrage for men and women.

The *New York Times* of August 20th in an interview attributed to a prominent citizen who has repudiated it, criticised and denounced Jane Addams for nominating me, and also criticised the Progressive Party for permitting women to be in the Progressive Convention. It attacked Miss Ad-

16. Payne, *The Birth of the New Party,* pp. 307–308, 309, has these two planks of the Progressive platform.

dams' conduct as "spectacular" and "in very bad taste," and also criticised me as being spectacular because I had "the bad taste to publicly compliment on her action and thank her."[17]

My only reference to Miss Addams was contained in the following sentence: "I wish to tell those who proposed and seconded my nomination that I appreciate to the full the significance of having such men and such a woman put me in nomination."[18] It will be noticed that in this sentence I did not even mention Miss Addams's name and if President Elliott [*sic*] really considers this allusion to Miss Addams as being spectacular and in bad taste I should feel a mild curiosity to know just what he would regard as non-spectacular and in good taste.

It would not be worthwhile to pay any heed to this article in itself; but it illustrates an attitude of mind sufficiently common to deserve consideration. Among the other sentences in the article were the following: "Women have no proper share in a political convention. We need women to bear children and attend to their homes. The men ought to be able to regulate their own politics and meet all needs without direct assistance of the women."

Of course it is entirely right to say that we need women to bear children and attend to their homes; just as it would be right to say that we need men to beget children and make the homes in which the women live and the children be brought up. One statement is as true as the other and both come under the head of the obvious. I have said not once but a score of times that I put the domestic life above every other kind of life, that I honor the good and wise mother as I honor no other woman and no man, and that the perpetuity of the nation depends primarily upon the average man and the average woman therein being the father and mother of healthy and happy and wisely brought-up children, children trained, boys and girls alike, in industry and decent conduct and to the habit of meeting with wisdom and with high courage the many and difficult problems that confront each of us in his every-day individual life and all of us in our collective life.

I think the highest life, the ideal life, is the married life. But there are both unmarried men and unmarried women who perform service of the

17. Charles William Eliot, the former president of Harvard University, had made the comments about Jane Addams (1860–1935) in the *New York Times* story, which appeared on 21 August. "Criticizes Jane Addams," *New York Times*, 21 August 1912. Addams was the famous social reformer and peace advocate who supported the Progressive Party.

18. Roosevelt said those words when he accepted the Progressive nomination on 7 August 1912. "Roosevelt Named Shows Emotion," *New York Times*, 8 August 1912.

utmost consequence to the whole people and it is equally foolish and wicked for a man to slur the unmarried women when he would not dream of slurring the unmarried man. Bishop Brent in the Philippines is unmarried.[19] He has done admirable work there just as Jane Addams has done at Hull House. When the *Times* says that it dislikes to see Miss Addams "held up in the limelight as an example for all other women to follow," it speaks offensively, and its words are true only in the sense that they would be true if it had used them about Bishop Brent or the late Phillips Brooks.[20] Again and again I have heard Bishop Brent held up as an example, and I have held him up as an example myself and so of the late Phillips Brooks. And in just the same way, I am heartily glad to say, I have heard Jane Addams held up as an example and have thus held her up myself. The cases of the three stand on the same plane: all three by their lives have added to and are adding to our heritage of good in this country, and it is an absurdity to say that in recognizing this fact as regards any one of them we are in any shape or way explicitly or implicitly failing to take the position that we ought as a matter of course to take about marriage and the happy married life.

Now for the statement about women having no proper share in a political convention, and that men ought to be able to regulate their own politics and meet all needs without direct assistance from the women. That man knows little of our political, social and industrial needs as a nation who does not know that in political conventions the politics that ought to be "regulated" are the politics that effect [*sic*] women precisely as much as they effect men; and he must be unfortunate in his list of acquaintances if he does not know women whose advice and counsel are pre-eminently worth having in regard to the matters affecting our welfare which it is of the most consequence to have dealt with by political conventions. I suppose that the trouble is that the *Times* fails to understand that we intend from now on to make participation in "politics" a method of applying ethics to our public life and both ethics and economics to our industrial life. Such a theory of public conduct is wholly incomprehensible both to those who dominated the Republican convention at Chicago and to those who dominated the Democratic convention at Baltimore. The Progressive Party is the one Party which since the War has dealt with real issues, and these real issues affect women precisely as much as men. The women who bear children and attend to their own homes have precisely the same right

19. Charles Henry Brent (1862–1929) was the Episcopal bishop in the Philippines.

20. Phillips Brooks (1835–1893), an Episcopal clergyman, was bishop of Massachusetts when he died. He never married.

to speak in politics that their husbands have who are the fathers of their children and who work to keep up their homes. It is these women who bear children and attend to their homes and these men, their husbands, who work for their wives and children and homes, whom the Progressive Party is endeavoring to represent and in whose interest the Progressive Party proposes that the governmental policy of this nation shall hereafter be shaped. Such being the case it is eminently wise that women should share in the political conventions, and that they should join with the men in regulating the politics, which are in no proper sense only "the politics of the men" as the *Times* says, because they are of vital concern to the women as to the men.

I doubt if there ever was a convention more really representative of the people, and with a higher average of individual character among the representatives, than was the case with the Progressive National Convention at Chicago. The spirit in which it met was a spirit of deep and genuine religious fervor, using the word religious in the broadest and truest sense—a spirit which found expression in singing the Battle Hymn of the Republic, a hymn by the way, which was written by a woman, Mrs. Julia Ward Howe, who as wife and mother, and in all her relations of both public and private life, was one of the best citizens this republic has ever brought forth.[21] I am glad to say that among the representatives in our Convention were a number of women; and not only in high purpose, but in wisdom, in character, in cool headedness and in far sighted understanding of the minds of the nation, they stood on an exactly equal footing with the men. Our National Committee will publish Jane Addams's speech. I ask you to read it for yourselves and then yourselves pass judgment on the good taste and wisdom of the *New York Times* in denouncing that speech. One of the memories of the convention which I shall always cherish is the fact that Jane Addams seconded my nomination.

I grew to believe in Woman Suffrage not because of associating with women whose chief interest was in woman suffrage, but because of finding out that the women from whom I received most aid in endeavoring to grapple with the social and industrial problems of the day were themselves believers in woman suffrage. For a long time I have been interested in such questions as the betterment of tenement house conditions, the abolition of sweat shop factories in tenement houses, the betterment of the conditions of work and life of working girls in industry, the establishment of chil-

21. Julia Ward Howe (1819–1910), author and social reformer, had written "The Battle Hymn of the Republic" during the Civil War.

dren's courts, the establishment of playgrounds, the putting a stop to the employment of children in industry and dozens of other like matters. Now the way I got into touch with each different kind of such work was to get hold of some man or woman who knew about it and could guide and instruct me and enable me to see for myself what the facts were. The man to whom I owe most in this matter is Jacob Riis, and I shall never forget all he did for me during the time I was Police Commissioner.[22] In exactly the same fashion I have profited by the teachings and experience of Judge Ben Lindsey of Colorado, of Judge De Lacey of Washington, of Charles Stelzle, of Father Curran, of Homer Folks, of Paul Kellogg, of Mannis [Mannes], of Raymond Robbins, of Weyl and McCarthy and Kingsbury,[23] of many many men connected with the work of organized charity and with private or religious charity, and of many clergymen, priests and rabbis—I cannot begin to enumerate all of them. Well, in precisely the same way I grew acquainted with women who were doing the same kinds of work, with Miss Addams, with Miss Kellor, with Mrs. Kelly[24] with many others. I talked to them and worked with them just as I did with the men. I found that they had the same zeal and earnestness and judgment that the men had, and differed among themselves just as the men did. I found that as a result of their actual experience they felt that working girls would be helped by suffrage just as working men are helped, and that in our warfare against certain dreadful evils of our social life the help of the women

22. Jacob Riis (1849–1914), author and social reformer, had known Roosevelt since the 1890s. He became famous for his book *How the Other Half Lives* (1890), which depicted urban poverty.

23. Benjamin Barr Lindsey (1869–1943) was the judge of the juvenile court in Denver, which he had founded in 1900. He was a fervent supporter of the Progressives in 1912. William H. De Lacy had been named judge of the juvenile court in Washington, D.C., by Roosevelt in 1906. Charles Stelzle (1869–1941) was a union machinist who became a Presbyterian minister and advocate of the Social Gospel. He wrote about the problems of the urban poor. Homer Folks (1867–1963) was president of the New York State Probation Commission and a leading opponent of child labor. Paul Underwood Kellogg (1879–1958), a social reformer, edited *Survey* magazine. He had studied in depth industrial life in Pittsburgh, Pennsylvania. David Mannes (1866–1959), an American violinist, founded a music school for African-American children in New York City. Raymond Robins (1873–1954), a writer and social reformer, was active in Illinois politics at the time and a supporter of Roosevelt's candidacy. Walter Weyl (1873–1919) published *The New Democracy* (1912) and wrote extensively on social problems. Charles McCarthy (1873–1921) was the director of the Legislative Reference Library in Wisconsin. Although he publicized Robert M. La Follette Sr., a senator from Wisconsin, in his book *The Wisconsin Idea* (1912), McCarthy supported Roosevelt for the presidency. John Adams Kingsbury (1876–1956) was active in addressing the condition of the poor in New York City.

24. Frances Allen Kellor (1873–1952) served with the Bureau of Industries and Immigration, which she had helped to create, from 1910 until she resigned to join Roosevelt's campaign. Florence Kelley (1859–1932) was affiliated with the Consumers Union and had been a major figure in social reform for two decades.

would be of particular value. Very much of what I learned to believe from them they were quite unconscious of having taught me, and it was this largely unconscious teaching of theirs and my study of what had been done in the states where suffrage exists that gradually turned me into a believer that women should have the same right to vote that men have. I do not believe that there is identity of function between men and women, but I do believe there should be equality of right. I see no reason why voting should interfere with women's home life any more than it interferes with the every day work of the man which enables him to support the home.

Typed manuscript, Roosevelt Papers, Library of Congress; "How Women Won Roosevelt to Them," *New York Times*, 31 August 1912, indicates that Roosevelt followed the text in his remarks.

After speaking in Vermont, Roosevelt spent the next two days in Connecticut in rainy, cold weather with speeches to large and enthusiastic crowds. Reporters noted that the audiences paid close attention to Roosevelt's remarks. His speech at Hartford was delivered in what the New York Times *called "a hard rain."*[25]

A Speech at Hartford, Connecticut, 2 September 1912

My friends and fellow Americans, men and women of Connecticut, it gives me great pleasure to be here at your fair and I am only sorry that you should have to suffer so from the weather, but I am glad, at least, that progressives never suffer from cold feet. I have come to ask the support of Connecticut for the progressive platform and I appreciate the greeting you have given me, but this is not a personal fight; if it was only for me, I wouldn't be in it. I am in this simply as your instrument, the person chosen to stand for your principles. Take a man and use him as your instrument, break him if necessary and throw him aside then and you won't hear any complaining from me. This movement is an effort to bring the government back to the people. Most men will agree that the people ought to be governed but they are not so ready to say that the government should be by the people and for the people.

Q. "Why didn't you advocate this seven years ago?"

25. "Crowds Brave Rain To Hear Roosevelt," *New York Times*, 3 September 1912.

Why bless you I did, and I am delighted to find that you have awakened to the fact that I am doing it now. Pretty soon you will come over on our side.[26]

I noticed recently that the *Hartford Courant,* of blessed memory, has recently accused me of "scuttling the ship," of trying to wreck the Republican party. As a matter of fact the *Courant* and its allies caused the scuttling at Chicago last June. They made a pirate ship of the party and it had to be scuttled. Suppose any ship in the United States navy should hoist the black flag and skull and crossbones what else could be done with it but to sink it?

We are trying to hold to the principles of Lincoln and his colleagues. Can you imagine Lincoln, if he were alive today, allied with Penrose and Barnes and Guggenheim? What we are attempting to do is to apply the principles of Lincoln to present day issues and thus to meet the issues of today and of the days to come. A friend of mine once said that he did not care much whether a man stood so long as he was going in the right direction, and we are trying to go in the right direction; some of us farther along than others but all of us are headed the right way.

I invite your special attention to the fact that both the old parties are arrayed against us, while non-partisan Wall Street is ready to aid the one which can make the most headway against the progressives. There are some good respectable and well meaning men too, opposed to us. I notice that Jacob Schiff according to the *New York Times* has just declared that he shall vote for Wilson and urges others to although he says that he has been a life-long republican.[27] He says a vote for Taft will be a vote thrown away, and I agree with him there, and then he goes on to say that the only way to perpetuate the republican party is to elect Wilson.

He knows it is impossible to elect Taft, but he hopes to see Wilson elected and to keep up the old see-saw between the two parties, both supporting whatever Wall Street is willing to stand for. The same attitude has been shown in the Penrose and Archbold testimony, and a precious pair they are! Mr. Archbold, in a burst of reminiscent agony, told of the horrible treatment he received at the hands of the Roosevelt administration. I thought the Standard Oil Company stood in need of such treatment, and if

26. According to the *New York Times,* what Roosevelt said at this point was, "The answer to that is that I did advocate it seven years ago. I am glad that we have got you along in your slow procession to where you know we advocate it now. You'll be with us before you know it." "Crowds Brave Rain to Hear Roosevelt," *New York Times,* 3 September 1912.

27. Jacob Schiff (1847–1920), a prominent German-American banker with Kuhn, Loeb & Co., had declared for Wilson in mid-August. See Naomi W. Cohen, *Jacob H. Schiff: A Study in American Jewish Leadership* (Hanover, N.H.: Brandeis University Press, 1999), p. 151.

I ever have the chance it will get it again. Men like Penrose and corporations like the Standard Oil Company are quite right in taking the attitude they do. They are willing to see either of the old parties win, but they do not want to see the progressives triumph, because you are really the people they are afraid of. They know if we get the government back to the people the day of bosses and special privilege will be at an end. We may make mistakes if we come into power, but we shall not make the same mistake twice.

I wish you would look at the old platforms and compare them with the progressive. I want to say here that every promise we make will be made good and if any office holder fails to live up to the platform I will take the stump against him myself. I am sick and tired of platforms that are simply rhetorical efforts.

Now, at this fair, I want to say a word to the farmers concerning our platform and its effect upon them. We have proposed a definite course of action. When I went to Europe I was unpleasantly surprised to find that the old monarchies of Europe were in advance of us in dealing with the farmers and to find that the farmers in Germany and Denmark were better organized and cared for by the government than ours. Our purpose is to adapt the methods of Germany and Denmark, with such modifications as may be necessary, to our conditions. Again, we declare for the parcels post bill, and if I am elected we are going to have it. If I were President and Congress failed to pass a parcels post bill I would call it back until it did. We have made definite promises and I feel that they are to be kept as an honorable business man would keep his pledges.[28]

Our platform favors efficient control of the issuance of securities. The post office department reports that over $170,000,000 is lost to the people through fake financial promotions. We favor a blue sky law on the lines of the Kansas enactment, which will protect the people. Again, one of the chief causes of the high cost of living is the fact that farm products have to pay three or four profits between the producer and the consumer. Denmark avoids this to a large extent and we can do it here.

Q. How would you do it?

Our purpose is to regulate the farmers for cooperation in selling and secure government control of market places and railway terminals so that the products of the farm may pass from the farmer to the consumer without paying two or three profits while on the way.

28. Parcel post or parcels post was a program for having the post office deliver packages to rural areas without charge. Private express companies and merchants in rural areas, who previously had handled mail, opposed the change. Congress adopted legislation to put the service into effect on 1 January 1913 through the Parcel Post Act.

I want to see the government engaged in aiding all the people governed. Our forefathers builded better than they knew when they dotted the land with school houses. I want to see these school houses used all the time, not standing idle when school is not in session as they do now. I want to see them used as polling stations, where men exercise their highest rights as citizens. Is it not just as seemly to cast a vote in a schoolhouse as in a shed or a barber shop or a saloon? I would open them for political meetings for any party, where arguments may be made to enlighten the voters. It would tremendously reduce campaign expenses if this were done and everything which will reduce the expenses of political campaigns will be a good thing for the country. At first blush this plan may strike you as revolutionary, but it already has been tried out and has worked well. We can make each school house a senate chamber of the plain people and the people need what information they can get.[29]

I wish the newspapers would tell the truth; I don't care what they say in their editorial columns if they would only give the news. Until the time when they do we need every opportunity to bring the truth before the people. I wish to speak a moment, and I think you are awfully good to stand here in the rain and listen, on another matter. I see here before me some men who fought in the Civil War, in the great war. I took part in a little war myself. It was a small one, but it was all the war there was. The men of fifty years ago won imperishable glory for themselves and our boundless gratitude because they faced and directly faced, the issues of their day. If they had contented themselves with fine speeches about the valor of Washington's Continentals we should not have put down the rebellion in a hurry. Let us face our issues as they did and as fearlessly as they did. This can't be a good government for some of us until it is a just government for all of us.

I recently received a letter signed by various socialists in this city who said, among other things, that the progressive party has taken some of the planks from the socialist platform. I answered the most of that letter at Bridgeport, but I want to say that if anything is right I am for it and I don't care who backs it up.[30] I have no use at all for some socialists—for those who hate a big man because he is big. What I want to see is love for the little man and help to make him big. If a man has given up his life to social service and has been just in his dealings, I honor him for it. If he has been

29. For more on this issue, see "The Political Use of School Buildings," *Outlook*, 102 (14 September 1912): 51–52.

30. "Crowds Brave Rain to Hear Roosevelt," *New York Times*, 3 September 1912, discusses the letter from the socialists and his response.

unjust and has oppressed his employees, I will help pull him down, not because he is big but because he is crooked.

I am opposed to some of the socialists, to those who preach hatred, but there are many who see existing evils and who are trying to find a solution for them. Their trouble is that they are trying to take about 200 steps at once. I am in favor of taking two or three now and then, perhaps we shall see our way clear to taking two or three more when we can meet the next needs.

We advocate an eight hour day for women and minors. The reason why I became interested in woman suffrage [is] because I had seen the treatment which unorganized women and girls were accorded in some establishments by employers who did not have their consciences aided by outside help. We have declared for one day's rest in seven for men engaged in continuous employments those which go on twenty-four hours a day, seven days in the week and fifty two weeks in the year. I am no believer in idleness whether it is practiced by the hobo or the son of a multi-millionaire, but the man or woman who works too hard has his or her life crushed out just as sure as the pursuit of idleness crushes out the soul. I believe in pleasure, I have had a good deal of it in my day, but I think it ought to be a by-product. I have no idea of promising the millennium because, after all the laws which human wisdom can devise have been passed, the success of the individual must depend greatly upon himself. Our purpose is only to give the ordinary man and woman a better chance to make good.

One law which we propose may not strike you as of so much importance as it does me. It provides that a man in prison shall have his earning there go to the support of his family if he has one. When I was a police commissioner I often came across some brute of a wife-beater who was sent to jail where he was well fed while his family was starving. I want to have such men working so that their families will be cared for and I think that's pretty practical.

We want a workmen's compensation act, and when I say we want it and propose to have it I do not mean that if it is declared unconstitutional by the courts we shall content ourselves by saying we are sorry. The constitution belongs to you. Your fathers made it and fashioned it and why should not you say whether it is or is not now just and adapted to your needs? Take it in New York; we have had a compensation act, an act limiting the hours of labor and safeguarding dangerous employments, all declared unconstitutional by judges who know more about the law than they do about men. I contend that in a case of that sort the people should have a chance to vote on the law and say whether or not it is just.

I have lived among men myself; on the ranch we used to go to market with a trainload of cattle and, when the train stopped, go along and punch up the steers that were lying down. Then we would get on the car nearest the engine and worked our way back on the roofs of the car to the caboose. I know the danger when the weather is cold and snowy, and yet a judge once told me that if a brakeman fell off it was his fault. I know one case, a brakeman with a wife and two or three kids, who was getting on well until he fell from a train and lost both legs. The next winter his wife, I found, could not leave the house because she had no shoes to wear. This condition of things is unjust and I contend that the state of New York has a right to a law like that of Iowa or Washington or Massachusetts.

I feel that we have the right to ask you in Connecticut to be with us in this fight. Every crook and every boss, including the bosses in your own state, is against us. Let us stand for the people, not a part of the people but for all the people.

Typescript in Roosevelt Papers.

3

Campaigning in the Middle West

After concluding his campaign swing through New England, Roosevelt embarked on his nationwide tour. During the first two weeks of September, he stumped through the Middle West. He addressed conventions of the Progressive Party where his supporters were selecting candidates for state offices. At the same time, he and Woodrow Wilson began their exchange of charges and countercharges about the tariff, trusts, and social justice legislation. Roosevelt opened this part of his White House run with a speech to the Missouri Progressives in St. Louis on 3 September.

Remarks to the Progressive State Convention, St. Louis, Missouri, 3 September 1912

Yesterday Mr. Wilson alluding to the third party platform asked, "With that programme who can differ in his heart, who can divorce himself in sympathy from the great object of advancing interest of human beings wherever it is possible to advance them."[1]

I am very glad that Mr. Wilson should be with us in his heart, but if his party sympathizes with us in its heart why didn't they in their platform make a programme at least remotely resembling ours? Our sympathy for the programme is not only with our hearts—it is with our heads and our hands, also.

When he comes to the tariff Mr. Wilson attempts to quote me, but he is

1. For Wilson's remark, see "A Labor Day Address in Buffalo," 2 September 1912, in Arthur S. Link, et al., eds., *The Papers of Woodrow Wilson, Volume 25, 1912* (Princeton, N.J.: Princeton University Press, 1978), p. 71.

singularly unsuccessful. He states, for instance, that I am not concerned with the general interest of the taxpayer or the general public. If he would take the trouble to read what I have said or to read our platform he would find that the commission principle which we propose and to which he and his party are hostile has for one of its special objects the careful consideration of the needs of the general public.

We are advocating the commission system which has been tried in Germany and which has been one of the pieces of governmental and industrial mechanism that has been so extraordinarily successful in building up the great prosperity of the German empire.

I believe in protection. I believe that if Mr. Wilson's free trade policy or tariff for revenue policy is in good faith adopted and not merely treated as a campaign cry, widespread disaster could result to American life.

But, I do not for a moment believe that a protective tariff by itself offers in any way or shape the solution for the economic and social injustice against which the progressives are striving.

Let Mr. Wilson study what has happened to industry in England and in Germany during the last forty years. During that forty years England has been under a free trade system, and Germany has adopted a high tariff system. During that forty years the conditions of labor have grown worse in England and better in Germany. Germany has advanced relatively to England all along the line, and especially in the standing of her people.

As to what Mr. Wilson says about the minimum wage I can only say that I disagree with him in toto. We are only advocating what we are sure can be done and ought to be done. Evidently Mr. Wilson has not studied the conditions about the labor of women in many factories in big cities.[2]

Mr. Wilson comes squarely against our proposal to regulate the trusts. He has not anything to put in its place except a statement that he stands by the great democratic thinkers who have made the democratic platform on this subject.

Mr. Wilson is now governor of New Jersey and has been such for nearly two years. If the Baltimore platform really offers any hope for the trust solution why during these two years has nothing whatever been done by New Jersey under Mr. Wilson's lead or even attempted by Mr. Wilson in New Jersey for the regulation of trusts? The answer is because the states by themselves cannot meet the difficulty, and it is pure toryism of the most

2. Wilson criticized the Progressive proposal for a minimum wage because, he said, it would lower wages as employers reduced wages to approach that level. Ibid., p. 72.

backward kind to suppose that they can; and incidentally any such policy would have the grinning support of every lawbreaking trust.

Mr. Wilson seems to forget that part of my programme is to give the people themselves direct control over their government, that is, put them over the governmental system and their agents of government. When the people themselves thus effectively control their own government and the government in its turn controls the big corporations it seems to me the veriest folly of fear to express apprehension lest under such a system the chief employers, as Mr. Wilson says, because they have "this tremendous authority behind them" may oppress the wage workers.[3] We have a genuine constructive policy. Mr. Wilson's plan as far as I can gather is merely to continue the present futile system, adding fresh and empty protestations of hostility to the trusts, but giving no hint as to any method by which these protestations can become more than protestations. We must supplement the anti-trust law by the kind of real and efficient governmental control advocated in the progressive national platform or we will not have made even one step toward solving the trust question.

Des Moines Register and Leader, 4 September 1912. A similar version of Roosevelt's remarks appeared in the Duluth *News Tribune,* 4 September 1912.

A Speech to the Iowa Progressive State Convention, Des Moines, 4 September 1912

Mr. Chairman, and you, my fellow citizens, fellow progressives, men and women of Iowa: I am glad indeed to have the chance of coming to this convention, and I come less to speak to you than to learn from you and get inspiration from you, for, friends, I have long looked to Iowa for leadership. I have long held up Iowa as an example to my own state of New York, as an example to the rest of the country. And now, friends, I should feel very sorry indeed if I felt that Iowa was not to give us leadership in this great crisis of our national affairs, and I am more pleased than I can say that you have nominated my friend Judge Stevens here, and that you are going to make a straight out fight for a new progressive party.[4]

I feel that we have the right in this contest to appeal for the support of every good citizen without regard to his former political affiliations, with-

3. I have not been able to locate this Wilson quotation.

4. John Loomis Stevens (1850–1933) was the Progressive candidate for governor of Iowa.

out regard to his birthplace or his creed if he is a straight out American, if he believes in the elementary principles which lie at the basis of decent American citizenship.

Friends, I appeal to you for your support, I appeal to this great state for its support not only because of that for which we stand, but because of what the forces are that are behind our opponents in this contest. And remember it is only nominally a three party contest. In reality it is between the party of the people on one side and on the other side the bosses, the representatives of privilege who will throw their weight for whichever of the old parties they think is the best instrument with which to beat us.

As a matter of fact I believe that you will find long before election day what there are already symptoms of, that the republican party is swept completely aside, that the fight is between us, between the progressives and the machine democracy. And I feel that the situation warrants us in appealing to every former republican who is a progressive, and I mean by that to every former republican who is loyal to the principles of Abraham Lincoln, to come with us, and to every former democrat who is loyal to the principles of Thomas Jefferson and Andrew Jackson to come with us.

And now a word first to the former members of the republican party. The official republican party of today bears to the party of Abraham Lincoln the same resemblance that a ship that has been captured by a gang of pirates does to the ship before it was captured. In the June convention at Chicago, the republican national convention, the bosses stole the machinery away from the people and friends, I speedily found that there was no point to which they were not willing to go in order to prevent my nomination and the reason was not so much that they disliked me, although they did, but because they dreaded you; you are the people of whom they were afraid. You men and women here and those like you throughout this country, you are the people of whom the Penroses, Barneses and Guggenheims stood in dread and they were willing to scuttle the republican ship rather than to see it pass under your control and the reason is simple.

These men I have named—Penrose, Barnes, Guggenheim, Crane and the rest of them—they care nothing for republican principles; they would not have known what they meant if they had met them or heard of them that prompted these men on the historic day when the Republican party was born.[5] Imagine them upholding the hands of Abraham Lincoln. They took no thought or care for the principles the party was founded to main-

5. Winthrop Murray Crane (1853–1920) was in his second term as a Republican senator from Massachusetts. He was a close political adviser of President William Howard Taft.

tain. Their interest was to perpetuate their own grasp and perpetuate their own rule, and perpetuate also the day of the great special interests that stand for privilege in business as well as privilege in politics.

These men were fighting for their political lives. They did not care for the success of the republican party unless it meant their own political and financial success. They represented the crooked alliance between crooked politics and crooked business which has been the curse of American political life and they cared nothing for the welfare of the party when weighted in the balance against their own desires. They were perfectly willing to see the party defeated if they could keep their grip on the party machinery. They didn't care. They expected to see democracy go into power and they thought they would retain control of the party machinery and that you would find it wise to put the other set of bosses in power, and then after four years of that would put them in power again.

There is nothing that these men so much desired as for the average man who revolts against crookedness to make his revolt take the shape of punishing the set of bosses which the day after tomorrow he will equally dislike. Of course each set would prefer to take the government all the time, but they know they can't do that so they are content to keep it jointedly all the time. That is half of them at one time and half of them at the other and nothing is gained by changing the whips of Penrose, Barnes and Guggenheim for the scorpions of Murphy, Taggart and Sullivan.[6]

All bosses look alike to us and we stand against them all and that is the reason why they make common cause against us and you will find that every great political boss in the country, every great crooked business and every great crooked representative of crooked business will stand against us and support either party which they think has the best chance of beating us. I believe, progressive men who have been republicans, I believe that you cannot as honest men help coming with us and in politics the most important of all the commandments is, "Thou shalt not steal," and woe to the man who practices or profits by or condones theft.

I see that Mr., what is his name, the congressman from St. Louis, Bartholdt, who was one of the highwaymen, has asked Senator Cummins to debate the Texas, Washington, Arizona, and California cases with him.[7]

6. Charles Francis Murphy (1858–1924) was the Democratic leader of Tammany Hall in New York City.

7. Richard Bartholdt (1855–1932) was a conservative Republican congressman from Missouri who served on the Republican National Committee. He was a staunch defender of Taft during the seating of the disputed delegates at the national convention. The four states Roosevelt mentioned were the most contested ones at the convention and the Roosevelt forces had identified them as the clearest ex-

I hope the senator will refuse, for this reason. I won't debate with a pickpocket the ownership of my watch. If the police are handy I will turn him over to them and if they are not I will attend to him myself, but I won't go into a joint debate with him. There is not any more room for debate as to the action of the committee of which Mr. Bartholdt was a conspicuous part last June, and I mean that literally, there is no more room for debate than there is for debate of the average offender who has just been sentenced in one of the minor criminal courts here in your city or in mine.

Unfortunately, what they did was in a convention which has no standing before the law, so there was no action under the law that could be taken against them, but the exact truth was stated by Frank Heney who was counsel in those great cases in San Francisco, when, after the committee at Chicago perpetrated some unusually frank bit of scoundrelism, Heney came up and said, "Why, we sent Abe Ruef up for twenty years for doing less than you gentlemen have just done."[8]

I wish to state this as emphatically as I can that any man who, with knowledge of the facts or who is in such a position that he ought to have knowledge of the facts, by that I mean any congressman, any senator, any man, any candidate for governor who supports Mr. Taft after the way the nomination was obtained, gives us a legitimate right to say that he is not competent to pass judgment on honesty in public life. And that is why, as far as I am concerned, I will not take part backing any man who now supports what was done in the Chicago convention, for I believe that such a man is sinning against the cardinal principles of American political life.

I want to say a few words to men who were formerly democrats, to the progressive democrats, as to why they should come to us too. In the first place I call your attention to this great difference between Baltimore and Chicago. The victory for Mr. Wilson at Baltimore was achieved because the bosses finally concluded that they would name him because his victory would mean theirs. The result in Chicago was determined because the bosses had been taught by the preceding four months' campaign that our victory meant their defeat. If democracy is successful in the national campaign it means that every boss in the democratic party will be entrenched in power in his state. If democracy is successful in this campaign it means that the powers that prey on business, that the representatives and benefici-

amples of fraudulent behavior on the part of the Taft supporters. Albert Baird Cummins (1850–1926) was a progressive Republican senator from Iowa who endorsed Roosevelt for the presidency but did not leave the party.

8. Francis J. Heney (1859–1937), a close friend of Roosevelt, had prosecuted graft cases in San Francisco. His main target was the "boss" of city politics, Abe Ruef (1864–1936).

aries of privilege will feel that they have another lease on life granted them. It means precisely that.

Now friends, I ask you to accept on that my point not on my say so, but the unwitting testimony of the beneficiaries of privilege themselves. Some of the men in Wall street who represent privilege and plenty of them are entirely respectable men who think they are doing what is right, but they are blinded by their surroundings and training, but I have no question that they mean as well as anybody else. These men, their feelings were given expression the other day by Mr. Jacob Schiff, who has done some good philanthropic work. He has been a republican all his life. The other day he came out for Mr. Wilson, for the democratic party and his reason interested me greatly and it ought to interest more the progressive democrats, every independent citizen, no matter what his political affiliations, who believes that the time has come to shut off both of the old time political machines.

Mr. Schiff said he was going to vote for Mr. Wilson—I am now giving his opinion as given in the *New York Times,* a pro-Wilson paper, which I presume is speaking correctly, on that point—Mr. Schiff said that he wanted everybody, all his friends, to support Wilson because it was the only way of beating me. That is, if they divided their votes and some of them went to Taft the idea was that then I might get in. They could not afford to throw votes to Taft, they must all rally to Wilson and then followed the very curious statement which at first I could not understand but finally I did understand it. He said that the only way to perpetuate the republican party was to elect Mr. Wilson.

At first I could not grasp what he meant. Then I saw of course what he meant was that the alternative of electing Wilson was electing the progressives and if the progressives came to power both of the old parties would be goners, that would definitely establish that the people should have the power to rule themselves, whereas what he wants is what he thinks would be obtained by the election of Mr. Wilson, that is that the progressives having failed would be eliminated and Mr. Schiff would come back to what he likes, which is the see-saw between the old political machines, each one dominated by the same type of beneficiary.

In other words, every machine man of both parties will give their support to either of the old parties that they think can beat us. Every machine man and every big boss man who represents crooked business, who represents a business that fears the law, will do whatever is necessary in order to secure the triumph of the old parties, they don't care which, so long as they can beat the one party that really represents the people, because the only party they are afraid of is the people's party. They can get along with the bosses perfectly well and whether they are democratic or republican bosses it is the same thing to them.

They will get along with the bosses, they can't get along with the people, they can't get on where the people really rule themselves.

And that idea of Mr. Schiff's I find everywhere. For instance, just today Judge Stevens was telling me of an old standpat machine politician of the steam-roller type here in Iowa who had said to him the other day that "I am going to vote for Wilson. I am going to throw the lever clean over, I am going to beat the progressives anyway."

Now where Mr. Wilson is getting that kind of support, where the democratic party has to rely for its chance of victory upon the support of these men we have a right to ask every independent democrat, every progressive democrat, every man who has believed in the principles for which the democracy nominally stood to come with us and join with us in a new movement, in a new party, a real party, a party which is emphatically the party of social and industrial justice, a party which is emphatically a party of the people themselves.

Now, friends, I want to call your attention again to some testimony given a week last Friday and Saturday by Senator Penrose of Pennsylvania and Mr. Archbold and one or two or three of the moving spirits in the Standard Oil trust, testified before the senatorial committee. They testified on Friday and Saturday. On Saturday I telegraphed requesting to be heard on Monday myself. Senator Clapp, the vice chairman of the committee, stayed in Washington, but every standpat senator, democrat and republican, all of them scattered to the four winds of heaven; and Mr. Archbold went to Europe and it was announced to me that I could be heard a month or two later on.

So I wrote a letter to Senator Clapp which he published.[9] In this I went over the matters which Mr. Archbold and Mr. Penrose had testified to in detail. But what I want to call your attention to now in their testimony is this: Mr. Archbold said at one point what he thought of me and these words you will find on page 123 of the printed testimony. He said: "Darkest Abyssinia has nothing to show compared to the treatment given to the Standard Oil people during the Roosevelt administration."

He was quite right. I did give it the Abyssinian treatment because I thought it needed it, and if I ever get into power again and the Standard Oil does not reform its ways I will give it the Abyssinian treatment again.

9. Roosevelt to Moses E. Clapp, 28 August 1912, in Elting E. Morison, et al., eds., *The Letters of Theodore Roosevelt* (8 vols., Cambridge: Harvard University Press, 1951–1954), 7:602–625.

I will try to administer the Abyssinian on Senator Penrose too, and Mr. Archbold knows that and that is why he appeared and testified. He didn't complain he had had any Abyssinian treatment under the present administration. The stock went up 20 or 30 points and so did the price of oil and gasoline and so on.

He has no fear of Abyssinian treatment under either of the old parties if they come into power again—perfectly indifferent to that. His fear is of the progressive party and of me merely because I happen at the moment to stand as the representative of the progressive party. If I had not accepted the progressive nomination you would never have heard a word from Mr. Archbold or Mr. Penrose and I want to call your attention again to the testimony in so far as it affects themselves. In so far as it affected me it was really not directed against me but against a dead man. They testified that the dead man had tried to blackmail them and that the dead man said I knew of it. They waited seven years during which the dead man was alive and never ventured to bring an accusation against him. He is dead now and they bring it.[10]

I need not say I do not believe their testimony as far as Mr. Bliss is concerned or their testimony so far as it concerns me, through the testimony against the dead man, but it was very interesting testimony so far as it affected themselves.

The curious shamelessness of the two men was what interested me. Mr. Penrose testified that he had advised the Standard Oil to make a heavy contribution for fear it would incur hostility in high quarters. He must have meant in the administration, by me. I could not be hostile to the Standard Oil as long as the Standard Oil behaved itself. If Standard Oil obeyed the law I could not do anything to it.

Standard Oil had no more reason to fear me as long as it obeyed the law than any of you have to fear a policeman as long as you don't do something for which he can arrest you. If you find a man paying something to a policeman and another man advising him to pay for fear he will incur the policeman's ill will, you can make up your mind he has done something shady. Isn't that so? Exactly. It was the same way with Penrose and Archbold and, mind you, Penrose, a United States senator, testified to that about himself. If in a police investigation you found a policeman against whom it was proved that he had advised a law breaking liquor seller or gambler to pay blackmail because he feared he would incur hostility high

10. The dead man to whom Roosevelt referred was Cornelius N. Bliss (1833–1911), who served as treasurer of the Republican presidential campaign in 1904.

up, if you found that policeman had given such testimony, you would have him turned off the force, and when a United States senator bears such testimony against himself he ought to be thrown out of the United States senate.

And Archbold's complaint was what? Archbold's complaint was not that he had been blackmailed, he didn't complain about that, it was that having paid money improperly for an improper reason to get an improper favor, he had not got the goods. He testified of Cornelius Bliss that he went to him when he began to administer the Abyssinian treatment and asked Bliss to interfere, and that Bliss said to him, "I have no influence with Mr. Roosevelt. I can't help you in any way."

Now I have no doubt that testimony was partially true. It is more, I will say, than some of the other testimony. It is not true that Mr. Bliss did not have influence with me. He had a great deal. I had a very high regard for him and any proper question upon which Mr. Bliss came to me I would listen to him with the utmost respect. I would have paid the utmost heed to his opinion, but neither Mr. Bliss nor any other human being could have had or ever attempted to exercise any influence over me when the question was of treating an offender against the law, corporation or individual, as the offense warranted.

And Mr. Archbold and Penrose testify as they do at this time because they hope to defeat, not me personally, but the progressive party of which it happens that for the moment I am chosen as leader. They testify because they want to help both or either of the old parties and their concern is to see the progressive party beaten. Friends, when the Archbolds of finance and the Penroses of politics act in that nonpartisan way in favor of either or both of the old parties and against the progressives we have the right to ask the plain every day citizen, the ordinary decent American without regard to what his political affiliation may have been in the past to come with us because we are the only party organized which offers to the people the chance of permanently and definitely relieving themselves of the control of the Penroses and the Archbolds in our political and business life.

I want to take up for one moment just one or two of the accusations made against me—I can't take them all up because there are too many. They have spoken as if this was a party whose only object was to elect me, as if I somehow engineered it to gratify my personal ambition.

Friends, if this was a one man party I would not be in it, I would not have anything to do with it, if the only object was to elect one man, me or any one else, I would not touch it. I would not be concerned with it or be supporting it. I am standing for this party because it has formulated the principles in which I believe with all my heart and soul.

I believe in the very strongest fashion that in this contest the people must treat every public man the same as an instrument to be used in achieving the purposes of the people. You use the instrument that is most useful at the time, when the instrument gets useless, throw it to the one side, when a better instrument offers itself take the better instrument, and if a man is worth his salt he will never complain. If a man is worth his salt he will feel that in this cause the reward is ample to spend and be spent in the service of the cause itself.

I never had, I never knew and I never shall have one ounce of power that you, the people, do not give me. I never had it while I was president. People have said I was a dictator while I was president, but if I dictated, to whom I would like to know. Not to you. Not for a moment. And I did not dictate to senator or congressman who represented the people because I could not. The only people I ever dictated to were the men who did not represent the people, and the only way I dictated to them was to go over their heads to the people behind them. Then if I could convince the people that my stand was the right stand they did the dictating themselves. And I ask you to look at who the men are who are afraid of the dictatorship. Mr. Penrose, Mr. Archbold, Mr. Barnes, that is the crew, they are the men who are afraid of the dictatorship, afraid of me, only as I represent you. Why, friends, I could have got these men simply by raising my little finger. All I would have to do would be to make them convinced that I would go their way, that I would leave you and they would turn with whoops of delight.

They object to me because I represent you. They object to me, as I say, they don't like me. I don't blame them for that. That is not the real reason they don't like their privileges interfered with. They object to me because they dread you, because they do not wish to see you able to exercise your honest ability to make the weight of your opinion felt in our governmental life and that is all. Dictation—it is exactly like the statement that I acted in an unconstitutional manner.

With your permission I will give you just two anecdotes to show you what they mean by my acting in an unconstitutional manner. There are veterans here, men who fought in the great war—you say 300, and you are fighting again in the great cause of righteousness.

I was in the Spanish war, it was a little war but it was all the war there was. And I had a regiment down here and after the first fight in Cuba we got short of food, there was a break in the commissary, we had nothing but salt pork and hardtack and not much of that. So I thought I would get some more, and I heard they were landing supplies at siberly [Siboney?]. And I took forty of my men and marched them down there and when we got there the supplies were being landed higgledy-piggledy on the beach.

I hunted up the commissary officer and told him I needed supplies and he asked me what I wanted and I asked him what he had got. He told me to look around. I looked about and pretty soon I found a lot of sacks of beans, about 1,100 pounds of beans, and I asked him to send them down and he wanted to know how many and I told him I wanted 1,100 pounds of beans. He picked out a little book and showed me the section 3, division 7, subdivision X, or whatever it was, which said you could only have beans for the officers' mess. Well, I told him, my officers and men are all alike when they came down to hard tack. He said he was very sorry and I told him he was not as sorry as I was. He said he could not give them to me—he would have to refer me to Washington—that would have taken about two months, and two months is a long time between meals.

I said no, and I went back and thought it over and then I came back with a requisition and I made a requisition of 1,100 pounds of beans for the officers' mess and he looked at me and said, "Colonel, your officers won't eat 1,100 pounds of beans," and I says, "You don't know what appetites they have." "Well," he said, "the department will take that out of your pay." I said, "I guess it will." Finally, he said, "I think I will have to send that requisition to Washington," and I said, "All right, but you give me the beans."

So finally, we established a working compromise, he got the requisition and I got the beans. By the technical letter of the law I had no right to do that, but the spirit of the law was that I should keep my men fed when they were doing Uncle Sam's work and I will appeal to every veteran here and I know they will say I would not have been fit to be colonel if I had not seen that my men—I never mollycoddled them, made them work—if I had not seen that they had the best there was coming, if I could get it for them.

In the same way when I was president if I had found that Uncle Sam needed 1,100 pounds of beans I would have got them for him. Take for a moment the Panama canal and at present everybody is, I think, pretty glad we got that canal, but during the time when I got it a considerable section of the people said I ought to have been impeached for it. What happened was this: When I became president I found that negotiations had been going on with great decorum at Washington about the Panama canal as they had been going on for twenty years.

The Spaniards had discovered the isthmus four centuries before and they had said what a nice thing it would be to dig a canal and there had been four centuries of conversation on the subject, and I thought the time had come to reduce it to action. I did my level best to get Colombia to allow us to dig it not only justly but more than generously and then finally made up my mind they would not do it and that they intended to hold Uncle Sam up and I think Uncle Sam is a bad man to hold up and so I had two courses of action open.

One was to send a masterly report on the subject to congress. If I had done that congress would have held a series of able debates on the masterly report and we would have had half a century of more conversation and the canal would have been fifty years in the future now.

Well, I didn't do it. I took the isthmus and started the canal and then had congress debate me instead of the canal. It would have hurt a great deal to have had them debate the canal, whereas it didn't hurt anybody to have them debate me and the debate about me goes fitfully on, and I see no signs of its ending until long after I am dead and the canal will be finished year after next. There again we had a working compromise, congress got the debate and the United States got the canal.

Now, friends, in that they said I acted unconstitutionally. They can't show a section of the constitution or a line of law that I violated. All I did was that when an emergency which was a vital emergency arose where there was no provision made for it in the constitution, I gave the people of the United States the benefit of the doubt.

You recall, the older among you, the veterans, how President Buchanan towards the end of his administration sent a message to congress in which he ably discussed secession and showed first that there was no constitutional right to secede and second that there was no constitutional right to put down secession. Lincoln came in and put it down. He found the constitution all right. We are all of us small men, but we can try to tread afar off in the footsteps of Abraham Lincoln.[11]

I wish you would examine, indeed I know you have examined, but I wish we could make other people as well, examine the progressive platform. No such platform has ever been put before our people since the close of the civil war. Never has been such a document put before the people since the days of Abraham Lincoln. With that we are facing the future, we are facing the social and economic needs of our generation and the remedies that ought to be applied. We have not done it in any false spirit. I think I can say that we have shown in that platform that while we intend to go

11. For a good modern treatment of Buchanan's annual message in 1860, see William C. Harris, *Lincoln's Rise to the Presidency* (Lawrence: University Press of Kansas, 2007), p. 281.

forward, to be progressive, that in the proper sense of the word we are the real conservatives.

You recall in the days of Lincoln his opponents kept calling themselves conservatives and they called Lincoln radical. He was radical of course, but he served the nation, he served the United States. He was the real conservative of his generation because he dared go forward for righteousness' sake.

We have dared to go forward for righteousness' sake and we are the true conservatives for we are striving to do away with the abuses which if left uncurbed will some day bring our mighty republican fabric down with a crash on the heads of our children or our children's children, and, oh, friends, if I could only persuade the men who take the lead against us, many of whom I know and like and respect my multimillionaire friends, if I could only persuade them that if they were wise they would come with us, that we are the true friends of their children, we are the true friends of their descendants in the future, for if they had their way, these men had their way and the abuses of today were left uncurbed, then a generation would grow up with sullen hatred and discontent, feeling it was suffering unmerited wrong and when a generation in America thus grows up woe be to those to feel the effect of the public uprising that will follow.

We are acting as the true friend of the children and grandchildren of the great moneyed men of today when we strive to bring about justice in the land, for in the long run this country will be a poor place for anyone to live in unless we make it a fair place for everyone to live in.

Our opponents have said that I preach class hatred and discontent. Class hatred! I never preached hatred of any class in my life, excepting the class of crooks—that is all. It has been said I preached discontent. I have preached discontent only with what is wrong—and I should esteem myself a poor citizen if I sat down in supreme content in injustice. I would think but ill of you, I would not care to work with you if you did not have in your hearts the plain hatred of injustice, the feeling for righteousness, if you did not feel your soul burn with an endeavor to make this country a better place for men and women to live in.

The reason I can work with you is where your hearts are hard your heads are good. Afar off many of us small men of small days, are trying to follow in the footsteps of Abraham Lincoln; we are trying to emulate his life, his firm determination to do away with evils, his patient and long suffering charity, his freedom from vindictiveness and his clear-headed good sense. I ask you again to look at the planks in our platform. None of them preaches hatred. We still stand up for a man of wealth, if he is menaced with injustice, just exactly as we will stand up for anyone else, but we intend we shall have justice ourselves.

I see here the placard, "Let's pass prosperity around." Now it is necessary that we should take thought for the economic well being of the average man. It is a prime necessity. You cannot do any permanent good to any man if he lives under such conditions that his wife and children are dying in want. We have got to take thought for the man's body. We have got to shape things so that he shall have, if a wage worker, a living wage, if a farmer an opportunity to get for himself not for any middleman the best there is on the farm, if a business man or professional man he shall have the chance to earn what his abilities honestly exercised entitles him to earn. We realize that. We do not propose to do anything that will interfere with prosperity, but we want it passed around.

Now the question of the tariff, I have remained attached to the doctrine that the progressives taught three years ago.[12] I do not believe in free trade. I think you would abolish too much prosperity in some people, but you would do it by the simple expedient of abolishing all prosperity for everybody. On the other hand I equally disbelieve in the standpat republican theory of the tariff. I believe that under the Payne-Aldrich Tariff bill a great wrong was done our people and I think a part of the wrong was done by the shams and humbugs of the bill and among the shams and humbugs was the tariff board.

The tariff board was appointed under a section of the law which was meant to be a sham. While the republicans under the lead of Messrs. Aldrich and Cannon were in power they did not give a real commission which the progressives demanded, but finally made a little sham board. I think it was better than nothing myself but it was not much, and the trouble was having exhaustive power, being constituted as it was, it worked with such extreme slowness that nothing concrete ever came out of it.

Our proposition is that there shall be a real commission composed of experts with ample power who shall report speedily on the different matters that come up so that in a few months if a progressive administration gets in they will be able to take up schedule after schedule of the important schedules under adjustment, and lower each in accordance with the recommendations of that tariff commission, being based, not as a result of log rolling and not as the result of any appeal of any special interest.

12. Roosevelt is referring to the opposition of progressive Republican senators such as Beveridge and Robert M. La Follette to the Payne-Aldrich Tariff during the Senate's deliberations about the measure in the summer of 1909.

There is another thing that commission is to do if the progressives come in. I believe as I say, in the policy of protection, but it is to be the protection of the farmer just as much as any one else and he is not to bear the only burden of reduction. He is to have fair play, no favors, but just as much favor as anyone else and the commission is to consider the interests of the consumer and it is to investigate and see that in giving protection to an interest the benefit of the protection doesn't stop at the front office, that a reasonable share goes into the envelope of the wage earner, and if it don't go there take off the protection.

In that matter we stand as against both of the old parties. We stand against the doctrine, the republican party's tariff doctrine, that is a tariff for privilege. We stand against the democratic doctrine which is a tariff for destruction and we believe in a tariff for labor, a tariff to help our wage workers and the justification for which is to be found in the actual way in which it does help the wage earners.

And now, friends, I appeal to you here to see that in all that you do you make it evident that this is a genuine new party, and that the ex-democrat and the ex-republican will come into it on equal terms and are equally well treated and have an equal share and equal voice in the management and make it evident also above all that we are really standing for the interests of the people and be broad minded with those [of] our neighbors who have not gone as far as we have but whose faces are set toward the light.

I was very much pleased yesterday to see that Senator Cummins had announced that he intended to vote for me, but I see that he intimates he doesn't think our movement will be permanent, but he was going to support it this time anyhow. I differ from him about the movement being permanent. I think this is a permanent movement. I know it is a permanent movement. We have put our hands to plow and we will not look backwards.[13]

While I would want to see everyone I can of the boys crowd in with us on the basis of being a permanent movement, yet I welcome every man who supports us, even though he thinks that a year or two hence he may go back to either of the old parties, but my belief is that when he once gets in our company he will stay and he will be glad to stay. And so I ask every former republican, every republican yet hesitating who believes in honesty and decency, who believes in the principles of the republican party as Abraham Lincoln understood them, I ask him to stand with us. I ask every democrat who honestly believes in the rule of the people and in social and in-

13. "Senator Cummins Is for Roosevelt," *Des Moines Register and Leader*, 4 September 1912.

dustrial justice to come with us because every representative of privilege, every boss, every representative of social interests in financial life is going to his side. I ask him to come with us and we will welcome him on the fighting field, glad to stand shoulder to shoulder with him in this fight for the rights of the people and I ask all good citizens everywhere to stand with us for that work against unrighteousness.

As far as it is given to us to know our own souls, we have no feeling of hatred to any man, we have no hostility, no vindictive purpose towards any man, but we work to uplift the humble and work to make this in every way a government of the people, we work to make this a country in which from one great ocean to the other justice shall be done to every man and every man within the limits of the nation.

Des Moines Register and Leader, 5 September 1912.

From Des Moines, Roosevelt moved on to North Dakota, where he delivered two speeches on 6 September in Grand Forks and Fargo. As he got nearer to the Canadian border, his attacks on Canadian reciprocity increased. Though voters in Canada had rejected the proposal in September 1911, the laws implementing the agreement on the American side remained in force.

A Speech at Grand Forks, North Dakota, 6 September 1912

Mr. Chairman, my regret was you didn't speak longer, for the chairman was stating as well as could be stated what the fundamental principles of this party are, and if he had been permitted to go on I have no doubt he would have stated why we found it necessary to start the party.[14]

A party is an instrument for the good of the people. As soon as the managers of any party forget that fact, as soon as they begin to think that the party exists for their benefit, then the time has come to break with the party so controlled. And friends, I see in this audience men who wear the button that shows that they fought in the great civil war and that in their youth they came forward to defend all that we prized most in this country when Abraham Lincoln called to arms. Now, friends, at that date a new

14. E. J. Lander, a prominent insurance executive who chaired the Roosevelt executive committee in North Dakota, had introduced the presidential candidate.

party had just been founded, the progressive party of that time—it was the republican party then founded by Abraham Lincoln and the men in association with him. Lincoln had been a life-long whig. It was a wrench to him and to many others to leave the old whig party, to others to leave the old democratic party, but it had to be done, because each party had proved disloyal to the principles which it was founded to maintain. The democracy of that day claimed heirship from Jefferson, but Jefferson had founded it as a party of liberty, of freedom, and it had been perverted into being a party that stood for slavery. In the same way, friends, today we who belonged to the republican party witnessed in June last at Chicago, the theft of the party machinery by the bosses away from the people, and friends, the men who thus stole the party organization—the Penroses, the Barnes, the Guggenheims, the rest of them—they haven't any right of kinship with Abraham Lincoln and his men (Applause). If you seek to find the principles of Lincoln, if you seek to find the principles for which the men in the early sixties fought and risked their lives for, you must find them in our ranks. Ours are the purposes of Abraham Lincoln; we are the men who are trying to apply to the present day conditions the eternal principles of right for which Lincoln and the men of his day applied to their conditions. And friends, the easiest of all things is to praise virtue when virtue is dead; the easiest of all things is to try to show your adherence to principle by applying it only to the issues that have vanished. We were all of us progressives about 1860. Now there isn't any body that isn't glad that slavery was abolished and the union preserved, but when you, and the men like you, started in to preserve the union there was plenty of opposition then. You recollect the assertions made that you were acting in an unconstitutional manner. (A voice: "I do.")

You remember, you remember. Any argument advanced now against the progressives was advanced with even greater force and bitterness against the progressives of 1860 to 1865. And friends, I want to give all of you here in North Dakota this word of warning too. Remember that sometimes in the name of progressiveness you will be asked to oppose the only progressivism that counts. That again is just what happened with Lincoln and the men of Lincoln's days. In 1864 there were some men calling themselves radical republicans, who insisted that the republican Party under Lincoln had not gone far enough; and you remember they wanted to nominate Freemont [*sic*] against him in 1864. That was at the time that Wendell Phillips spoke of Lincoln as "the slave man of Illinois." It seems rather queer language to us to use about the great emancipator. So I want you to remember here that any man claiming to be a progressive, who doesn't heartily support the progressive party is merely the ally and tool of the reactionaries.[15]

Understand the fight is now on, perfectly fair, and people must be with us or against us. And loyalty to progressive principles can be shown in but one way, and that is by supporting the progressive party today. Neither of the old parties are capable of grappling with the great and real issues of the present time. Each is boss-ridden, each is privilege controlled. Neither of them represents the party of the people. Now friends, I ask you to compare our platform—the progressive platform—with the two platforms put forth by our opponents, the regular republicans, the machine republicans, the Barnes-Penrose-Guggenheim republicans (applause), the pirates who captured the republican ship and sail under false colors on it, compare it with their platform and with the platform adopted at Baltimore and then I will ask you to judge our faith by our works. I want you to look at my administration while I was president, and while I was governor of New York, and I want you to look at Hiram Johnson's record as governor of California. (Applause.) Now, I have been a governor myself. Mr. Wilson is a governor, Mr. Marshall is a governor, and I wish to state as my sober and deliberate judgment that no governor of any state since the Civil War has while governor had such a record of achievement to his credit as Hiram Johnson has had as governor of California, and the national progressive platform is largely a demand for just what Johnson has actually done as governor of California. If you print his record of achievements as governor—the record of achievements made under his administration—you will find that you have just about printed the national progressive platform. The worth of a platform is—exodus a small bull moose (as a father removed a crying baby from the audience). You know my views on the baby question.

Now, the worth of a platform must be gauged by its sincerity. The capital crime that can be committed against the people is the crime on the part of a public man saying one thing and doing another, and that crime is of course an aggravated crime when it takes the shape of a party platform being insincere. I want just to touch on the platforms of the two old parties first—and as regards the republican platform it will literally be only a touch. Because when a convention is organized by theft and declines to pay heed to anything that that convention puts forth in the way of a promise—the homily—a homily upon honesty by a pickpocket detected with the

15. John C. Fremont (1813–1890) had been the first Republican presidential candidate in 1856 and was discussed as a possible alternative to Lincoln's reelection in 1864. Wendell Phillips (1811–1884), an abolitionist orator, called Lincoln "the slave-hound of Illinois."

goods upon him doesn't tend toward edification. And the republican platform isn't worthy of serious discussion, because the men who adopted it were at that moment engaged in the successful theft from the people of the people's rights. Now mind you, nominally they stole the nomination from me. That is of no earthly consequence to anyone. The real fraud was that they stole the nomination from you. Now, they did me the honor to dislike me, but after all that wasn't their real feeling. I could have gotten them over to my side by moving my little finger. All I had to do was to let them know I would play their game. It would have come to me like that (Snapping his finger). Was it me that they really minded? Those whom they dreaded were you, and those like you. The reason they were bound to defeat my nomination, even if it wrecked the republican party, was because it happened that I stood at the head of a movement which was to give to the people themselves the real control of their nomination conventions, as well as the control of the legislative and executive officers. They knew the Penroses, the Barneses, the Franklins, the Murphys, the Cranes, the Guggenheims.[16]

They knew that if we win, their power was at an end in the republican party. More than that friends, if we won in that party the bosses of the other party knew that their power was coming to an end, and all of the bosses, all the beneficiaries of big privilege, were banded together to see if they couldn't beat us in any way. In Ohio, for instance, I was struck by the fact that the machine Democratic papers were doing everything they could in the primary to help the regular republicans beat us, and the big representatives of privilege were joined hands to see if they couldn't beat the new party. They are doing that same thing now.

I shall come to it later on.

Now, so much for the republican platform. Now for the democratic and here I want your special attention. Some days ago Mr. Wilson stated—it was in his letter of acceptance—that the Democratic platform was not a program and he did not expect to see it adopted by the people of the United States. Well, if it wasn't a program, why was it put up? Our platform is a program, and it isn't only a program, it is a covenant. There isn't a promise we make in that platform which we do not hold ourselves bound to execute exactly as an honest man in private life executes his business engagements with his neighbors. We have promised nothing we cannot perform. Instead of making loose promises to try to catch votes and then not

16. Roosevelt was referring here to Franklin Murphy (1846–1920), the Republican governor of New Jersey from 1902 to 1905 and a staunch Taft supporter in 1912.

intending to keep them after election, we have promised not one thing which we cannot perform; and if any man elected on that platform as a progressive fails to do his utmost in good faith to see that every promise therein made is kept, I will take the stump against him myself. Now friends, contrast that with the attitude of our democratic foes. Mr. Wilson says that the platform is not a program. You men of the Civil War will remember that in 1864 the democrats announced in their platform that the war was a failure. You remember. And the candidate had to hustle and explain that that wasn't a program either. Mr. McClellan was a high-minded, upright man who had rendered service to the community just as in the case of Mr. Wilson, but Mr. McClellan stood as Mr. Wilson stands on a platform that he had to repudiate, had to say it wasn't a program, because otherwise he couldn't get before the American people.[17] And I do not believe that the American people will, and I know that the American people ought not, to expect to put in power any party which initiates a declaration of principles which must be immediately repudiated by the party's candidate, or which the party's candidate must immediately announce is not a program before he appealed for the suffrages of the people.

Friends, we can get along pretty well with a man with whom we differ if he will tell us just what he means to do and will stand by it. The one party, the one individual and the one party with which it is impossible to get on with is the individual or aggregate of individuals who say what their principles are and then explain to you that they do not really mean that those are their principles. And that is exactly what is meant when you say that a platform isn't a program. Either it is a program or it is a falsification of the truth. If a man has to repudiate his platform, then it is high time that he got a new party or that that party suffered a radical change of heart.

Now, let me give you just one illustration of what I mean as applying to your own interests here. The progressive party has declared outright in favor of the repeal of the reciprocity treaty. And a great many of us, including myself, were originally in favor of reciprocity, because we were assured that it was fair to all our citizens, that it was done in such a manner as to do justice to all of our people. We then discovered that it was a jug-handle arrangement under which the farmer was expected to bear the whole burden. When we made up our minds definitely to that point we came out against it, and the progressive party, and only the progressive party declared outright for the repeal of the reciprocity party [treaty?].

17. George B. McClellan (1826–1885) was the Democratic nominee in the 1864 presidential election. He distanced himself from the platform that advocated a negotiated peace with the Confederacy.

Now, Mr. Wilson's party—the democratic—in their platform has declared that the entire tariff is unconstitutional. Either they mean that or they don't. If they don't mean it, then we can't trust them in anything. If on that subject they say what they don't mean, then we can't tell that the next thing they say will not be something they don't mean. Then we can't trust any promise they make on any subject. If they do mean what they say, then you will not only get the reciprocity treaty, you will not only have the tariff abolished as regards Canada, you will have it abolished as regards all other countries. Now I want you to think of that. You object to the reciprocity treaty. You are quite right. We propose to repeal it so that if at any time Canada changes its mind, the treaty won't be there for it to change its mind about. We propose to repeal the treaty. The democratic party in its platform declares that all protective tariff duties are unconstitutional. If it means what it says—and it isn't entitled to support anywhere unless it does mean what it says—if it means what it says, the duties that are taken off in that reciprocity scheme as against Canada will not be only taken off as against Canada but will be taken off as against every other nation in the world. Now you think over that. Think over that yourselves and see if there is any flaw—if there is any flaw in my statement.

And you can turn to the democratic platform and to ours and see for yourselves. Now what is the difference—I think I can put it in a nutshell—of the three platforms on the tariff. The republicans advocate a tariff for privilege, the democrats advocate free trade—a tariff for revenue only; that is, a tariff for destruction. We advocate a tariff for labor. We hold to the position taken by the progressives in the senate, and in the lower house three years ago, that there should be a substantial reduction of duties—a substantial lowering of the tariff downward on certain industries, but we feel that the farmer, instead of being the first, should be among the last to feel any such reduction; that it should be notably certain great interests as to the duties affecting which should be lowered. We wish to have that done by a commission of experts—not like the last little board which was largely used as a means of delaying action, but a genuine commission with sufficient equipment to enable it to speedily report as to exactly what reduction should be made. And part of the duties of that commission should be to say that where there is a protected manufacturing interest, the benefit of the reduction shall not stop in the front office, that a legitimate share shall get into the pay envelopes of the working men, and that if it doesn't the duties will be taken off. A perfectly feasible principle.

Now, friends, I don't see how North Dakota, if it was sincere in its opposition to reciprocity, can fail on that point alone to support the progressive ticket and with its eyes open support the democratic party which endorsed a plank which, if carried into effect, would mean the taking off of all duties on farm products, not merely as against Canada but as against all other nations of the world. There again I mind you, don't accept merely my words. Take our platform and the democratic and republican platforms and look them over for yourselves. Again friends, I feel that you of North Dakota should be with us in this contest because of the enemies we have made. (Applause.) Now I want to say right at the outset, I should hold myself unfit to come before you if I objected to any man merely because he was right, to any business merely because it was big. You men who fought in the Civil War, you know that what you cared for in your bunkie was not whether he was a banker or a bricklayer, not whether he had much money or little. What you wanted to know was whether he would stay put. That is what you wanted to know. In other words, if the man did his duty on the march and in camp, and if when you got into a fight you didn't have to look over your shoulder to see if he was still there or not, he was all right. You would stand for him. Now in just the same way, if a rich man or big business—I don't draw the line against size, I draw it against conduct. I don't object to the crooked, big man because he is big. I object to him because he is crooked. (Applause.) In other words, if a big businessman earns six cents by rendering real service to the people, why I would be ashamed to grudge him his six cents. I am glad he got it. What I object to is the big businessman who earns his success not by serving the people but by swindling the people. That is what I want and he is the man I am after.

Now, unfortunately, not only the big businesses who swindle, but I am sorry to say a lot of respectable businessmen who simply get frightened or have been misled by others have turned against us. There are a few who are far-sighted enough, a few who have children and realize that we are trying to make this country a country in which it will be worthwhile for their children to grow up in, but it isn't going to be good country for them to live in if we don't make it a pretty good country for everybody to live in. But most of them have gone against us. Now, I am going to quote from one who represents the respectable side of Wall Street but who looks upon me with much dread, and then from a couple of gentlemen who represent—well, I won't say what side they represent. The first is Jacob Schiff, who is one of the big noted men down in Wall Street, who has been a lifelong republican, but who has come out enthusiastically for the democratic party this year—for the election of Mr. Wilson, and in an interview—a statement given in the *New York Times* which is supporting Mr. Wilson. I was much interested in the reasons given why Mr. Schiff was supporting

Mr. Wilson. In the first place he explained that to fight for Mr. Taft was to throw your vote away, and that nobody could afford to throw his vote away when he ought to try to beat me with it. And then he went on to say, and this at first puzzled me, he said that the election of Mr. Wilson was the only way to perpetuate the republican party.

Well, now, I didn't understand that at first. Then I saw what he meant. He means that if we, the progressives, that if we carry the elections the old corrupt machine is broken into pieces, that we are done for good and all with the kind of politics which triumphed last June in the Chicago convention, and what he wants to do is to beat the progressive party. He is simply willing to beat it with the democratic or republican, whichever is handy. He may have slight individual preferences between democrat and republican, but those preferences are so slight compared with the bitterness of his dislike for the progressive that he won't allow these preferences to come in and wants, if he can, to beat the progressive with the democratic party then he will have us, he hopes. I think he is mistaken, but he hopes that they will get back to the same old see-saw, the two parties nominally against each other, each under the control of the bosses, each under the control of privileges, one going up, the other going down, but the man in the middle who teeters the see-saw controlling both. (Applause.) And Mr. Schiff and Wall Street wants to stand in the middle and teeter the see-saw so as to let the republican end of the see-saw come up, then the democratic end of the see-saw come up, but to keep the progressives from getting aboard. Now our proposal is that we won't any longer allow Wall Street to act as a teeter on the political see-saw between the two parties, that we are not any longer going to permit two parties nominally opposed to one another but each alternately coming up accordingly as the big interests choose to bear down heavier with one foot or with the other.

Mr. Schiff and all those like him—are perfectly well meaning men only they don't know our people. They are afraid of you. They don't know what you are like. They think you would do something dreadful to them. You wouldn't. You would treat them squarely and make them treat other people squarely. And they will do anything they can to keep you out of power—to keep a party which really represents you from getting in power, and the progressive party intends to put an end to the Wall street teeter of the political see-saw. Now friends, so much for the perfectly respectable Wall street men, who simply haven't got an idea of what the American people want or need or what the American people are determined to have.

Now, I want to touch on just for a moment representatives of another type of element there. Senator Penrose and Mr. Archbold of the Standard

Oil company. A week ago last Friday and Saturday they appeared before the Senate committee and testified—the testimony being intended to attack me, and the object of the testimony being to withdraw attention from Mr. Penrose's record. Mr. Penrose is a modest man and he doesn't like anybody to look at his record; and he thought the effective way to prevent an inquisitive disposition about what he had done was to see if he and his side partner, Mr. Archbold, couldn't create a diversion by attacking me. That was on Friday and Saturday. On Saturday I telegraphed to the committee asking to be heard on Monday. It was Saturday, and Monday was the earliest day to be heard on. The chairman of the subcommittee, Senator Moses E. Clapp, stayed in Washington. Every reactionary senator, republican and democrat alike, scattered to the four winds of heaven, and Mr. Archbold went to Europe. (Applause). And I was notified I would have to wait a month or two before I could be heard. So I wrote Mr. Clapp a letter which was published Monday and which I shall ask—it will be furnished in full to all the progressive committees and I want you to get copies of that letter, as many thousand of them as you wish from the central committee and have them distributed here among all of our people who take any interest in the subject. I went over everything in that letter.

Now, today I only want to call your attention to just two or three features of it. Mr. Penrose and Mr. Archbold attacked nominally me. Really they attacked Mr. Bliss, the treasurer of the republican committee eight years ago, who had been treasurer under McKinley for his two canvasses and who was continued in my campaign. They attacked Mr. Bliss. Mr. Bliss is dead. He had lived for seven years during which they had never said a word against him. When he died they attacked me. They said that Mr. Bliss tried to blackmail the Standard Oil Company and it had been done in my interest. I published my own letter to show that I had especially forbidden any contribution to be received from the Standard Oil, but I won't touch on that now. But what I want to call your attention to is the testimony of Mr. Archbold and you will find it on page 133 of the printed report of the Senate committee. Mr. Archbold suddenly was overcome by a memory of his ways. And he said, "Darkest Abyssinia has nothing to show compared with the treatment awarded the Standard Oil Company under the Roosevelt administration." Now on that point he told the truth. After careful investigation I came to the conclusion that the Standard Oil Company needed Abyssinian treatment and it got it. If ever I were president again, unless the Standard Oil Company mended its ways, it would get the Abyssinian treatment again. And Mr. Archbold and Mr. Archbold's side partner, Mr. Penrose, know that. Mr. Penrose knows that there is danger of the Abyssinian treatment being applied to him too. And that is why they come forward at this time to bear testimony. If I hadn't been chosen as the head of the progressive party, you wouldn't have heard a thing about that testimony. They don't give a rap for me as a private individual. The only reason they want to hound me now is because it will hound you; they want to prevent you from coming into power. They don't complain that they have had any Abyssinian treatment under the present administration. They haven't had. And they are obviously entirely at ease as to either the democratic or republican parties. They haven't the slightest fear of Abyssinian treatment from either of them, if they should come into power. They make no attack on them. Penrose and Archbold are nominal republicans but they come to attack the progressives.

Both of them are sensible men and know they can do nothing with Mr. Taft. They can't elect him, can do nothing toward electing Mr. Taft. They come to attack the progressives because they wish to see the democratic party come into power, although nominally they are opposed to each, they wish to see the democratic party come into power rather than to see the progressive party take control of the government, rather than to see the government restored to the people themselves. And there was just one other bit of testimony which Mr. Archbold gave that interested me. Here again I think he probably told the truth. It is a guess on my part. He said that when the administration began to act against Standard Oil he went to Mr. Bliss to get me to stop it and he said that Mr. Bliss said: "I have no influence with Mr. Roosevelt. I can't help you in the matter." Now that isn't true, stated in such extreme fashion. Mr. Bliss was an honorable, upright man and had influence with me. I had a great regard and affection for him and at any time had Mr. Bliss come to me on any subject of legitimate discussion, any question where honesty was not involved, where it was simply a matter of policy, I would have listened to him with the utmost attention, and if I hadn't agreed with him it would only have been because I honestly could not. But it is true that neither Mr. Bliss nor any other human being had any influence with me when the question was of holding to account either a law-breaking individual or a law-breaking corporation. That is true. (Applause)

Now, friends, I wish I could stay here and make you an address about three times as long. But I am working on a schedule. I am trying to visit most of the states of the union because the channels of information that ought to be open to the people are choked, especially in the metropolitan centers. Our newspapers in the big metropolitan centers, notably New York, are for the most part so controlled that we cannot get information before the people, and I have got to trust largely to put it before the people myself. Therefore I have to make a big campaign and keep many engagements.

And now I appeal to you to stand with us, because we stand for the right of the people to rule and for their right to rule as to promote social and industrial justice throughout this land. (Prolonged applause.)

Grand Forks Daily Herald, 7 September 1912; another version of this speech with different capitalization and paragraphing appears in James F. Vivian, ed., *The Romance of My Life: Theodore Roosevelt's Speeches in Dakota* (Fargo, N.D.: Theodore Roosevelt Medora Foundation, 1989), pp. 87–96.

Roosevelt made a second speech in North Dakota along the lines of his remarks at Grand Forks. The Outlook *magazine published this excerpt from what he said about antitrust policy.*

The Taft-Wilson Trust Programme: An Address at Fargo, North Dakota, 6 September 1912

During my Administration, and since, I have first directed and tested, and then studied the working of the Sherman Anti-Trust Law. When I came into office that law was dead; I took it up and for the first time had it enforced.

We gained this much by the enforcement: we gained the establishment of the principle that the Government was supreme over the great corporations; but that is almost the end of the good that came through our lawsuits.

Take the Northern Securities case.[18] Under me that suit was brought to a successful conclusion. I at first thought that we had secured a definite and real solution of the difficulties, and my opponents thought so too at first, and were very sore; but in the end it proved that all we had accomplished was what is said above. As one of the greatest magnates concerned afterwards remarked: "Well, when the smoke cleared away, I found that

18. *Northern Securities Co. v. United States* was the case the Roosevelt administration filed against a railroad combination in the Northwest in 1902 under the Sherman Antitrust Act. The Supreme Court ruled in favor of the government in 1904. This litigation established Roosevelt's reputation as a "trust-buster."

George W. Perkins, a former partner of J. P. Morgan, was a major financial backer of the Roosevelt campaign. Roosevelt defended his supporter on several occasions during his swings around the country. (Library of Congress)

whereas formerly I had to prove my ownership by one bit of paper, I now have to prove it by two."

Take again the Standard Oil decision.[19] The Standard Oil Company was nominally dissolved as a result of the suit against it. It was divided nominally into thirty-four different companies. For a moment there was a great deal of fright in Wall Street; and under the stress of that fight the big magnates for the time being thought they would come round and advocate the policy of control that I had advocated because, while that control would really control them, would hamper and limit them, at least they thought that they would thereby escape death. Then they found that it was only make-believe death to which they were exposed. And as a result of the suit for dissolution Mr. Rockefeller's property rose in value to a higher degree than it ever had gone before, and to an already sufficient fortune he had

19. *Standard Oil Company of New Jersey v. United States* in 1911 brought a Supreme Court decision ruling that the oil company should be broken up.

some eighty or ninety millions of dollars, while the price of oil went up to the consumer. Men who purchased Standard Oil stock on the curb in New York tell me that the sole difference is that, whereas formerly the broker would give them one slip of paper, now he gives them an envelope containing thirty-seven slips—that's all.

You recollect Mr. Pierpont Morgan said, "You can't unscramble the eggs in an omelet."[20] This particular instance of trying to unscramble them didn't help anybody but the owners of the eggs, for it increased the value of the eggs indefinitely and made the omelet cost more to the general public. Now our proposal is not to try to unscramble the eggs by a mere succession of lawsuits, but to exercise such administrative control by the Government as will prevent the eggs from ever being scrambled.

Mr. Wilson in a recent speech in New York said that "no body of men would have the wisdom necessary to enable them to regulate the industrial processes of the country."[21] I was very much interested in that remark because it represents the exact attitude always taken by the respectable ultraconservative in matters of this nature. Word for word it is what some of the great railway magnates used to say before the passage of the Inter-State Commerce Law. They used to say that "no body of men alive could undertake to regulate the complicated railway business." Other big men used to say the same thing when the proposal was to establish Public Utilities Commissions.

I appeal from the prophet of to-day to the way the facts have refuted the prophets of yesterday. There is no more difficulty in regulating the Standard Oil or the Steel Corporation than in regulating a big railway. We have actually made the Inter-State Commerce Law work. We have found by the test of actual work that the way to control the railways lies through increasing the power, and especially through increasing the application of the power, of the Inter-State Commerce Commission, by regulating and controlling those railways and not by any development of the Anti-Trust Law. Real control of the trusts can only come through the adoption of similar expedients. What I want to see done with our industrial concerns is to see an Inter-State Industrial Commission established, which shall handle the Standard Oil, the Steel Trust, the Tobacco Trust, and every such big

20. J. P. Morgan (1837–1913) was the famous investment banker who had financed many of the corporate mergers about which Roosevelt was speaking.

21. I could not find this Wilson quotation, but he expressed a similar thought in a speech on Labor Day in Buffalo, New York: "I have never known any body of men, any small body of men that understood the United States." See John Wells Davidson, ed., *A Crossroads of Freedom: The 1912 Campaign Speeches of Woodrow Wilson* (New Haven, Conn.: Yale University Press, 1956), p. 80.

trust, through administrative action, just as the Inter-State Commerce Commission handles the railways, and with a power extended beyond that of the Inter-State Commerce Commission.

And Mr. Wilson need not bother himself about finding men to administer such a law. If he cannot find them, I can and will. I will guarantee to find men who will be able to understand and supervise and regulate the business of these great industrial corporations.

Some of Mr. Wilson's supporters have said that our purpose is to "legalize monopoly" and his to "regulate competition."[22] On the contrary, our proposal is to abolish monopoly and to restore competition where possible, and where this is not possible then absolutely to control the monopoly in the interest of the general public. His proposal is in effect to leave the present system unchanged; and the present system has just resulted in legalizing the monopoly of the Standard Oil and Tobacco Trusts. Substantially this has been the sole result, the only result Mr. Wilson's policy would achieve. His proposal is to do precisely nothing; his proposal is to continue in exactly the same course that the Taft Administration is now continuing; for the differences between the Republican and Democratic platforms on this matter are merely differences of sound and fury, and not of sense.

Mr. Wilson's proposal is to regulate competition by "dissolving" trusts in the way the Standard Oil and Tobacco Trusts were "dissolved." You know the prayer in Wall Street now is "Give us another dissolution." Wall Street likes to have its property dissolved in that way. Every one of those dissolutions has been accompanied by a great rise in the value of stocks, has legalized monopoly, and has conferred upon the trust magnates the great boon of being fortified by the law in their intrenchments.

On the contrary, the proposal of the Progressives is to put a stop to the continuance of the Taft-Wilson programme of further legalization of monopoly under the guise of a make-believe assault on monopoly. We propose by administrative action to control the conditions which, if left uncontrolled, lead to monopoly. We propose to restore competition where possible. But where this is not possible, we propose to have a real remedy instead of a sham remedy.

The talk about really controlling the trusts by regulating competition merely by lawsuits along the lines of the Anti-Trust law, or an amendment

22. Roosevelt is referring to Louis D. Brandeis (1856–1941), who provided Wilson with the distinction between "legalizing" monopoly and regulating competition. For a discussion of Brandeis's economic thought, see Thomas K. McCraw, *Prophets of Regulation: Charles Francis Adams, Louis D. Brandeis, James M. Landis, Alfred E. Kahn* (Cambridge, Mass.: Belknap Press of Harvard University Press, 1984), pp. 109–112.

proposed to it by the Stanley Committee or by any one else—all such talk is the veriest nonsense. The proposals in the Democratic platform, so far as they could be enacted into law, would be of no help whatever. They would not change the present situation one little bit, except for the worse.

There is not a Wall Street man engaged in big business of the kind to which our people object, there is not a trust magnate, who doesn't regard with utter derision the talk of interfering with monopolies along the lines indicated by Mr. Wilson and his supporters. The only thing they fear is the kind of regulation that we Progressives propose to give them. Mr. Wilson's proposals are entirely satisfactory to them, quite as satisfactory as the actions of the present Administration; indeed, Mr. Wilson's proposals are so vague that they can hardly be called proposals at all, and the proposals of his supporters are either impracticable to adopt, or, if practicable, would work no real change in the present conditions. Accordingly, the enormous majority of the Wall Street men who have been guilty of the obnoxious practices in connection with the trusts, having given up the hope of electing Mr. Taft, are now supporting Mr. Wilson; for they dread us as their only real foes, and know that the policies advocated by Messrs. Taft and Wilson represent not real hostility, but only mock hostility, to the crooked trusts—although these same policies do contain a serious menace to every kind of honest business, big or little, which does not rely for protection on adroit use of the chicanery of the law.

I call attention of those who doubt our ability to regulate big business to what has happened with the insurance companies. Nine years ago the effort was made to limit them in size, much as the Stanley Committee proposed to limit industrial concerns generally. In actual practice this worked so badly that the effort had to be abandoned. At present the insurance companies are not limited in size, but they are supervised and controlled. There is plenty of competition among them, and the policy-holders are so well protected that they are entirely satisfied, those in the big companies more than those in the others.

The sum of the matter, therefore, is this. Mr. Wilson, like Mr. Taft, has no improvement to propose in this matter, for the difference between the proposals in the Republican and the Democratic platforms on the trust question are merely differences of declamation. Both sets of proposals indicate nothing but vague, puzzled, and hopeless purpose feebly to continue the present futile policy of attempting to regulate the trust by nothing but a succession of long-drawn and ineffective law suits; and if actually put into operation both sets of proposals would produce exactly and precisely nothing.

On the contrary, our proposals are definite and concrete, and are based on successful action along kindred lines in the past. If we are allowed to put them into action, we will immensely benefit the honest business man by making the law certain, and by punishing misconduct and not merely size; and we will effectively, and not merely nominally, curb and control the big trusts which are actually or potentially guilty of anti-social practices.

I do not wonder that, in view of these facts, every big crooked financier is against us and in favor of either Mr. Wilson or Mr. Taft in order to beat us. I am sorry to say that the great majority of the respectable men of great wealth seem to be against us, not realizing that it is really in their interest that we should exercise supervision over the business men of their great wealth. I feel that every honest and far-sighted businessman, big or small, should be with us, for our purpose is to help energy and power in business life, so long as the energy and power are used honestly and the public treated fairly; and all the secondary business men, the moderate-sized business men, should give us their hearty aid.

We are proud of the energy and initiative and success of our business men; we wish to see them prosper and build up American business to the highest pitch of efficiency, both at home and abroad, both in internal trade and in international trade. It is because we war intelligently against dishonesty in business, it is for the very reason that we efficiently oppose crooked business, that we have the right to ask the support of all honest business men; for the Progressive party in its platform offers the only really good platform that the honest business man has had offered him, and makes the only efficient proposals that any party has made for the elimination of evil business practices and the control of big business so that it shall not be used against the business interest either of weaker business rivals of the employees and other wage workers, of the shareholders, or of the general public.

Outlook, 21 September 1912, pp. 105–107.

4

The Pacific Northwest and the Pacific Coast

After Roosevelt completed his day in North Dakota, his train moved west into Montana and then on to Idaho, Washington, and Oregon. In these speeches, the candidate sounded his now-familiar themes about the third party, the tariff, and Woodrow Wilson's ideas on the trusts. The latter issue came into sharpest focus when Roosevelt reached California. During a major address at San Francisco on 14 September, he pounced on Wilson's statement about the role of government, issuing his strongest attack on the Democratic nominee.

As his trip proceeded, Roosevelt endeavored to bolster Progressive candidates across the country. He spoke out for the party's nominee for governor of New York, Oscar S. Straus, and he still endeavored to pull progressive Republicans over to his side. Roosevelt had only moderate success in these efforts. The need to make a national appcal wore on the Progressive standard-bearer as his journey progressed.

A Speech to the Montana State Progressive Convention, Helena, 7 September 1912

A couple of days ago Mr. Wilson in a speech in New York said that a body of men would not have the wisdom to enable them to regulate the industrial processes of the country. There is no more difficulty in regulating the Standard Oil or the Steel corporation than in regulating a big railroad.

We have actually made the interstate commerce law work. We have found by the test of actual work that the way to control the railroads is by increasing the power of the interstate commerce commission—by regulating and controlling those railroads and not by any development of the anti-trust law.

What I want to see done with our industrial concerns is to see an interstate industrial commission and board, which shall handle the Standard Oil, the Steel trust, the Tobacco trust and every big trust through administrative action, just as the interstate commerce commission handles the railroads, and with a power extended beyond that of the interstate commerce commission.

Mr. Wilson need not bother himself finding men to administer such a law. If he cannot find them, I will. I will guarantee to find men who will be able to understand and supervise and regulate the business of these great industrial corporations.

Mr. Wilson's proposal is to continue in exactly the same course that the Taft administration is now continuing, for the differences between the Republican and Democratic platforms on this matter are merely differences of sound and fury and not of sense. Mr. Wilson's proposal is to regulate competition by "dissolving" trusts in the same way the Standard Oil and the Tobacco trusts were "dissolved."

You know the prayer on Wall Street now is "Give us another dissolution." Wall Street likes to have its property dissolved in that way.

On the contrary the proposal of the Progressives is to put a stop to the continuance of the Taft-Wilson programme of further legalization of monopoly under the guise of a make-believe assault on monopoly.

There is no Wall Street man engaged in big business of the kind to which our people object, there is not a trust magnate, who does not regard with utter derision the talk of interfering with monopolies along the lines indicated by Mr. Wilson and his supporters.

The sum of the matter, therefore, is this, Mr. Wilson, like Mr. Taft, has nothing to propose in this matter for the differences between the proposals in the Republican and the Democratic platform on the trust question merely are differences of declamation. Both sets of proposals indicate nothing but a vague, puzzled and hopeless purpose feebly to continue the present futile policy of attempting to regulate the trusts by nothing but a succession of long drawn and ineffective lawsuits. On the contrary, our proposals are definite and concrete, and are based on successful action along kindred lines in the past.

New York Tribune, 8 September 1912.

Brief Remarks at Hathaway, Montana, 7 September 1912

I am accused of wanting to rule the country with an iron hand. I always feel inclined to answer that the people who make this statement don't know kings or else they would not put it down as my ambition to be one. They don't know things as I do. Other things I might like to be, but not a king. The constitutional monarch of the present time comes nearer being a cross between a perpetual Vice-President and the leader of the four hundred than anything else I know.

Mind you, I am not saying anything against the job of king, but I just wouldn't have it.

New York Tribune, 8 September 1912.

Comments on the Nomination of Oscar S. Straus as the Progressive Party Candidate for Governor of New York, 8 September 1912

The Progressive Party is to be congratulated, not only on the platform of principles for which it stands, not only because of the character of the men and women who took part in the conventions that started it, and are making its campaign, but also because of the character and achievements of the men whom it has put forward as candidates in the several States.

Next in importance to the nomination of the Vice President is the nomination for Governor of New York. And it seems to me that Hiram Johnson and Oscar Straus symbolize what this movement stands for. One is an ex-Republican, the other an ex-Democrat; they both stand for what is highest in American citizenship.

Mr. Straus is not merely a high-minded and able man, a man of incorruptible integrity and great ability, but also a man who has kept abreast of the great movement from which sprang the Progressive Party.[1] He is eminently fitted to be one of the leaders in this movement. On every point of our platform he represents an intense earnestness of conviction for all the

1. Oscar Solomon Straus (1850–1926) had been secretary of commerce and labor from 1906 to 1909. The Progressives in New York had nominated him to run for governor.

things for which we stand. His attitude toward business, his attitude toward the complicated, and the vitally important social and economic problems which are dealt with in our plank concerning social and industrial justice; in short, his position on Governmental matters has been such as to warrant our saying that he is already in practice applying the very principles which we preach.

New York State has a right to be proud of the fact that in this first State Convention of the people themselves Mr. Straus's nomination was, in the most emphatic sense, a nomination by the people themselves, a nomination representing the desire of the people to have the very best man take the office, although that man was himself sincerely desirous to escape having to take it.

I have known Mr. Straus intimately ever since I was Governor of New York. When he was in my Cabinet I leaned much upon him, and a more loyal and disinterested friend no man could have, and, what is more important, no man could have a more loyal, disinterested and sanely zealous supporter. As head of the Department of Commerce and Labor Mr. Straus himself, by study and administration of the law, was one of those who reached conclusions as to the needs of our handling of the anti-trust and inter-State commerce and similar laws, which I set forth in message after message to Congress, and which were substantially embodied in the Progressive platform, and in his attitude toward labor, toward immigration, toward the duty both of public and private employes, he foreshadowed that part of the Progressive platform which has dealt with these same matters.

Moreover, by his disinterestedness, his unselfish devotion to the cause of good government, and of sound progressive doctrine for economic and social reform, and by his willingness personally to sacrifice his own interests to those of the cause he espouses, he is, I am happy to say, typical of all the men who are in the new movement.

Exactly as it is a real sacrifice for Hiram Johnson to accept the nomination for Vice President, so it is a real sacrifice for Oscar Straus to accept the nomination for Governor of New York. Each has accepted because he is not thinking for himself. He is thinking of his duty to the people as a whole; of his duty to the great Nation to which he belongs. Oscar Straus's nomination is not only a most fortunate thing for the New York Progressives but it is also a piece of real good fortune for the Progressive movement throughout this Nation.

I wish to take this opportunity of again expressing my obligations to the commercial travelers. Everywhere I go I find evidence of the admirable work they are doing for the Progressive movement. The Progressive movement has no machine behind it, and the organization is as yet necessarily imperfect, so that we are almost entirely dependent upon the disinterested zeal of volunteers who serve the cause for no motive save their belief in it, and their desire to do what is best for their country.

Among all these volunteers the commercial travelers occupy a peculiarly important position. They, by the very nature of the case, are peculiarly fitted to do the kind of missionary work which the cause needs. And they are doing it in masterly fashion. I wish to extend to them my hearty thanks and acknowledgments on behalf of the genuine Progressives of the United States.

New York Times, 9 September 1912.

When he reached the Pacific Northwest, Roosevelt spoke to large crowds in Spokane and Seattle, Washington. Once again, the Outlook *provided its readers with an excerpt of the Progressive candidate's remarks about the minimum wage and his differences on the subject with Woodrow Wilson.*

The Minimum Wage: Comments at Spokane, Washington, 9 September 1912

Mr. Wilson has distinctly stated in his speech of acceptance that he does not regard the Democratic platform as a programme. We Progressives are more fortunate. For we regard our platform as a very practical programme, and we intend to put it into effect if the people give us the power.

Mr. Wilson, while expressing general approval of the Progressive platform, has made specific mention only of those parts which he condemns. Among the things which he condemns is our minimum wage plank.

As reported, he states that he opposes this plank because he thinks that employers, if such a law were enacted, would reduce the wages of their employees to the minimum prescribed by law. Such a fear is so groundless that I do not believe it would be expressed by any man who has studied the conditions of life and work at first hand among the workers. The objection is purely academic; it is formed in the school-room; it will not have any weight with men who know what life actually is. Those employers who now pay their lowest-paid employees a starvation wage prove by that very fact that they are paying to all their employees the very least they can get them to take. They have already brought them down as far as possible; if it were possible for them to reduce the wages of their higher-paid employees, they would do so. It is a wholly needless apprehension that they have let any wages stay up by an oversight and would reduce them to a minimum only in case the minimum for the poorest paid were raised by law above the starvation point.

The minimum wage plank is peculiarly in harmony with the general spirit of the Progressive platform. The portions of that platform dealing with social and industrial justice are meant especially to help the men and women who are wage-workers in industrial pursuits. The promises of the platform are specific and reasonable. They are promises which can be kept, and which will be kept if power is given to the Progressives. We stand, in the Nation and in the several States, for the abolition of child labor; for the reduction of hours of labor for women in industry to eight a day; for workmen's compensation laws; for laws guarding the health of workers in factories and protecting them against accidents to life and limb; for laws securing proper conditions of life to wage-workers; for laws providing that in continuous industry there shall be one day's rest in seven, and three eight-hour shifts per day; and for a law establishing a minimum wage for women workers. No proposals such as these are to be found in the platforms of either of the old parties; and no such platform, we believe, would be or could be enacted into law by either of the old parties.

The Progressive proposal regarding a minimum wage is not an ultra-radical one. It is both modest and conservative. We do not at the moment take up the question of a minimum wage generally; we know that in all matters like this it is necessary to proceed slowly so that we may test each experiment, and then, if the test is successful, proceed further along the same line. The men and women who framed this plank and who advocate it have studied the conditions of life and labor among girls and women in industry and know the dreadful suffering and misery, know the crime and vice, that are produced by a wage that is insufficient to enable the girl or woman to keep body and soul together in surroundings of ordinary decency. Any man who goes to the night session of such a court as the Jefferson Market Women's Night Court in New York City, and who follows up some of the cases brought before that court, will soon learn for himself just what misery and immorality are produced among women when they receive less than a living wage. We are faced with the actual fact of doing away with the heartbreaking misery which now exists in the concrete, and we are not to be frightened from our purpose by suggestions of a purely academic kind, however well meant they may be, as to highly improbable possibilities. We intend to put a stop to the misery which now actually exists, and we believe that a minimum wage plank is a humane, practical, and effective method of attacking that misery.

We shall sedulously safeguard the rights of property and protect it from all injustice. But we hold with Lincoln that labor deserves higher consideration than capital. Therefore we hold that labor has a right to the means of life—that there must be a living wage. I doubt whether the protection of the workers from the evils of overwork, unemployment, sweat-shop wages, and child labor will really enhance the cost of production; but, in any event, I would rather see the cost of production enhanced than see it kept low by unpaid labor, physically and morally unhealthy and socially unstable. For, as the great scientist Huxley has pointed out, a society based on such labor, whatever temporary success it obtains, must in the end fall through hideous misery and degradation to utter ruin.[2]

I believe that Mr. Wilson, whose sincerity of conviction in this matter I do not for a moment question, and the other worthy and respectable men in the name of conservatism who oppose the minimum wage plank are misled by the fact that they get their information from study of the laws laid down by political economists who wrote when the social and industrial conditions were utterly different from what they have now become. Under present industrial conditions, to leave wages in all cases to free competition now sometimes means that under the pressure of the competition the freedom left to the laborer is to starve out right or else to starve slowly by accepting a wage insufficient to sustain life as it should be sustained. We in this democracy must shackle force and cunning and fraud alike and we must not permit the weak to remain and the mercy of the strong who are also brutal.

The men and women who are broken by the hard strain of modern industry, and are driven lower and ever lower until they accept wages which will not allow them to be decently fed and clothed or comfortably housed, cannot render to the community the services which should be demanded of American citizens. Idleness is a curse and hard, reasonable work a blessing. But wearing overwork, long continued, destroys the body and the soul, and under-payment will achieve the same end and more rapidly.

It is bad enough to exploit men, but it is inhuman to exploit women in

2. Thomas Henry Huxley (1825–1895), the English biologist and social thinker, was the great defender of Charles Darwin and evolution.

such fashion, to force them to sell their labor power at a wage which reduces them to a condition incompatible with the public welfare. I am not at the present time going beyond the platform of the Progressive party as announced; whether ultimately we shall or shall not do so is for the future to decide. But most emphatically I am standing for the announcements in the platform, and it is my judgment that one of the best things in it is the declaration for a minimum wage for women workers.

Outlook, 28 September 1912, pp. 159–160.

Roosevelt left Washington and on 11 September made two speeches in Portland, Oregon. The longer of the two lasted for an hour and ten minutes at the Gypsy Smith Auditorium in Portland.

An Address at Portland, Oregon, 11 September 1912

Judge McGinn, You Men and Women of Oregon and of Portland:

My friends, I listened with great interest to Judge McGinn's introduction.[3] I thank him very deeply for what he has said, and I wish to continue for a moment on the very argument he made. We are appealing to you all here, without regard to your past political affiliations to come with us, just as in the late '50s and the late '60s, the appeal was made by Abraham Lincoln and those connected with him, to leave the old parties that had become useless, to leave the old parties that no longer represented the will and interests and the high aspirations of the American people and come with the Progressive party of that day—the Republican party of Abraham Lincoln—and so, friends, we ask you to come with us now—ex-Republicans, ex-Democrats alike—for we are true to the principles which every party in the United States has served, just so long as it was able to serve the people.

We are true to the Democracy of Andrew Jackson, just as we are true to the Republicanism of Abraham Lincoln, and the same staunch [words omitted?] friends, were leveled against these men in their youth when they stood for the new party that are leveled against us now. The Whigs were

3. Henry E. McGinn (1859–1923) was a local lawyer and former district attorney in Portland.

asked why they had remained loyal so long to the old leaders and now cast them aside.

Lincoln was asked why he no longer served the men whom he had served in the past: why he abandoned men whom he had followed or by whom he had stood. His answer was that he was bound to be right, that he followed any man so long as that man was right and served the people, and when he ceased to serve the people, and ceased to lead in the fight for righteousness then it became his (Lincoln's) duty to leave him and he did leave him, and, friends, it has been no easy task, no light work for men to leave the parties with which they had been throughout their lives affiliated.

They err who fail to see that for years the signs have been such that had the politicians had the eyes to see they would have seen them. It has been said by my enemies that this is a one-man movement, this movement is in my interest. If it were a movement for any one man, for me or anyone else, I wouldn't be in it myself. I am in it because it springs, as every great movement must spring, from the hearts of the people themselves.

Friends, this movement was to come any way. The people for some years had been growing more and more discontented with the way in which they had been represented by men in political life. The people have for a number of years been growing more and more discontented with the failure of men in public life to grapple with the evil conditions in the economic and industrial life of the day. They were prepared to shatter the old machines and they were preparing to come together in a new party that should really be a party of the people.

They were tired of seeing an insincere fight waged on hollow issues between parties neither of which greatly believed in the convictions it expressed or greatly disbelieved in the convictions expressed by its foes. The time was ripe. All that I in any way did was to bring the movement about a little quicker than it would otherwise have come. It would have come any way shortly. The part that I played was gradually to bring on a little sooner than it would otherwise have come, and the occasion of its coming was furnished by the bosses at the Republican National convention held in Chicago last June.

When I went into the primaries I did so very reluctantly and only because a conviction had been forced upon me that men whom I had earnestly believed would serve the people had not served the people, and only because the conviction came to me, reluctantly, that those whom I had believed would carry the cause of the people forward had deserted the people, had turned about and looked backward. Then, and then only, I came out myself as a candidate, but only when I found that the people who I had thought would serve the people had deserted them and were serving the enemies of the people; and, friends, when I was then forced to make the choice there was no room for hesitation.

I couldn't hesitate when the choice was between those who I thought would serve the people and who had deserted the people, and on the other side, the people themselves.

I had to go with the people.

I had to stand by the principles that I have always held.

I had to stand by the people of the United States; and now, to clear away any possible misunderstanding, let me say a word about the future.

We progressives have declared for a given platform which we say is our programme, our covenant with the people. If any man elected on the Progressive ticket fails in good faith to do everything in his power to carry out the principles of our platform, I will turn against him. I will do my best to defeat him, for my fealty is to the people themselves and not to any man who misrepresents the people. And whether now I am supporting such a man or not will not alter the way I behave if the man proves false to the people who put him in office. In other words, friends, I hold that every public servant, and I, just as much as any other public servant, that all of us are instruments with which the people are to work. Take a given instrument and a given task, use the instrument as long as it is the best instrument available, and when it breaks, or another more fit is at hand, throw aside the old instrument and go ahead with the task.

Throw aside the public man when he no longer represents you, or when another man can represent you better, throw him aside. Whether I am the man or whether anyone else is the man matters not. The cause matters everything and the personality of the man is of no consequence whatever, excepting as for the moment it may make him of use in advancing the cause.

In the civil warfare of today act as Lincoln acted in the Civil War. Some of you men have served in the Army of the Potomac, undoubtedly, and you know Lincoln had tried man after man at the head of that army, instrument after instrument he took, because it seemed to be the one with which he could work, and he used it until it broke in his hand and with sorrow he cast it to one side, took up another instrument as it was his duty to do, and continued to do the work as best he could until that instrument broke; and finally after testing man after man his choice settled on the great silent captain, on Grant (hearty applause).

And so, friends, as Lincoln did in his day we must do in ours, and I know

William A. Barnes, Jr., was a conservative leader in New York State who had kept the delegation in line for Taft at the Republican National Convention. He was an object of Roosevelt's scorn in several speeches. (Library of Congress)

that the men who wore the blue will be the first to welcome into the new movement their fallen foes who wore the gray. Nothing could be better, for not merely the new movement but for the new country, a rejuvenated country which will spring from the new movement.

In the August convention we had ex-Confederates standing shoulder to shoulder with the Union men in making the new party, and the sons of ex-Confederates like Judge Ben Lindsay [*sic*], joining with the sons of ex-Union men to serve the common country, knowing no rivalship, save the rivalship of seeing which could serve their common country best; and, friends, the only place in which a veteran of the Civil War, the only place in which the men who voted from Freemont [*sic*] to Lincoln, can feel really at home is in the Progressive party.

You can't be true to the principles of Lincoln if you surrender your souls into the keeping of Penrose, Barnes and Guggenheim. You can be true to the principles of Lincoln only if you are supporting the party which at Chicago in the Progressives National Convention put forth the best and bravest platform that any National party has put forth since the close of the Civil War; and friends, I want to call your attention to the fact that we are only nominally fighting two parties. We are really fighting the same representatives of interest in both the old parties.

Well meaning but foolish people have proposed to rebook [rebuke?] to the bosses who shattered the Republican party at Chicago by voting for the bosses who triumphed at Baltimore. Now there isn't anything that the bosses of both parties more cordially appreciate than the action of the well-meaning so-called independent who strives alternately to punish each set of bosses by putting the other set in power.

Judge McGinn—True, indeed.

Now, whether these bosses are called Penrose, Barnes and Guggenheim or Murphy and Sullivan and Taggart, doesn't make any difference. It is the same old boss. Republican or Democrat, whatever his name may be, our proposal is to do away with the boss definitely and for good. Our proposal is not merely to smash the individual bosses, but to destroy the conditions which have made boss-ship practicable, and in doing that also to destroy conditions which have made possible the triumph of special privilege in our National life in business and finance; and we propose, and our programme is brief and simple and we have lived up to it in the primaries last year in every state where there was a primary, and we forgot the bosses that were against us.

And at Chicago they were willing to wreck the Republican party rather than to see me nominated, and now, friends, I want to call your attention to just what that meant.

It was not primarily because of me.

They didn't like me. I know that, and I am a little proud of it; but that wasn't the reason that actuated them mainly.

They didn't like me and they dreaded you, you, the people here (applause).

The theft of the nomination really wasn't really from me. It was from you.

They stole the nomination from the people without any reference to who the individual man was whom the people at the moment happened to want.

They regarded as all important that there should be no upsetting of the existing conditions of the political life. And the two old parties, the Republican party and Democratic party, each in its internal organization, is perpetuating the old conditions, the conditions which can be kept up by the successful alliance of the crooked politicians with the crooked man of business, and, finally, with the newspaper that is controlled by such politicians, by the newspaper that is controlled by such politics and by such business or is directly or indirectly so influenced by the bosses and the big beneficiaries of privilege who stand behind the bosses. That paper is no longer a free organ for the expression of the popular will.

Shouts from the audience—The *Oregonian.*[4]

I can name some newspapers in New York of that kind, but I will leave you to do the naming here.

Now, friends, remember what this fight in its essentials is.

It is a fight of both of the old parties against us. It is a fight of both the old parties to continue the old system against the men who are seeking to bring into effect here in America a new system, a new system, so old, the system of having the people rule their own Government, a rule that will bring about a real and not a nominal system of justice, not only in politics, but in our economic and social life as well; and, friends, I want to call your attention to two significant actions recently.

Among the leading Republicans of New York was a number of big—was the head of the big banking house of Kuhn-Loeb & Company, the second most important banking house in New York, Mr. Jacob Schiff.

Now, mind you, Mr. Schiff is a thoroughly respectable and well-meaning man. I am sure that he means to do what is right. The trouble is that he doesn't know you and that he is afraid of you. He thinks of you as the mob and his idea is that you should be controlled decently and owned by the boss and the big financier who is allied with the boss. Recently Mr. Schiff announced that although he had been a Republican all his life he was now going to support the Democratic ticket, and he gave two reasons.

They were given in the *New York Times,* which is supporting Mr. Wilson, and is opposing me with a fervor of spirit that makes hydrophobia seem calm. Mr. Schiff announced in the first place that he hoped all his friends, that means all of Wall Street, some of them are able on the moment to conceal their friendship, that his friends would all support Mr. Wilson and not throw away their votes on Mr. Taft, because the essential thing was to beat me.

That means to beat you, and then came the statement which at first puzzled me.

He said that the only way to preserve the Republican party was to elect Wilson. I studied over that a minute and then I saw what he meant. He meant that if we would triumph we would smash not merely both of the older machines but the system that produced the old machines as well; and

4. The audience was shouting out the name of the local paper, the *Oregonian,* which was strongly pro-Taft and anti-Roosevelt in its news coverage.

that therefore it was to the interest of every man who represented the kind of interest that he did, who felt as he did, to support the party that they thought might beat us, because they thought that if we were beaten that would re-establish the old see-saw between the two old parties which was controlled by the old type of boss and political machine.

You see what Mr. Schiff's theory is, that our political life ought to consist of this see-saw, a plank—the same plank—labeled Republican at one end and labeled Democratic at the other end, and the labels of the two ends different, but the same plank; the Republican party with a lot of Republican bosses on one end of the plank, and the Democratic party with a lot of Democratic bosses on the other end of the plank, and then see-saw; one end of the plank up, and then the other end of the plank up, the Republican party up and then the Democratic party up, but the same boss always up, and see-saw, with Wall street teetering in the middle, putting up whatever end of the plank it thought at the moment would serve its purposes.

Now, friends, that is briefly an exact description of the present situation of the political situation which our foes wish to see perpetuated.

The type of man, the Mr. Taggart, the Mr. Penrose and bosses of that kind, the financiers who stand behind bosses of that kind, they have each a tepid preference for one party over the other, but it is a very tepid preference compared to the intensity of the burning zeal with which he wishes to keep either party in power rather than see you come to power. In other words, those bosses and the big men in finance behind them do precisely as two corporation lawyers on opposite sides of a corporation suit do. Both fight with each other in the suit, but they will come together as one man against the common foes, and you are the common foe. They are against us not because we are against some one particular man, but because we are against the system which produces such men. They are against us because we fight the political and economic system today, as in your day you fought against slavery.

And now, friends, I ask your attention to another matter to which Judge McGinn alluded. There were Messrs. Archbold and Penrose—Penrose at the head of the Pennsylvania machine which we smashed in the primaries; Archbold at the moment the biggest leader of the Standard Oil trust—they appeared before the Senate committee and testified against me. Let me point out the fact that if I had been in private life they never would have come in and testified against me. They didn't care for me, myself, so far as I was concerned. They testified against me because for the moment it happened that I was leading your fight and they wanted to do anything they could to damage your cause. They can't do it. After they testified I said: "The Lord hath delivered them into my hands."

Judge McGinn—That is correct. (Great applause).

They have asked for the sword. They shall have it. Now I can get at them in open field. They testified on Friday and Saturday. On Saturday I sent a telegram to the chairman of the sub-committee, Senator Clark [Clapp], asking that I be heard on Monday; you see they stopped testifying on Saturday. The only reason I didn't ask to be heard on Sunday was because I couldn't be heard on Sunday. Senator Clark [Clapp] stayed there in Washington. Every standpat Republican or Democrat scattered to the four winds of heaven, and Mr. Archbold went to Europe. I wrote at once to Senator Clark [Clapp] a letter which is now published at the progressive headquarters and which I would like everyone here to get because I went into the thing at length. I don't want to go into it at the moment, into the accusations against me, except to point out this fact. These accusations are really not against me at all, but against Mr. Cornelius Bliss, who is dead. Mr. Bliss lived for seven years after the event happened, but they never brought the accusation against him during those seven years. He is dead.

They say that Mr. Bliss blackmailed them and that he told them that I knew it. This accusation against me is that those two worthy citizens, Penrose and Archbold, say that a dead man told them eight years ago that I knew something about what he was trying to do. That is not the kind of evidence that would be received in court, is it, Judge McGinn?

Judge McGinn—The witness would have to be bolstered up, Colonel.

I will bolster them (applause). And what I want to call your attention to is the curious side-lights that their testimony gave on themselves and what my administration had done. In the first place, as regards themselves, Mr. Penrose and Mr. Archbold testified that Mr. Penrose advised the Standard Oil Company or Mr. Archbold to make a blackmailing contribution in order that they should avoid being punished for wrongdoing. The exact expression of Penrose, which is found on page 164 of the printed testimony, is, "I advised him," Archbold, "that it was a mistake not to contribute; that if he didn't, the Standard Oil Company might incur hostility in certain circles." That meant me. Now I want to call your attention to this. The Standard Oil Company couldn't incur my hostility unless it broke the law. So long as the Standard Oil Company didn't break the law it would have no more to fear from me than anyone of us here today would have to fear from the police. If you find a man paying a couple of hundred dollars you can guarantee that it is not from motives of philanthropy, and if he says it is, that he may not incur police hostility, you may be sure that he is doing something that the police ought to be hostile to. Now in regard to Mr. Archbold's testimony: In that did he protest against being blackmailed? Not a bit. He didn't protest that at all, and he had no idea that he was accusing Mr. Bliss of bad conduct or bad character. He said Bliss was a splendid man and that he had a splendid character. Not that I, Judge McGinn, accuse Bliss for a moment of having a bad character, nor do I say his conduct was bad. Archbold said that he didn't mind being blackmailed. What he objected to was that he didn't get the goods (applause). There was one refreshing bit of testimony when his feelings suddenly overcame him. This is on page 133 of the testimony:

"Darkest Abyssinia has nothing to show comparable with the treatment administered to the Standard Oil Company during the Roosevelt administration."

Now, he was right about that. I did administer the Abyssinian treatment to the Standard Oil Company, and if ever I am President again and the Standard Oil Company doesn't mend its way, or any other corporation behaves as the Standard Oil Company then behaved, I will administer the Abyssinian treatment again, and that is just what Messrs. Archbold and Penrose know. They don't complain of any Abyssinian treatment under the present administration and they haven't the slightest fear of the Abyssinian treatment under either of the old parties. They recognize their foes and you are their foes. They fear the party of the people themselves. They know they can make their terms with the bosses. They know they can't make their terms with the people of the United States, and so Messrs. Penrose and Archbold, and the Penroses and the Archbolds throughout this land are willing to help Mr. Taft, and if, as they have grown to see that it is hopeless; then to help Mr. Wilson if they can only beat us, if they can beat the Progressive party, if they can beat the candidates of the Progressive party and the people who stand behind these candidates. They can't do it.

And now, friends, I wish to ask your support because of the enemies we have made. I ask your support because of the principles for which we stand. We are standing for social and economic justice, and our proposals are not mere abstractions, but they are concrete. One of these proposals, friends—it seems strange to appear to argue for it here on the Pacific slope—one of our proposals is to give women the same right to vote that men have, which represents a step toward industrial and social justice which I have come to believe in, not because of my study of it alone, not because of what I have read in books, but primarily because I have known life, because more and more as I have studied life, and as I have gotten over the prejudices which we all inherited. I have grown to realize that while there must be a wide difference of function between men and women there should be equality of right. I have grown to feel that there are certain cruel wrongs of which women are too often the victims and which cannot be righted unless we give the women not only the power to defend themselves by the ballot, but their right to the respect of men. Now, friends, this is only one of the incidents in which we are trying to secure social and industrial justice. We should help the cause of the farmer and make it our own. We have been content too long in this country to permit a haphazard neglect for the farmer's rights and interests and a haphazard interest on the part of the Government to the welfare of the men who live in the open country. We must turn the Government more and more into an agent for the betterment of those who live in the open country and make it an agent for the betterment of the man, so that he may get more out of his soil and may join with his fellows to do in common the work that ought to be done in common, and especially to market his goods in common, so that the price paid by the consumer shall go from his pocket into the pocket of the farmer and not stop in some other pocket between.

This is the most efficient way in which to deal with the problem of the high cost of living. So, with the wage worker our proposals are perfectly definite. We take the position that no community is in a healthy condition if the less fortunate members of it are crushed under social and industrial conditions. We are our brother's keepers. It would be the rankest kind of injustice to give equality of reward when there is gross inequality of service. We should see that there is a living wage paid to the wage workers of this country men and women alike. We propose to do away with child labor everywhere, and while we wish to work through the states we are more fortunate than our opponents in the sense that we decline to make a fetish of the states' rights.

We are for states' rights. Where the people's rights means states' rights, we are for states' rights, and where they mean National rights we are for National rights. We are for the people's rights in every case. We propose to establish in continuous industries where they labor seven days a week and 24 hours a day, we propose to establish by law that there shall be one day's rest in seven and that, inasmuch as in those industries there must be either two 12 hour shifts a day or three eight-hour shifts a day.

In those industries we will establish by law an eight-hour day for labor. We propose to provide for the safeguarding of dangerous machinery, for a workmen's compensation act and for all similar types of legislation; and, friends, in doing this we are acting not merely in the interests of the wage-worker, but we are acting in the interest of all of us, for our assumption is that this country won't be a good place for anyone to live in unless we make it a pretty good place for everyone. Friends, in these reforms we have been asking that the lead be taken not primarily by the men and women who are most to benefit from them and above all in no spirit of hatred, of sullen anger and revenge, but that the lead should be taken by the men and women who have no immediate personal concern, but who have it borne in on them that they cannot see their less fortunate brothers and sisters beaten down in the stress of modern industrial life. I ask for the leadership of the man to whom much has been given that they may themselves freely, as a matter of justice and duty, take initiative in righting the wrongs of their brethren to whom less has been given.

My plea is for a disinterested leadership. My plea is for the recognition by each of us that the other is indeed his brother and that none of us has done his duty if he hasn't striven to make the condition of his neighbor a little bit better off. Now, friends, I am not asking the impossible and I am not promising the impossible. I am not promising the millennium. You men of the Civil War didn't bring the millennium before your victory, but you saved the Union and you abolished slavery. You rendered one of the greatest services to humanity ever rendered by any men of any generation and you left the ground cleared of the party's wrong so that your children could act with unhampered hands to grapple with the wrongs that arise in our day. Now that is all that I expect that we can do if successful. We won't bring the millennium or anything like it.

We can do away with the mass of existing wrongs and we can clear the way for a better and truer life for our children not to stagger under the accumulated burden of wrongs that their fathers permitted to exist, but grapple with the wrongs that arise in their day with the same spirit with which we will have to grapple with the wrongs of our day. That is all I am promising.

Friends, our opponents have said that I go about the country preaching discontent and class hatred. I have never in my life preached hatred of any class except the class of crooks, and I have never preached discontent with anything except that which was wrong. My experience has been that the same qualities which make a good big man make a good little man, and vice versa. I don't admire a little crook any more than I admire a big crook. It is merely that the big crooks are more dangerous, but both are equally bad. My experience has been that any man who preaches hatred, envy and jealousy, any man who tries to arouse the wicked and ill-feelings toward those who are better off is just the kind of a man who would oppress those who are less well off.

There is substantially the same feeling at the bottom of hatred and envy by the poor man toward the rich man. They are just two sides of the same evil feeling and one feeling is to be condemned as much as the other. I am bound to strive with all the strength there is in me to try to make conditions better, juster and fairer and do what I can toward helping up men and women whom I see struggle painfully along because the road is needlessly hard for them. I am also bound to work in Abraham Lincoln's spirit of malice toward none with charity toward all, and if I fail to work in that spirit my work will not be good, and I know no law, friends, that the wit of man can devise that will make any man succeed if he hasn't got the right stuff in him. If he is weak, vicious or drunken, if he is foolish, you can't make him succeed. You know that. You know that after we have done everything that can be done to bring nearer the day when there will be justice, there will still be men and women who will fail. I am not expecting to make everyone succeed, but I am hoping and believing that if we progressives are true to our principles and true to our platform, and if the people give us a chance to apply these principles of our platform, the covenant into which we entered for an actual purpose, I hope and believe that we can make things measurably better, that we can smooth some of the rough places for those with whom life comes undeservedly hard; that we can make conditions of life such that it can be easier for the next man and the next woman to live their lives under proper conditions; to earn their daily bread in such a manner that they shall bring up their children to be fit for citizenship and the exacting duties of citizenship in this great Republic of ours.

I don't expect to get the millennium, but I do believe we can measurably better the economic, the social and the political condition of this Republic; and therefore, friends, I appeal to you, as I appeal to all our fellow-countrymen, to stand with us, for we stand for the two basic principles of the right of the people to rule themselves and duty so to rule, as to bring nearer the day when there shall be social and industrial justice for every man and every woman within the borders of this great land of ours. (Great applause.)

Portland *Oregonian*, 12 September 1912.

Roosevelt's next speech, at San Francisco, brought one of the most dramatic moments of the campaign against Wilson. On 9 September, speaking at the New York Press Club, Wilson had attacked Roosevelt's idea of having the federal government regulate large corporations along the lines of the New Nationalism.

Such a union of business and government, Wilson said, would raise the prospect of absolute power. "Has justice ever grown in the soil of absolute power? Has not justice always come from the press of the heart and spirit of men who resist power?" These words did not appear in the account of the speech the New York Tribune, *a Republican newspaper, sent out across the country.*

Wilson then added sentences that were in the news reports Roosevelt received. "Liberty has never come from the government. Liberty has always come from the subjects of the government. The history of liberty is a history of resistance. The history of liberty is a history of the limitation of government power, not the increase of it." Roosevelt decided to make this statement the keynote of the speech he would give in San Francisco.[5]

An Address at the San Francisco Coliseum, 14 September 1912

Mr. Chairman, and you, my fellow citizens, men and WOMEN of San Francisco:

I put the emphasis where it belongs. It is a very great pleasure for me to be here this evening and I esteem myself especially fortunate in having Mr. Heney preside over this meeting.

He and I have fought in communities and many places together and in all the United States I know of no man who, whether in victory or defeat, fights with an equally undaunted soul against the powers of evil. And friends, it means very much to me to come here to California here to San Francisco to see you and to greet you and be greeted as you have greeted me this evening and I come before you not so much to give inspiration as to get it.

Nothing would have made me miss coming to California in this campaign, for I feel that this is peculiarly California's campaign. California has led the entire nation in this movement, and the first thing I wish to do here in this speech to-night is on behalf of the entire Progressive party of the Union, to express our profound obligation to California. I tell you when we saw those flags that are here now coming along with the delegation at Chicago in June it gave new heart to every man, and there was no delegation there which kept as united a front and showed as the Californians showed; they showed not the least little trace of wavering at any time.

5. For a discussion of this episode, see John Wells Davidson, ed., *A Crossroads of Freedom: The 1912 Campaign Speeches of Woodrow Wilson* (New Haven, Conn.: Yale University Press, 1956), pp. 129–130.

Roosevelt made his campaign tours by train in 1912. As a candidate and political celebrity, he traveled with an entourage of aides, a doctor, and a bevy of journalists. (Theodore Roosevelt Collection, Harvard College Library)

You actually have done in this State what we promise to do in the nation, and your achievement is the guaranty that our promise will be made good. The Republicanism of Abraham Lincoln, which was the progressivism of its day, is to be found in the Republicanism of California under Hiram Johnson, and it is to be found in the national Progressive party.

It has not one thing in common with the sordid baseness of the present national Republican organization which has abandoned the people and has abandoned every principle of honesty and of popular rule and surrendered itself to servile subjection under the bossism of the Penroses and the Barneses.

But the great beneficiaries of privilege and the believers in boss rule have now abandoned the idea they can elect Mr. Taft and the Republican ticket. They are concentrating their efforts upon electing the Democratic National ticket and Mr. Wilson. Some of them prefer Mr. Taft and some of them prefer Mr. Wilson, but it is a tepid preference in either case compared with the intensity of their desire to beat the Progressive party with either Mr. Taft or Mr. Wilson. And every true Progressive in the country will support us against both Mr. Wilson and Mr. Taft. In view of the Democratic platform and of the utterance of Mr. Wilson no man can claim to be a Progressive who supports Mr. Wilson on that platform and backed by that party.

The other day in New York Mr. Wilson came out in a sweeping assault on the Progressive platform and programme, and defined his own position as to social and industrial justice. According to the stenographic report of his speech in the "Tribune," Mr. Wilson stated that there is no hope for social reform through the platform of the Progressive party, saying: "In the very platform itself is supplied the demonstration that it is not a serviceable instrument. They do propose to serve civilization and humanity, but they cannot serve civilization and humanity with that kind of government. The history of liberty is a history of the limitation of governmental power, not the increase of it." And he then continues to uphold what he calls "representative government" and "representative assemblies" as against the platform that we propose, and also to uphold the Democratic proposal for dealing with labor and the trusts as against the Progressive proposals.[6]

Mr. Wilson is fond of asserting his platonic devotion to the purposes of the Progressive Party. But such platonic devotion is utterly worthless from a political standpoint because he antagonizes the only means by which those purposes can be made effective. It is idle to profess devotion to progressive principles and at the same time to antagonize the only methods by which they can be realized in actual fact.

The key to Mr. Wilson's position is found in the statement I have quoted where he says that "The history of liberty is a history of the limitation of governmental power, not the increase of it." This is a bit of outworn academic doctrine which was kept in the schoolroom and the professorial study for a generation after it had been abandoned by all who had experience of actual life. It is simply the laissez-faire doctrine of the English political economists three-quarters of a century ago. It can be applied with profit, if anywhere at all, only in a primitive community such as the United States at the end of the eighteenth century, a community before the days of Fulton, Morse and Edison.[7] To apply it now in the United States at the beginning of the twentieth century, with its highly organized industries, with its railways, telegraphs and telephones, means literally and absolutely to refuse to make a single effort to better any one of our social or industrial conditions. Moreover Mr. Wilson is absolutely in error in his statement, from the historical standpoint. So long as governmental power existed ex-

6. The news account had fused two sections of Wilson's speech that were originally some distance apart. See for the first two sentences, Davidson, *A Crossroads of Freedom,* pp. 131–132, and for the third sentence, Ibid., p. 130.

7. Robert Fulton (1765–1815) developed the steamboat. Samuel F. B. Morse (1791–1872) invented the telegraph, and Thomas Alva Edison (1847–1941) had numerous inventions, including the electric light and the phonograph, to his credit.

clusively for the king and not at all for the people, then the history of liberty was a history of the limitations of governmental power. But now the governmental power rests in the people and the kings who enjoyed privilege are the kings of the financial and industrial world and what they clamor for is the limitation of governmental power and what the people sorely need is the extension of governmental power. If Mr. Wilson's statement means nothing, then he ought not to have made it. If it means anything it means that every law for the promotion of social and industrial justice ought to be repealed, and every law proposed should be abandoned, for without exception every such law represents an increase of governmental power.

The Interstate Commerce Commission law represented a great increase of governmental power. Does Mr. Wilson mean to repeal it? If not, does he deny that it represents a great increase of governmental power over the railroads? Let him take whichever horn of the dilemma he chooses. Either his statement is not in accordance with the facts or else he is bound, if it is in accordance with the facts as he sees them, to include in his programme the repeal of the Interstate Commerce Commission act. Again, every Progressive State in the Union has passed laws for factory inspection; every such law means an increase in governmental power.

Is Mr. Wilson in favor of repealing such laws? If he is not, then what does he mean by saying that the history of liberty is the history of the limitation of governmental power? The fact is that his statement is a mere bit of professorial rhetoric, which has not one particle of foundation in the facts of the present day. If it were only a bit of professorial rhetoric, I should not pay any heed to it, but Mr. Wilson is a candidate for President and we have a right to know just what his intentions are and just whether he means what he says.

Again, we propose to limit the hours of working girls to eight hours a day; we propose to limit the hours of workingmen in continuous industry to eight hours a day and to give them one day's rest a week. Both of these proposals represent an increase in the exercise of governmental power, an extension of governmental power. Does Mr. Wilson mean that he is against this extension? If not, then his sentence which I have quoted, and which represents the keynote of his speech, means nothing whatever.

In other words, Mr. Wilson's promise is either a promise that is not to be kept or else it means the undoing of every particle of social and industrial advance we have made and the refusal to go forward along the lines of industrial and social progress. He stands for a policy which necessarily means, if that policy is honestly put into effect, that he must be against every single progressive measure, for every progressive measure means an extension instead of a limitation of government control.

We propose to do away with occupational disease. Is he against this proposition? He must be if he believes in limitation of government control. We propose a women's [workmen's] compensation act. Is he against this proposition? He must be if he sincerely means that he is in favor of the limitation of government control. We propose to regulate the conditions of work in factories, the conditions of life in tenement-houses, the conditions of life and work in construction camps—every one of these proposals means an extension of government control. Is he against them?

Either he is against his own principles or else he is against these reforms. He can choose either horn of the dilemma he wishes; but one of [or] the other he must choose. He has definitely committed himself to the use of the taxing power only for the purpose of raising revenues. In that case he is against its use to put out of existence the poisonous-match industry. He is against its use for the purpose of preventing opium coming into this country. He is against its use for preventing wild-cat banking.

In short he is against its use in every case where we now use it to tax out of existence dangers and abuses.

The trouble with Mr. Wilson is that he is following an outworn philosophy and that the history of which he is thinking is the history of absolute monarchies and oriental despotisms. He is thinking of government as embodied in an absolute king or an oligarchy or aristocracy. He is not thinking of our government which is a government by the people themselves. The only way in which our people can increase their power over the big corporation that does wrong; the only way in which it can protect the working man in his conditions of work and life, the only way in which people can protect children working in industry or secure women an eight-hour day in industry or secure compensation for men killed or crippled in industry, is by extending instead of limiting the powers of government.

There is no analogy whatever, from the standpoint of real liberty, and of real popular need, between the limitation of an irresponsible monarch or a dominant aristocracy and the limitations sought to be imposed by big financiers, big corporation lawyers and by well-meaning students of a dead and gone system of political economy on the power of the people to right social wrongs and limit social abuses, and to secure for the humble what, unless there is an extension of the powers of the government, the arrogant and the powerful will certainly take from the humble. If Mr. Wilson really believes what he has said, then he has no idea of our government in its actual workings. He is not thinking of modern American history or of present day American needs.

He is thinking of Magna-Charta, which limited the power of the English King because this power had before been absolute. He is thinking of the Bill of Rights, which limited the power of the governing class in the interest of the people who could not control that governing class. Our proposal is to increase the power of the people themselves and make the people in reality the governing class. Therefore Mr. Wilson's proposal is really to limit the power of the people and thereby to leave unchecked the colossal, embodied privileges of the present day. Now, friends, you can adopt one philosophy or the other. You can adopt the philosophy of laissez-faire, or the limitation of governmental power and turn the industrial life of this country into a chaotic scramble of selfish interests, each bent on plundering the others and all bent on oppressing the wageworker.

This is precisely and exactly what Mr. Wilson's proposal means; and it can mean nothing else. Under such limitation of governmental power as he praises every railroad must be left unchecked, every great industrial concern can do as it chooses with its employees and with the general public; women must be permitted to work as many hours a day as their taskmasters bid them; great corporations must be left unshackled to put down wages to a starvation limit and to raise the price of their products as high as monopolistic control will permit. The reverse policy means an extension, instead of a limitation, of governmental power; and for that extension we Progressives stand.

We propose to handle the colossal industrial concerns in interstate business; and we propose to go forward in the control of both, doing justice to each, but exacting justice from each, and we propose to work for justice to the farmer and wage-worker in the same fashion.

Let me give you a concrete instance of what Mr. Wilson's policy, if applied, means as compared with ours. The Stanley committee, the Democratic committee of the Democratic House of Representatives, has just practically applied its interpretation about trusts, which is substantially the Republican platform, the Wilson-Taft platform. Some time previously under Government suit the Standard Oil Trust was dissolved. Under the decree of the court the Standard Oil Company was split up into a lot of smaller companies, precisely as the Stanley report proposes that similar trusts shall be split up. What has been the actual result?

All the companies are still under the same control, or at least working in such close alliance that the effect is precisely the same. The price of the stock has gone up over 100 per cent, so that Mr. Rockefeller and his associates have actually seen their fortunes doubled by the policy which Mr. Wilson advocates and which Mr. Taft defends. At the same time the price of oil to the consumer has gone up by leaps and bounds. No wonder that Wall Street's prayer is "Oh, Merciful Providence, give us another dissolution."

The Progressive proposal is the direct reverse of this. If we had our way, there would be an administrative body to deal radically and thoroughly with such cases as that of the Standard Oil Company. We would make any split of the company that was necessary real and not nominal. We would step in in such a case as this, where the value of the stock was going up in such enormous proportion, and forbid any increase of the price of the product. We would examine thoroughly and searchingly the books of the company and put a stop to every type of rebate and to every practice which would result in the swindling either of the investors or competitors or wageworkers or of the general public.

In short, the Taft-Wilson plan has actually resulted in enormously benefitting Mr. Rockefeller and his associates and is causing serious damage to all consumers. Our plan—the plan to which Mr. Archbold of the Standard Oil Trust so feelingly objects as "Abyssinian treatment"—would result in preventing any increase of cost to the consumer and in exercising the kind of radical control over the corporation itself which would prevent the stock-gambling antics which result in enormous profits to those on the inside—to those who, in the parlance of the street, know that "there is a melon to be cut."

Now, gentlemen, I have stated to you as fairly as I know how what Mr. Wilson's plan is, if his words mean anything, and what our plan is. And I ask every workingman, every farmer, every professional and business man to say for themselves which is best. I do not wonder that the crooked trusts and the great bosses are rallying to a man behind Mr. Wilson. They know that they can do nothing with Mr. Taft; that he is dead. And they are now rallying with enthusiasm to the cause of Mr. Wilson, and their organs and mouthpieces in the metropolitan press are supporting him with delight because they know that his principles, if carried into effect, meant that every great crooked trust in this country will flourish.

But the honest business man, the honest man in every branch of industry, and especially the small and the moderate size business man and professional man, the wage-workers and the farmers have nothing to hope from such a programme. It may be that in a period of great prosperity for a few years they could not appreciate the damage it was doing to them. But sooner or later they would find that under such a programme privilege was enthroned and special interest fortified, and that the big man left uncontrolled by governmental action, had profited to an enormous and incredible degree at the expense of the smaller man.

The people of the United States have but one instrument which they can effectively use against the colossal combinations of business—and that instrument is the Government of the United States (and of course in the several States the government of the States where they can be utilized).

Mr. Wilson's proposal is that the people of the United States shall throw away this, the one great instrument, the one great weapon they have with which to secure themselves against wrong. He proposes to limit the governmental action of the people and therefore to leave unlimited and unchecked the action of the great corporations whose enormous power constitutes so serious a problem in modern industrial life. Remember that it is absolutely impossible to limit the power of these great corporations except by extending the power of the Government. All that these great corporations ask is that the power of the government shall be limited. No wonder they are supporting Mr. Wilson for he is advocating for them what they hardly dare venture to advocate for themselves.

These great corporations rarely want anything from the government except to be let alone and to be permitted to work their will unchecked by the Government. All that they really want is that governmental action shall be limited. In every great corporation suit the corporation lawyer will be found protesting against extension of governmental power. Every court decision favoring a corporation takes the form of declaring unconstitutional some extension of governmental power. Every corporation magnate in the country who is not dealing honestly and fairly by his fellows asks nothing better than that Mr. Wilson's programme be carried out and that there be stringent limitation of the Government's power.

There once was a time in history when the limitation of governmental power meant increasing liberty for the people. In the present day, the limitation of governmental power, of governmental action, means the enslavement of the people by the great corporations who can only be held in check through the extention of governmental power.

In another recent speech Mr. Wilson has taken his stand squarely on the Democratic platform about the tariff. The Democratic platform says that the tariff is unconstitutional in so far as it gives protection and that therefore it must be entirely removed. Mr. Wilson states that the protective tariff is a "malignant growth that requires a surgical operation"; and he explicitly promises to be the surgeon to "cut out the deadly thing."[8] Here again, if language means anything, either in the platform or the speeches of the candidate, there is a direct promise to destroy the protective tariff. This is not a promise to reform it, to reduce it, to do away with it where it is excessive, to see that the wage-worker is benefited by it, that it operates to the advantage of the producer and at the same time benefits the consumer. These are the promises of the Progressive platform.

Mr. Wilson's promise is a tariff for destruction. If a protective tariff is unconstitutional; if a protective tariff is a "malignant growth," which he proposes to "cut out," then it is disingenuous to say that the operation shall be done in a slow and leisurely fashion so as not to damage the patient. A malignant growth must be cut out at once; an unconstitutional law must be repealed at once.

Either Mr. Wilson and the Democratic party are promising what they do not intend to perform or else they are solemnly pledged at once to destroy our whole protective system. Now, friends, if men state in their platform and speeches what they do not intend to carry out, what they do not mean, then surely they are not entitled to trust. We are bound to treat them as sincere and, therefore, to assume that they mean what they say; and if such is the case, and if Mr. Wilson and the Democratic party, in good faith, endeavor to keep their pre-election pledges about the tariff, they will throw this country into widespread industrial panic and chaos. The Republican proposal is a tariff for privilege; the Democratic proposal is a tariff for destruction; the Progressive proposal is a tariff for labor; a tariff which shall give to the American business man his fair show, both permitting and requiring him to pay the American laborer the wage necessary to keep up the standard of living in this country.

Mr. Wilson's attitude toward the tariff is exactly in keeping with his attitude toward social and industrial reform. He is against the minimum wage for women exactly as he is against protective tariff. His principles would prevent us from effectually helping labor or effectually regulating and controlling big business. He is against using the power of the Government to help the people to whom the Government belongs. We take flat issue with him. We propose to do in the nation as you here in California have actually done. We propose to use the Government as the most efficient instrument for the uplift of our people as a whole. We propose to give fair chance to the worker, and to strengthen their rights. We propose to use the whole

8. Wilson used that image, if not those precise words, in a speech at the New York State Fair on 12 September. See Davidson, *A Crossroads of Freedom*, pp. 142–143.

power of the Government to protect all those who, under Mr. Wilson's laissez-faire system, are trodden down in the ferocious, scrambling rush of an unregulated and purely individualistic industrialism.

San Francisco Examiner, 15 September 1912.

5

Returning to Oyster Bay

After he spoke at San Francisco, Roosevelt went on to Los Angeles, where he gave another version of his remarks about Woodrow Wilson and limited power for government. He then journeyed through Arizona and New Mexico before heading north to Colorado on 19 September. During the two weeks that followed, he stumped through Nebraska, Kansas, Oklahoma, Arkansas, Tennessee, Louisiana, Georgia, and North Carolina before heading home to Oyster Bay, New York, to prepare for the second national tour.

As he proceeded eastward, Roosevelt continued his long-range debate with Wilson about the trusts and the proper way to regulate them. He also discussed the problems of the Mississippi River and its periodic floods at the Levee Convention in Memphis. When he went south, he stepped up his attacks on Wilson and the Democrats. At places he encountered protests from his audiences for his criticism of Wilson, but he also drew large and enthusiastic crowds wherever he appeared.

Two Speeches at Pueblo and Trinidad, Colorado, 19 September 1912

Pueblo

Now, I want to speak of the object lesson here of your Fuel and Iron Company as offering a commentary on Mr. Wilson's proposition of yesterday as to the management of the trusts. Mr. Wilson yesterday attacked the Progressive plank, saying that our proposal to control and regulate the trusts would not benefit business, because you needed competition, that what should be done is to encourage competitors in business, and also saying that if the Government gained control over these great corporations it would be bad for labor.[1]

Now I am in a city where your own industrial experiences conclusively refute Mr. Wilson's statement. The trouble with Mr. Wilson's proposal is that it is a proposal only of the schoolroom; that it's a proposal put forward by men whose knowledge is gained through books, not through life. He doesn't know the actual phases of our industries. He doesn't know what workingmen need and how they actually live.

In this town you have a competitor of the Steel Trust and in this town the advantages that Mr. Wilson sees in competition are fully evident and a *Survey* reporting on the conditions of workmen in this particular plant—the plant which is doing what Mr. Wilson hopes will be done universally—the *Survey* reports that in no other plant in the country are the conditions for the laboring man worse than here.[2]

Mr. Wilson says that faith must be put entirely in competition; that what is needed is to establish competitors with the Steel Trust. Mr. Wilson and Mr. Wilson's followers and supporters wholly neglect the human element in industries; they wholly forget that they are men and women and not merely machines that are doing the work of industry. Our proposal is to give the Government, through an efficient National commission, power over all these great corporations, power over the Steel Corporation and power over the competitors of the Steel Corporation—a commission that so far as is humanly possible will effectively do away with the conditions that tend improperly toward a monopoly and that work a monopoly.

Nevertheless, the Government will exercise control over each sufficient to see that it becomes the servant and not the master of the people. We made certain definite concrete proposals affecting just exactly such industries as this competitor of the Steel Trust. We say that there shall be a minimum wage for all women engaged in industry. A woman is less able to protect herself in industry than a man, and we cannot afford to have women worked by great employers or by small employers for a wage that makes misery and a constant tendency to submit to be trampled down to a condition worse than misery.

1. Wilson made these statements in a speech at Sioux Falls, South Dakota, on 17 September and then repeated his comments at Minneapolis the next day. See John Wells Davidson, ed., *A Crossroads of Freedom: The 1912 Campaign Speeches of Woodrow Wilson* (New Haven, Conn.: Yale University Press, 1956), pp. 175–176, 182–183.

2. Roosevelt is referring to John Andrews Fitch, "The Steel Industry and the People in Colorado," *Survey* 27 (3 February 1912): 1706–1720, which looked at working conditions in these communities.

We have got to have a minimum wage for women in industry; but Mr. Wilson says "No."

Mr. Wilson says that liberty is to be secured by the limitation of governmental powers. He is quite right. Liberty for some people will be secured by the limitation of governmental powers.

Here you have two great industries in this town. In one Mr. Rockefeller is dominant; in the other Mr. Guggenheim—that's the information I am given. (A voice. 'That's right.') Very good.[3]

Now Mr. Wilson will preserve the liberty of Mr. Guggenheim and Mr. Rockefeller. Mr. Wilson's proposal is to preserve their liberty by preventing governmental action on behalf of the people whom they employ.

Trinidad

Mr. Wilson should be above misquoting facts in order to bolster up his arguments. Mr. Wilson has an entire right to defend his own platform if he feels bold enough to do so, and an entire right to assail the Progressive platform, but he should confine himself to telling the facts as they are. In his speech yesterday he stated that the method now proposed by the Progressives to regulate the trusts was suggested by Messrs. Gary and [George Walbridge] Perkins before the committee of the House of Representatives named to look into the Steel Trust.[4] And he stated it was done to save the United States Steel Corporation from the necessity of doing its business better than its competitors.

Neither of these statements is in accordance with the facts. Not once only, but again and again, in messages to Congress and in speech after speech while I was President, I advocated the method proposed by the Progressives for handling the trust question, which is practically the principle applied in the Inter-State Commerce Commission.

I wish to call attention at this time to the fact that, as far as I know, the overwhelming majority of men who control both the Steel Corporation and the Harvester Trust are supporting Mr. Taft or Mr. Wilson. They are certainly opposing me. Indeed, as far as I know, the only man connected with either organization who is supporting me is Mr. Perkins himself.

3. John D. Rockefeller (1839–1937) was the head of Standard Oil, which owned Colorado Fuel and Iron.

4. Davidson, *A Crossroads of Freedom,* p. 175. Elbert H. Gary (1846–1927) was chairman of the board of United States Steel.

Mr. Wilson has not offered any action differing in any essential point from the action taken by the present Administration against the Standard Oil Trust. I do not wonder that every crooked monopoly which wished to be legalized confines its opposition to the Progressive Party and to me.

Mr. Wilson says the legislation we propose would put the workingman in the power of the big industrial concerns. There is a very simple way of testing the worth of this statement. Has the inter-State commerce law put the workingman more in the power of the railroads? Let Mr. Wilson answer this question. If it has, then it is his business to advocate the repeal of the inter-State commerce law.

New York Times, 20 September 1912.

A Speech at Topeka, Kansas, on Woodrow Wilson, 21 September 1912

At Detroit yesterday Mr. Wilson made a statement which purported to be an answer to what I said in Colorado.[5] I say purported because it was in no shape or way an answer at all. Mr. Wilson did not venture to state definitely his own position. Moreover, so far as his utterances can be said to contain any statement at all, it is simply a misstatement of the facts. Now Mr. Wilson has before him the Progressive platform and my speech before the Progressive National Convention, and he can obtain any other speech that I have made without the slightest difficulty. If he will read what I have said and then attribute to me what I have said and not what I have not, he will save me the painful necessity of pointing out his misstatements. His language at Detroit, as contained in the press reports, is confusing, so that I am not quite sure how much of the obscurity is due to obscurity of thought and how much to obscurity of expression.

Mr. Wilson states in rather disingenuous form—for he says it is a matter of "inference" from what I say—that I have said that it was not possible to check the supremacy of the trusts. Now if Mr. Wilson does not know that this is an absolute misstatement it is due to his deliberate refusal to read what I have said and what the platform has said. My statement is the direct reverse of that which Mr. Wilson alleges. I stated that his plan, or rather no plan—which is in effect only Mr. Taft's plan with a slight variation of

5. Davidson, *A Crossroads of Freedom,* p. 507.

sound and fury in the preamble—would leave the supremacy of the trusts unchallenged, but that, on the contrary, our plan for an extension of Governmental power will establish the Government in absolute and complete supremacy over the trusts.

Mr. Wilson says that our proposed commission would not tell how other men should be admitted into the field of competition with the trusts. This is an absolute misstatement. If Mr. Wilson had read the Progressive platform he would have been spared making such a misstatement, and he would do well hereafter not to attempt to state our position without taking the trouble to find out what it is. Our platform says explicitly that our commission must attack unfair competition, false capitalization, and special privilege, and by continued trained watchfulness guard and keep open equally to all the highways of American commerce.

This is the language of the platform. If Mr. Wilson had taken the trouble to read it before attacking it would have saved me the necessity of showing that he has directly inverted the truth about it. He continues by saying that our proposal is to say to the trusts that they are "beneficent" and "big but not cruel." This is such a preposterous misstatement that I suppose Mr. Wilson must have had a theory he was being funny when he made it.

Mr. Wilson's followers know their case is weak, and they also seem to be indulging in misstatements. One of them is represented as saying in Massachusetts the other day that our platform did not favor the organization of labor. As a matter of fact [it] contains the following plank:

"We favor the organization of the workers, men and women, as a means of protecting their interests and as a means of promoting their progress."

In this platform we say that the commission that we propose is to "maintain permanent active supervision over industrial corporations engaged in inter-State commerce, or such of them as are of public importance, doing for them what the Government now does for the National banks, and what is now done for the railroads by the Inter-State Commerce Commission."

We further state that "the existing concentration of vast wealth under a corporate system, unguarded and uncontrolled by the Nation, has placed in the hands of a few men enormous, secret, irresponsible power over the daily life of the citizen, a power insufferable in a free Government and certain of abuse. This power has been abused in monopoly of National resources, in stock watering, in unfair competition and unfair privileges, and finally, in sinister influences on the public agencies of State and Nation."

This is what we said. And it is of this plank which Mr. Wilson speaks when he says that we tell the trusts that they are "beneficent," but "not cruel." If Mr. Wilson wishes to be funny I cordially advise him to let his humor find some other outlet than that of deliberate misrepresentation.

Mr. Wilson's knowledge of what I did as President was gained from the seclusion of the classroom at a time when he was still taking the position of an ultra-conservative, and was being carefully groomed for the President by George Harvey and other representatives of the Wall Street interests.[6]

At Columbus [Ohio] yesterday Mr. Wilson made another speech and again, I am sorry to say, in his inability to answer what we Progressives have said he takes refuge in what I of course assume to be unintentional misstatement. He says that the leaders of the Progressive Party have abandoned any serious attempt to meet the main issues of the campaign.[7]

He knows that this is not in accordance with the facts. There is not an issue in the campaign that we have not met with entire fearlessness and at length, from the tariff to the trusts. He says that every day "we seek new issues and shift the ground of debate." This again is not in accordance with the facts. Every issue he has raised I have met, and I have met it fairly by quoting his position, by stating it exactly, and then by answering it. I have shifted the ground of debate only where he has shifted it, so that I have had to get on the same ground with him. The trouble has been that as soon as I have gotten on his ground he realizes that he cannot meet me and hastily jumps to some other position.

In this speech Mr. Wilson has said that prices have risen all over the world much faster and very much higher in high tariff than in free trade countries. This statement is incorrect, and the slightest study of the conditions of Germany and England will show that it is incorrect. The strain of living has increased more in England during the last forty years than in Germany during the last forty years, and yet England is a free trade country and Germany a protective tariff country. The same holds true as between free trade England and protected France.

He states in this Columbus speech, speaking of the Progressives in connection with the control of the trusts, "They even propose to remedy the results by the very means by which they were produced, namely the partnership of the Government for the management of big business. I, for my

6. George Brinton McClellan Harvey (1864–1928) had been an early supporter of Wilson and used the influence of his magazine *Harper's Weekly* to promote the New Jersey governor's campaign. The two men split in 1911–1912 as Wilson became more progressive.

7. Davidson, *A Crossroads of Freedom,* pp. 218–219.

part, can never bring myself to accept the proposal that the Government by regulation shall act through the trusts for the people."[8]

Mr. Wilson seems unhappily unable to state facts as they are when speaking of what he does not like. It is sheer nonsense that there has ever been any partnership of the Government in the management of such great typical trusts of the day, as the Standard Oil Trust, and where there has been such partnership, it is the Progressives alone who propose in effective fashion to eliminate it.

A Federal examiner can go into a bank at any time and make the most minute examination, and can issue orders as to what the bank is to do as regards vital features of its business.

Now we propose to do with Standard Oil, for instance, practically what is now done with the banks. Mr. Wilson's proposal is to do nothing with the Standard Oil Company, but merely to continue the utterly inefficient type of action prevalent under the Taft Administration, for no amendment of detail will ever make this effort at regulation by lawsuits successful.

The Progressive proposition is to give to a Governmental commission substantially such power over the Standard Oil Company as that which the Controller of the Currency now exercises over the National banks. The Government cannot only control the issuance of stock of the bank, examine the accounts, and go minutely into every feature of the business, but it can close the bank up or appoint a receiver for it. It punishes the misdeeds of the banking officials by punishing them personally, sending them to prison in case after case. The most conspicuous recent instance of this action was the imprisonment of Morse, whose release I personally regard as a scandal and a miscarriage of justice.[9]

Now, in the case of the Standard Oil Company, if we had the power that I would advocate, the Government would be supreme, and as long as the Standard Oil Company behaved itself and met every requirement of the Government no interference whatever would be had with it, but if the Standard Oil Company persistently misbehaved itself, the Government authorities would appoint a receiver and run the concern until they received practical assurance that the directions of the Government would be thereafter complied with, and if a man high up in the Standard Oil Company be-

8. These sentences do not appear in the text of Wilson's speech in Columbus.

9. Charles W. Morse (1856–1933) had been convicted of misappropriating funds from one of his banks in 1908. After being told that Morse was on the brink of death, Taft pardoned the financier in January 1912. In the months that followed, Morse regained his health and prospered in his business affairs, much to Taft's chagrin.

haved in the manner of Morse, the Government would treat him as it did Morse, and if I were in power I would not pardon him afterward.

Mr. Wilson's position as regards the trusts and all industrial questions is precisely like that of Mr. Buchanan in 1860 toward the dissolution of the Union. Mr. Buchanan said that the Union ought to be preserved and then added that there wasn't any way to preserve it. He stated that secession was unconstitutional, but also all the methods for putting down secession were unconstitutional. Mr. Wilson says that it is good to have fine purposes for helping labor and regulating the trusts but he is against every practical expedient toward that end. Mr. Wilson is the Buchanan of the present industrial situation in the United States.

Now Mr. Wilson says that we seek new issues and shift the ground of debate. I have never sought a new issue. I have never shifted the ground of debate. But when he makes statements I understand he does not venture to reply to my answers. He stated the other day that under our proposal the wage workers would be more at the mercy of the big trusts than before.

This is, of course, on its face a sheer absurdity, because the Government representing the wageworkers would for the first time have power in the matter, but this need not rest on the assertion of either Mr. Wilson or myself. The Inter-State Commerce Commission law, as I have over and over again stated, represents in practice the line along which we intend to go with industrial concerns, although, of course, we intend to develop the power and efficiency of both the Inter-State Commerce Commission and the proposed Industrial Commission.

Now, under the actual workings of the Inter-State Commerce Commission, and the Bureau of Corporations (that is, under working of the direct reverse of the system of limitations of government which Mr. Wilson extols), the wage workers have been helped and not hurt. If Mr. Wilson does not know this then he doesn't know the elementary facts in the actual working of our Government. If he does know it, then he must know that the fears he expresses as to the effect of the proposed Industrial Commission are not merely groundless but absurd on their face.

New York Times, 22 September 1912.

As Roosevelt made his way through the Southwest toward the southern states, he took time out from formal campaigning to deliver a nonpartisan policy address at the Levee Convention in Memphis, Tennessee. During the spring a series of devastating floods in the Mississippi River Valley had left thousands of square *miles under water and produced financial losses of at least $100 million. All along the river, flooded communities looked for help from the state and national governments. Congress had not acted on these pleas by the time Roosevelt stopped in Memphis in late September. There he announced his ideas for an ambitious program to combat the results of the annual flooding and to develop the valley as a unit. Because the address did not feature the criticism of Wilson or Taft that marked his other speeches, the press barely mentioned his remarks. They are important, however, as an indicator of the reach of Roosevelt's plans for the nation in 1912.*

Levee Convention Address, Memphis, Tennessee, 26 September 1912

The United States rightly prides itself on the business ability, not merely of its business people, but of its citizens taken as a whole. It is to this business sense of the Nation that to-day I am about to appeal. It is not too much to say that the immense internal water system of the Mississippi Valley plays as great a part in the national life as the oceans themselves, the Pacific and the Atlantic. The waters of the Mississippi, at every stage, from their sources in the Rocky Mountains and the Alleghenies till they flow into the Gulf, condition the life of all our people who live in this giant drainage basin, just as the Atlantic and the Pacific Oceans condition the lives of the men of the seaboard.

In the past we have only vaguely recognized this fact and have tried to treat the problem it implies in haphazard and piecemeal fashion. I do not think that this method, or rather this no-method, will longer commend itself to the national judgment. More and more we are growing to think nationally. More and more we are growing to realize that many of our problems are by their very nature such that they can only be dealt with as a whole, and only by the exercise of the national power. Half the states of the Union have a vital concern in the treatment of the waters of the Mississippi and its tributaries, and a portion of the great basin drained by these waters is outside our own limits within those of Canada. It is evident that no one state can so much as make an efficient beginning in the endeavor to grapple with this subject.

Fortunately, the matter has become one of prime and pressing importance at the very time when this nation has learned by actual experience that it is amply able to undertake the most colossal engineering job and has, as an incident thereto, collected the plant with which it can undertake another job of the same size. The Panama Canal is now nearing completion and the skill and trained ability and the machinery used in its construction are available for use within our own borders in developing a proper national control of the waters of the Mississippi Basin in their entirety.

It is no use going into the matter at all unless we go into it on a broad scale and a thoroughly sound basis. To attempt only to prevent the breaking of the levees along the lower course of the river would in no shape or way meet the need.

The great floods of the Mississippi Valley come from the combination of the great freshets from the source streams. These freshets must be controlled; and they can only be controlled through the action of the Federal Government. In short, in dealing with the Mississippi, we ought not to think of levee work along the lower course as our only end. The problem is much greater than keeping the water off the lands of any one set of men. It really concerns changing the conditions under which half the continent is drained and turning our giant internal river system into one of the greatest of national assets. The problem is a national one, not one for the states, because what threatens each state with ruin is often not anything which can be made beneficial to that state. The Federal Government should harness the waters of the Mississippi River drainage basin; no one state can do even a small part of the work in first class fashion. Take Louisiana, for instance; although the great drainage ditch of the Mississippi flows right through Louisiana, the drainage of Louisiana herself does not flow into this ditch, but into the Gulf. Louisiana spends millions to keep the drainage of other states off her fertile cane and rice and vegetable plantations. She even maintains a great levee line wholly within the State of Arkansas as a necessary link in her protection. Yet she has no control over the states where the floods form. Only the Federal Government has such control; and the Federal Government must not shirk its duty. It must keep the drainage ditch in order and prevent the formation of the tremendous floods which threaten ruin to the entire region. In thus keeping it in order it is clearly good business policy to turn it into an asset of navigation, of power, of irrigation, and to make it pay huge dividends to all our people in the shape of a permanent prosperity. I do not ask that the Federal Government confine itself to building levees from Cairo [Illinois] to the Gulf. I ask that the Federal Government build these levees as part of a program to harness the river and its tributaries and make them useful agents of business in place of dangerous agents of destruction.

It is to this work that I would ask the United States now to turn its attention just as it has turned its attention to digging the Panama Canal. Let us use the expert knowledge and the plant itself for the control of the waters of the great inland basin which occupies over half of the area of the Republic. The source streams must be harnessed. The freshet waters should be kept in reservoirs to be used for irrigation and conserved for dry season navigation, while strong levees built from Cairo to the Gulf will hold the already partially controlled floods. As the Louisiana Legislature has said, the Nation cannot afford longer to permit its resources of soil, of power, of water, and of navigation to be carried as a wasteful and destructive flood to the sea. Since the states themselves cannot in the general interest prevent this waste, the Federal Government should treat the problem as a whole, and grapple with it in the only efficient way—by conserving such floods at their source and thereby subjecting them at every stage of their hitherto wasted existence to beneficial uses.

A few months ago this valley suffered from a pitiless flood. It was the last and greatest of a long series of similar disasters. Homes and fields were laid waste, cattle perished, and nearly five and a half million acres of land were overflowed. The damage it did has never been adequately appraised, but it certainly exceeds $100,000,000, and will probably reach a much higher figure.[10]

The loss from floods in the United States is almost unbelievable. The best evidence indicates that the direct annual flood damage in the Mississippi Valley alone averages more than Seventy Million Dollars, yet this direct damage is only a small part of what floods cost. The greatest single item of flood cost is not the actual injury to crops, animals, and buildings from floods that have taken place. It is the depreciation of property values, due to the standing danger of floods that are yet to come.

The lowlands along the Mississippi, when subject to overflow, have merely a nominal value. When properly protected and drained they are, or will be, worth from $50 to as much as $1,000. acre, according to location and access to transportation facilities. There are nearly 20,000,000 acres of such lands subject to overflow unless protected by levees or otherwise during the high floods of the Mississippi.

If we assume an average value of $10. per acre for unprotected low-lying lands, which is high, and an average of $100 per acre for these same lands when protected and drained, which will be an exceedingly conservative value when protection and development has been completed and the land

10. "Mississippi Flood Is Growing Worse," *New York Times*, 6 April 1912.

is under cultivation, the difference of $90 per acre on nearly 20,000,000 acres amounts to a total of nearly two billion dollars, the greatest part of which is the cost of future flood damage along the Mississippi River foreseen and discounted today.

For the people of the Mississippi Valley, relief from the danger of loss by flood is more clearly in sight today than it was before the tremendous loss of the last great visitation. The National contributions to feed the destitute, to patch the crevasses in your levees, and to continue the work which has been dragging along for years and which has proved to be inadequate, will do nothing to prevent the ravages of the coming floods. I repeat that with the awful lesson of April and May hanging over you the prospects for relief are no brighter than they were a year ago. This is true in spite of the fact that Congress was in session for five months after the beginning of your last disaster, that the House, which originates appropriation bills, was in the control of the Democrats, mainly southern men, during all of that time, and yet not one measure of permanent relief or lasting help was enacted in your behalf, and as long as the habit of doing things piecemeal, sometimes known as the States Rights doctrine, stands in the way, nothing effective will be done.

The loss from Mississippi floods is not confined to the states along the lower Mississippi. It stretches all the way from the head waters of the Missouri, Mississippi, Ohio, and other tributaries to the Gulf itself. On the Ohio watershed for example, in direct damage to Pittsburg alone during the last ten years has reached a total of $12,000,000, while if the depreciation of property from the threat of flood damage was removed it was estimated by the Pittsburg Flood Commission that $50,000,000 would at once be added to the value of property in Pittsburg.

The drainage basin in which the Mississippi floods originate includes more than half the area of the United States. Therefore the Mississippi is not and never can be a local issue. The loss from the floods is a national loss, and the control of the river is a national problem. The benefits from its control will be and are national benefits, and the duty to undertake it is a national duty. This duty the people of the United States are willing to accept. If Congress will act there is no reason why the National contribution to the Mississippi problem should be limited to sympathy and patchwork.

The last flood, while enormous in the amount of damage it caused, was by no means the highest that is likely to occur. The flood wave that came down from Cairo was not the result of any unprecedented rise on the Ohio, Missouri, or upper Mississippi. It was merely the result of a meeting of moderate flood waves on all three of these rivers. These flood waves took their rise far away from the region where the damage occurred. Where the trouble originates is the best place to apply the remedy. So long as we attempted to meet the ravages of typhoid fever and yellow fever merely by giving attention to the individual patient suffering from their attacks, there was no permanent relief. But as soon as we began to go to the root of the matter by destroying the mosquitoes which carry the germs of the yellow fever and by stamping out the sources of typhoid infection, the situation was utterly changed, and real relief began.

So with floods. We must deal not simply with the floods after they occur, as we have been attempting to do by means of levees, we must prevent the occurrence of floods by beginning to control them where they originate, that is, on the upper reaches of the streams.

The special lesson of the last flood, like that of many a flood before it, is that the levee system alone is insufficient. The height and strength of levees in the Mississippi Valley has been increased over and over again. Every new high water mark has compelled a raising of the levees to meet it, and after each reinforcement the people have settled themselves behind their strengthened defenses in hope renewed, only in due time to be deceived again. This year, at the price of eighteen crevasses and nearly 5,500,000 of acres of land overflowed, a new high-water mark was set. It was set, as I have said, by the meeting of three moderate floods at Cairo, and the height of it will certainly be surpassed in the future.

At Cairo, the flood this year reached the 54 foot mark, the highest in its history. It was the bursting of levees down below which saved the city from a still greater overflow. Here at Memphis you had a 45-foot stage, and if the St Francis levees had not broken in six places you would have suffered a far greater disaster, for without the crevasses, it is estimated that the water would have risen three feet higher.[11]

At New Orleans, the whole of whose enormous wealth lies below the level of even an ordinary rise, the last flood reached 21.4 ft., well nigh up to the crests of the levee. They would surely have been overtopped had not the levees above and below given way. The truth is that the safety of many cities along the Mississippi Valley last spring depended solely on the fact that the flood protection system failed at the right time.

Do not misunderstand me. Levees are absolutely necessary. But they are necessary as a part of a complete system of flood prevention and control and not as the whole of it. We must have levees below, but we must also have water storage in forests and behind dams above, if the floods are to be

11. "Save Seven As Boat Sinks In River Flood," *New York Times*, 1 April 1912.

controlled. But that is not the whole of the story. It is not enough to make the Mississippi do as little harm as possible. We must make it do all the good we can, render all of the service of which it is capable to all the people. The Mississippi River system is in fact a great industrial plant, which may be made to yield transportation, power, irrigation, and other valuable services, if we only take the trouble to set it at work. The River is waiting but we cannot set it at work with success if we consider only one use at a time.

Some of the people whom the river must serve require water power and others demand irrigation. To some, navigation is the consideration of highest value, to others the drainage of swamp lands, and to others again flood prevention outclasses every other object of public improvement. Therefore any plan for Mississippi control that responds to one need to the exclusion of any or every other, must be shortsighted, inadequate, and unworthy.

The majority of men in this audience are attached in some way to an industrial plant of one kind or another. Suppose one of these plants, while profitable in the aggregate, falls short of the high efficiency it ought to reach, and falls far short of returning its rightful profits. In one department there was a waste of raw material; in a second there is inefficient machinery; in a third the shipping facilities are not able to do work of the right kind and amount; in a fourth department the motive power is unsteady and inefficient. If you were to reorganize the plant you would not confine your attention to one department alone. Their work would embrace the plant as a whole, and in the final result you would have each department doing its share, with harmony and unity throughout the whole plant.

So with the Mississippi. In dealing with the improvement of any river, and especially with the greatest of all rivers, we can never afford to forget that a river is a unit from its source to its mouth. It is because we have overlooked and neglected this fundamental fact and have expended vast sums which have gone to the improvement of the Mississippi in a way that was both piecemeal and haphazard, a little here and a little there, with no great general plan controlling the whole, that we find ourselves facing a situation where the floods are increasing, navigation is dying out, and the finest natural system of waterways on the face of the earth is less used and less usable than it was fifty years ago.

We need a general plan for the development and use of our inland waterways. On February 26, 1908, I sent the report of the Inland Waterways Commission to Congress. The Commission said:

"We recommend that hereafter plans for the improvement of navigation in inland waterways or for any use of these waterways in connection with interstate commerce shall take account of the purification of the waters, the development of power, the control of floods, the reclamation of lands by irrigation and drainage, and all other uses of the waters or benefits to be derived from their control."

"We recommend that hereafter both local and general benefits to the people shall be fully considered in any such plans for the improvement of navigation in inland waterways, or for any use of these waterways in connection with interstate commerce; and that wherever practicable Federal agencies shall co-operate with states, municipalities, communities, corporations, and individuals with a view to an equitable distribution of costs and benefits."

"We recommend that Congress be asked to make suitable provision for improving the inland waterways of the United States at a rate commensurate with the needs of the people as determined by competent authority; and we suggest that such provision meet these requisites, viz: expert framing of a definite policy; certainty of continuity and co-ordination of plan and work; expert initiative in the choice of projects and the succession of works; freedom in selection of projects in accordance with terms of co-operation; and the widest opportunity for applying modern business methods."

In the message transmitting the report, I said:—

"This report is well worth your attention. It is thorough, conservative, sane and just. It represents the mature judgment of a body of men exceptionally qualified by personal experience and knowledge of conditions throughout the United States to understand and discuss the great problem of how best to use our waterways in the interests of all the people *****

"The improvement of our inland waterways can and should be made to pay for itself so far as practicable from the incidental proceeds from water power and other uses. Navigation should of course be free. But the greatest return will come from the increased commerce, growth, and prosperity of our people. For this we have already waited too long. Adequate funds should be provided, by bond issue, if necessary, and the work should be delayed no longer. The development of our waterways and the conservation of our forests are the most pressing physical needs of the country. They are interdependent, and they should be met vigorously, together, and at once. The questions of organization, powers, and appropriations are now before the Congress. There is urgent need for prompt and decisive action."[12]

12. Roosevelt to the Senate and House of Representatives, 60th Cong., 1st sess. *Congressional Record* (26 February 1908): 2518–2519.

Congress, however, not only failed to act favorably on these recommendations, but it passed a law which attempted to make it impossible to continue the work of commissions of this kind. The Republican and Democratic parties alike were content to trifle with the vital needs of our people.

The fundamental information necessary to formulate an adequate, well-considered and thoroughly complete plan for dealing with the Mississippi is not yet fully at hand. We have been spending large sums of money in the Mississippi Valley, but instead of using it, or a part of it, to get the physical facts upon which a sound general plan of development must be based, that money has been spent in the furtherance of small and disconnected schemes which never could measure up to a problem so large and so important.

We still have much to learn, but that is no reason for delay. Already we have far more information than we can get appropriations to apply, and there is work enough and to spare along lines which are known already to harmonize with the general plan to keep us fully occupied while the plan itself is being made.

We know already that every flood is not only a vast engine of destruction, but an enormous and useless waste of water as well. The water which deluged your valley last April served no useful purpose whatever. That part of it which came down from the hills ought to be back there again under natural and artificial control so that it would come down as fast and no faster than the people need it. It should now be helping to irrigate the deserts, to maintain your river at a navigable stage, and to increase the energy at the great water-power sites that it passed on the way down.

No one will deny that more water in a river means greater navigable depth. If the water wasted in floods were held back and used at low water, the Mississippi River Commission would not need to work its dredge boats overtime to cut for you a temporary 9-foot channel through the bars. Because of the uncertainties of this channel, your river shipping is only a tithe of what it should be and would be under stable conditions of channel depth.

How can the necessary storage be accomplished? Occasionally a moderate flood may have its origins in the lowlands. By far the greatest number, however, rise in the higher country, and here are found the two great means for their control, forests and reservoir sites.

One great reason why floods are becoming more and more destructive is that we have rapidly denuded our uplands of their forests. Some men of good repute have denied the relation of forests to stream flow. Others who have firmly believed in the truth of it have until recently not been able to produce figures their opponents could not deny. Now, however, the facts are proved beyond the shadow of a doubt by the work of the Government in the White Mountain region of New Hampshire. During three periods of high water last April, to use but one example, the flow from the deforested watershed was not far from double the flow from the forested watershed, area for area, while there was deep snow still in the forest after it had entirely disappeared from the open. Further investigations not yet published show still more strongly the effect of forests on stream flow. These conclusions confirm the results of the Forest Service. Therefore we may regard that question as settled beyond dispute.

As President, I repeatedly endorsed the bill to purchase National Forests in the White Mountains and the Southern Appalachians, and did my utmost to secure its passage.[13] I have always been glad I did so, but I am gladder than ever now that there exists a clear proof of our oft-repeated assertions that the removal of our forests has markedly increased the flood tendencies of our streams. The gradual acquisition of mountain lands to help in controlling stream flow will not only devote those lands to the highest purpose for which they are fitted by nature, but it will also check erosion, reduce the suspended matter in our river waters, and play a great and beneficial part in lessening the frequency and severity of our floods.

So much for forests. Now as to reservoirs for flood control. At the head of the Ohio, the Tennessee, the Cumberland, and practically all the large territories of the Ohio Valley, there are reservoir sites so numerous and so large that by the construction and operation of dams the great floods of the Ohio may be almost completely controlled.

The Upper Mississippi basin is also singularly well adapted to reservoir control, and the United States already has there four large reservoirs in operation. A recent report from the U. S. Engineer office at Rock Island, shows that if all the easily available sites on the upper Mississippi were utilized, not only would the floods be controlled, but a navigable depth of 12 feet from St. Paul to St. Louis would be assured throughout the year.

The Missouri is less well adapted to reservoir control of floods, but on the other hand its reservoirs will serve a doubly useful purpose. There are numerous reservoir sites on its headwaters, and many of them are now or will hereafter be used to store water for irrigating arid or semi-arid lands. In consequence the waste water will be utilized to grow crops and withdrawn from the volume of the floods. It is principally because the flood

13. Roosevelt to Ligon Johnson, 11 January 1908, in Elting E. Morison, et al., eds., *The Letters of Theodore Roosevelt* (Cambridge, Mass: Harvard University Press, 1951–1954), 6:902–903.

waters of the Missouri cannot be sufficiently stored that the levees of the lower Mississippi must be permanently maintained.

The cost of a complete reservoir system would be enormous, but even if the cost were to be as great as that predicted by the bitterest opponent of the plan, the results would be worth all the expense. The mountain lands in the proposed reservoir sites are usually of little value, and to devote them to reservoir purposes would result in making them more useful than they could possibly be made in any other way. But even if that were not true, the reservoir system would probably pay for itself in the water power it could develop. Of the 200,000,000 possible hydro-electric horse-power in the U.S. only about 6,000,000 has already been put to use. Nearly the whole of this has been taken and developed by private and monopolistic use on terms utterly unfair to the people, to whom in the beginning the water power rights belonged. The beneficiaries of the gigantic developments at Niagara Falls, for example, do not pay one cent to the Nation or to the State of New York for the enormously valuable privileges given to them by the people.

The people should keep for themselves a part at least of the benefit of water power development instead of handing them out to the great water power combinations. The National construction of this great system of reservoirs could be one method of doing so.

No general plan of river regulation can be complete unless it makes ample provision for the drainage of swamp and overflow lands. These lands, 75,000,000 acres in extent, will supply us with food when our population has increased so that the lands now under cultivation no longer suffice. Our farmers are leaving the country at the rate of more than 100,000 per year to take up lands in Canada not so rich and strong as these. We need a progressive national participation in the work of drainage as a whole.

Finally, the Mississippi problem is too big to be solved from any single point of view or any single interest. Flood water conservation by forests and reservoirs will meet many needs. When it is accomplished by the Nation, for only the Nation can accomplish it, you of the lower Mississippi Valley will never again be submerged in great floods. The present levee system, strengthened and maintained as it must be by federal aid, would insure you safety against whatever floods could escape from storage. The 14-foot waterway that you desire and need so much would become a reality less through artificial channel correction and canalization than because of increased summer and fall flow, and the benefits of the Panama Canal would find their way by water straight to the heart of the continent. The hydro-electric development of the country would be increased by many million horsepower, the benefits of which would go directly to the people; such action would mean literally to "pass prosperity around." Irrigation would be extended not only in the West but ultimately in the East also; and the rise in the cost of living shows how vitally necessary it is that the farm lands which produce our meat and grain should be increased, and made more productive. Flood erosion of soil means a steady decrease in the value of farms. On these two accounts alone the proposed reservoir system would be amply justified. Lastly, there will be ample water supply for our growing cities, and those streams which are now foul and unsanitary during low-water seasons would flow clear and attractive water under the reinforcement of mountain water that they would receive.

I submit that here is a program worthy to fire the enthusiasm, and enlist the best support that any man can give. It is the Progressive program for the Mississippi Valley.

Typed manuscript in Roosevelt Papers.

Excerpt from an Address at New Orleans, Louisiana, 27 September 1912

Mr. Roosevelt arrived on time. He entered from the Girod-Street side, and W. P. Luck first appeared, waving his arms. He was followed by General W. J. Rehan, Mr. Roosevelt and John M. Parker.[14]

Great cheering greeted the ex-president, and he stood some minutes and bowed and waved his hand, as the band played and the chorus sang "Hot Time In the Old Town." Cecil Lyon of Texas, and Mr. Terrell of Houston, were in the party.[15] Mr. Roosevelt finally sat down, and General Rehan spoke of Mr. Roosevelt as the most progressive American, and said that his friends were glad to see such a reception. He referred to the man who had done so much to put this state in the forefront, and presented John M. Parker. "Shoot it to 'em, Parker," shouted some in the audience.

Mr. Parker delivered some talk about attacks on the bosses and boss

14. William J. Rehan (1840–1928) had been the Democratic mayor of New Orleans from 1882 to 1884. He left the party during the mid-1890s and chaired the Republican State Executive Committee from 1900 to 1912. John Milliken Parker (1863–1939) was later elected governor of Louisiana as a Democrat, 1920–1924. William P. Luck had been appraiser of customs at New Orleans.

15. Cecil Andrew Lyon (1869–1915) had been the leader of the Texas Republicans until he broke with Taft in 1912. He accompanied Roosevelt on the national trip. Scurry Terrell was the physician who took care of the candidate's throat.

rule, and of the declaration of independence against their tyranny. Both the old parties, he declared, were antiquated and had outlived their usefulness. He then said that the party headed by the greatest American is so clear in its declarations of what it intends to do that there is no misunderstanding it. He urged all men to join for good government and honest government, and said that Louisiana is, more than any other state, under obligations to the man who has consecrated his energy in leading a fight for honesty and decency. He referred to 1905 when Mr. Roosevelt ordered the medical corps to come to Louisiana and stamp out yellow fever forever and, to show his contempt for fear, came here himself to see that it was well done. He also spoke of his help in floods and in the panic year and to the "creation of the Panama Canal." He spoke of him as the "most loyal friend the Mississippi Valley ever had."

When Mr. Roosevelt arose to speak there was another ovation, with a "Hip Hooray" from the platform. The speaker began by saying: "Mr. Chairman and friends, men and women of Louisiana, men and women of this great city," and continued: "There is no speech which I have made during this campaign which I felt so anxious to make as the one I am making now; because, friends, I am not willing to admit that you and I are on opposite sides, and I came down here to make my plea for the right to stand shoulder to shoulder with those who look face to face with the great problems from the standpoint I do."

Mr. Roosevelt then took up his party and said: "Friends, this movement was not started by me. So far from it I went into it with extreme reluctance, and when it became evident that unless I led it no one would, and it had to be led by me at this moment. This movement has been growing in strength during the last decade, with many blind and groping manifestations. It means that the people of the United States have slowly come to the conclusion that they are not served as they should be by their public servants and much of the industrial life of the nation has been permitted to go awry. If I had never existed the movement would have gone on the same, but would have come to a head a year or two later."

Mr. Roosevelt explained that none of the leaders saw at first just what the drift of the party would be. "A number tried the experiment of putting the machinery of the Republican party under the control of the people and went into the primaries and fought through, but the victory was stolen not from us, but from the rank and file of the voters. Then we lived up to the doctrines we preached. I despise an honest man who will lay down before a dishonest one and I always preached that a straight and decent citizen should be ashamed to submit to one that was not, and we made the bosses understand that if they stole the victory in the way they did it should be proved to them that it wasn't worth gaining. Then we made up our minds that it was not worth while to stop half way and we raised the banner under which men of all parties may gather in the great war for righteousness. We had one thing in view, to make it a national movement, so that Southerners and Northerners, Easterners and Westerners could come together bent on achieving a common purpose. Our declaration of principles applies on the shores of the gulf as on the lakes and at the Golden Gate as well as Sandy Hook, and I wouldn't have been contented if I hadn't made every effort to get men and women of the South, who felt as we did, to come in with us, and undertake in common the betterment of the politics and economic conditions in the republic, and the man with whom I communicated at once was John Parker because he had those qualities which I particularly admire and was doing the kind of work I wish to do in the nation-wide field."

"He's the boy to do it," shouted a spieler.

"He's all right," answered the speaker.

"When I preach good citizenship," continued Mr. Roosevelt, "I like to have a good example. I deplore any man who is crook and the abler he is the worse, and it gives me a keener desire to hunt him out of public life. I don't believe in lying down and have little use for an honest man who is afraid.

"What Parker has done in business and agriculture means the building up of the country, and it made me feel that he was the man with whom I would like to work and appear in this crisis of our national life."

Mr. Roosevelt indicated that the Progressive Party has come to stay, and has no more connection with the old Republican or Democratic parties. "It is through once for all with the Republican Party. We are through with it because it has become an unfit instrument for doing the national business."

Mr. Roosevelt then said: "When I stand with a new party of this kind, I am unwilling not to stand with the same kind of men managing in the South as in the North, and not willing that it be started, except as a national party. If you refuse to come I should want to feel that I had done everything I could to get you. We are going to make a success, we are going to put it through, and I want you to have your hands on the lever and your representatives as friends, guides and allies and not, as I have often found, your representatives opposing your own interests—your representatives opposing the South's interests because I championed them and they felt that it was regular to oppose me. I can't help feeling that I am to blame if I can't put our case before you properly as it is overwhelming. We want to establish a party on a healthy, nation-wide basis so that your ownership will be as great as that of the East or North or West, and it will respond to your interests as well and you will have an equal share in its guidance. I ask you to join with us on a footing of equality in dealing with the issues of the United States, all in common. If on any point you sincerely disagree and go against me, all right. I do not appeal to men who do not believe the things I do, but those who believe with me and are artificially sundered from me."

Mr. Roosevelt gave some illustrations. He said that as soon as he became president he became confronted with issues of great importance. The greatest affected Louisiana and the states near the mouth of the Mississippi more than any other group, except those on the Pacific. "They more affected the Louisiana interest than those of the Northeast, and yet when I came to deal with those I was obliged to do it on an unnatural line, and the representatives of the states concerned, as they did not belong to the party I did, antagonized me and the things I believed in. If they did not they would be denounced as traitors."

Mr. Roosevelt took up the Panama Canal plans and said that for sixty or seventy years it had been discussed, and statesmen of the South always took the lead to secure "what we have actually done. I tried to be president of the whole country, and would have felt ashamed if the interest of the Gulf States was not as dear to me as those of any other part."

Mr. Roosevelt then gave a brief history of the Canal scheme. He said that he thought it was time to reduce the conversation to action. He tried to persuade Colombia to let us treat her decently, and explained to her that she would not only build up complications, but put France on the isthmus in her place. He might have made a masterly report to Congress, which would have held able debates, and there would have been had a century more of conversation. "Instead, I took the isthmus and started the canal (applause), and allowed Congress to debate me instead of the canal, and the debate about me still goes on fitfully, and bids fair to last when I am dead, and you will have the canal in a couple of years. I had to get ratification of the treaty and the opposition came from the South." He spoke especially of Culberson and Bailey, of Texas, and said Clark of Arkansas only stood by him, and Mr. McEnery, of Louisiana, helped materially. If ratification had depended on the votes of the Southern senators it would have been defeated.[16]

16. Joseph Weldon Bailey (1863–1929) and Charles Allen Culberson (1855–1925) opposed ratification of the Panama Canal Treaty in 1903–1904. James Paul Clarke (1854–1916) of Arkansas and Samuel D. McEnery (1837–1910) had favored ratification in the Senate.

"These political lines of division were artificial. I didn't have any way of appealing to the sentiments of the People of the South. I think I represented the South better than its own senators. I am not here to ask for the support of any who think that the senators did right, but of those who think the canal is necessary, so that you and I can get together and act efficiently. If I state my case and you agree with me and feel that mine are your principles, I want to feel that some way you and I can get together and work efficiently for the common good. We want you to come with us on our entire platform."

Then the speaker took up the control of the Mississippi River, saying that the damage done by it was well known. "The most disastrous flood was last spring. Since then the Democratic House has been in session five months with a Republican Senate and president. You have held meetings and now, friends, I wish to say you haven't yet as a nation taken one single step that makes you any safer from floods in the future than you were a year ago. Not one thing has been done to prevent such a disaster or to formulate a real and great policy to deal with the whole question and make the Mississippi River at all points an asset to the whole nation, instead of at certain seasons worthless and at others a dire menace to the nation. I have a perfectly clear policy that we ought to follow. It is a folly to waste time and effort in patching up parts of the system of defenses against the Mississippi. You have built the lines higher, and in a dozen years the flood grew higher and came over. No one state can control it. Louisiana has to extend her lines into Arkansas. The drainage of twenty states, none of which Louisiana has any control over, forms the floods. Uncle Sam is now big enough to undertake any task no matter how big that the welfare of the nation demands. The biggest in the next few years will be the utilization of the Mississippi River and its tributaries. Fortunately we possess at the moment what we have unwittingly provided. We are just finishing the Panama Canal, and I purpose [propose?] to use the plant, experience and skill of Uncle Sam at Panama to solve the question of the great Mississippi Valley. There are some tasks that are subsidiary and can be undertaken at once. For the main task we need an able commission, and must have a big man who shows that he can handle any big task. Water should be stored at the head of the stream. Last spring it was shown that the junction of the floods at Cairo caused the damage below."

Storage reservoirs were advocated by the speaker and he said that the water power secured would pay the expenses and the supply of water would make up for slack-water times.

He opposed doing anything by piecemeal. "To do it means getting the national government to treat it as a continuance of Panama. If I was elected president I would fight that thing through. I would get our people to authorize it, and then I would put Goethals in charge of it.[17] If you are against me, all right, vote against me, but if you are with me I don't want you to feel that you have a platonic affection for me, but have to vote for the other fellow."

Mr. Roosevelt spoke strongly for the building of the levee system on the lower river and the protection of the terminals in connection with the plan to control the sources, and said that in this way the nation can render it impossible for such a disaster as that of last spring to ever happen again. It would mean the increased value of the lowlands of ten to twenty times and that may be an understatement.

He said that he hoped the people would feel free to support him if they agreed with his views and would not feel obliged to vote against him for ancestral, traditional reasons, and so put themselves and the nation in a position of economic impotence. "I am less engaged in pleading my cause than yours. I want you to emancipate yourselves so that you can vote as you desire."

The speaker referred to the men who argued in favor of building the levees six inches higher and waiting until a flood ten inches higher comes along. He said he expected all those men to be against him. The Progressive platform appeals to all men who want to see the country advance as it deserves, and he wanted them to support the party, not quietly and with reluctance to let their relatives know, but come out and do their part to control the wheels of the administration.

Then Mr. Roosevelt took up the sugar matter and pointed out that the Republicans want to manage a tariff for the interests of the capitalists and the Democrats wanted destruction. The Republicans wanted to let some prosper too much and the Democrats nobody at all.

He favored a tariff that would be equally beneficial to the wage-earner and manufacturer and the farmer, and wanted the tariff so regulated the benefit does not stop at the front office, but some of it gets into the envelopes of the employees. He said that the Bristow bill represented the Progressive idea.[18]

17. George Washington Goethals (1858–1928) was the army engineer in charge of the construction of the Panama Canal, which was nearing completion.

18. Senator Joseph L. Bristow (1861–1944) of Kansas had introduced legislation to lower tariff rates on sugar. The national Democrats, much to the dismay of their party colleagues in Louisiana, wanted to reduce the tariff on sugar even more. Roosevelt was arguing to protectionist sentiment in the state that the Bristow approach was preferable.

"If Louisiana believes in no protection, all right, go against us, but if you believe with us, I want to feel that you have a right to go with us, otherwise go with the other party, I mean the Democratic, because the Republican party is a negligible element."

Mr. Roosevelt then said that in 1904 a Louisiana man said to him that in a certain famous club the members were delighted at his election. He said that was strange, as the vote did not show it. Then the man replied: "Oh, we all voted against you, but we were all anxious to see you elected." Mr. Roosevelt said he wanted to free the nation from such ideas. "A party is good so long as it is an instrument of good, and the same is true of a public man—me as well as anyone else. Use him as long as he is an efficient instrument to do a given job, and if there is another job or a better instrument, throw the old aside." He asserted that both old parties were dead issues, "or if they deal with living issues they speak a dead language about them."

There was an indication that Mr. Roosevelt thought he was speaking long, and he said, "You are such a nice audience that you are a little responsible." He then took up the labor situation and argued in favor of trying to benefit those who are not in the most prosperous condition and make their condition a little easier and fairer than present conditions allow. He said he never preached class hatred except as applied to crooks. He hated crookedness but not the crook. He wanted him to stop being crooked.

John M. Parker stepped up to the speaker at this point and told him that his physician, Dr. Scurry Terrell of Dallas, Tex., the throat specialist, said that he would have to sit down now. Mr. Roosevelt continued with a very pretty peroration for a better and fairer and healthier life for the ordinary man and woman, to make their lives more healthful, wholesome, more satisfactory and useful. He appealed to the voters, if they thought he was right, to vote for him here in New Orleans as they would in New York or Chicago or San Francisco. If the people believed that the Progressive Party would help them here, as in California and Ohio and New York, he asked them in the name of their own manhood and independence to come and join with the party in making the republic one where the people rule and secure the industrial and social good of all.

At the conclusion of the speech there was great applause and Mr. Roosevelt was taken out through the Lafayette Street side and entered an automobile for the hotel.

New Orleans *Daily Picayune,* 28 September 1912.

Excerpt from a Roosevelt Speech at Atlanta, Georgia, 28 September 1912

A remarkable sight greeted Roosevelt as he appeared in the Auditorium at 8 o'clock. The great hall was packed to its corners already, and there were several hundred more who came in, forming an escort to the colonel. Scattered throughout the audience were several thousand women, many of them waving red bandanna handkerchiefs. Altogether there were at least 10,000 people within the doors at that moment.

Just after the audience had sang "Onward, Christian Soldiers," from the progressive hymn books distributed, someone ran down the aisle and cried, "He's coming." Immediately the audience rose and turned to cheer the ex-president of the United States, who was walking toward the platform with a majestic tread. Cheers lasted for almost two minutes while the band played "America" and "Dixie." Roosevelt himself seemed one of the most enthusiastic in the hall, and he flung up a waving hand time and again in response to a cry of "Hello, Teddy."

Roosevelt himself was a spectacular sight. His eyes sparkled with the fire of conflict as he faced the audience. After he had spoken for three quarters of an hour he climbed up on top of a table on the platform and planted his feet firmly as he gazed, at times stared, over the throng, while his fighting neck strained with the tenseness of his voice as he made his personal appeal for the support of Georgia voters in the coming presidential primary.

The cosmopolitan throng of men and women showed his sway clearly, now yelling commendation in his words, now drawing aloof with an unexpected stillness, now breaking out in yells of opposition.

The Wilson demonstration came as a big surprise, after Roosevelt had spoken about twenty minutes.

"Mr. Wilson has declared," said the colonel, and pandemonium seemed to break over his head. Cries of "Wilson" and prolonged cheers filled the hall for a solid minute and a half (by the watch) before the upraised hand of Roosevelt brought silence and attention once more.

"Mr. Wilson has declared," cried the colonel in a terrific voice, his whole body tense with feeling at the Wilson demonstration, "that the democratic platform is not a program; that he doesn't expect to see the American people adopt that platform. Now, why don't you applaud that?"

Again the audience broke out into prolonged cheers, this time with the cry of "Roosevelt" on their lips, as he declared in a thundering voice, "I stand for a platform that will become a real program."

In this Clifford Berryman cartoon published on 6 August 1912, Roosevelt tries to convince Uncle Sam about his reform medicine while Robert M. LaFollette calls it quackery. (Library of Congress)

Thus the great audience swayed to and fro, uncertain of its own mind. Above the wavering crowd stood the wonderful Roosevelt, mighty African hunter and student of men, calculating the spirit of his audience with a master political mind, and bringing into play every argument at his command in an effort to carry the crowd with his enthusiasm. The tenor of the throng, however, was as uncertain at the end as it was before Roosevelt entered the door—it was a typical American audience that applauded at words rather than thoughts.

Dr. Robert Stuart MacArthur, president of the World's Baptist alliance, and pastor of the tabernacle, introduced Colonel Roosevelt, and was himself introduced by National Committeeman C. W. McClure, who presided.[19] Dr. MacArthur reviewed their friendship of a quarter of a century and sketched Roosevelt's rise to the presidency. He told an illuminating incident how, on his recent mission to Russia, a letter from the ex-president opened every door and paved the way to kings and queens.

19. Robert Stuart MacArthur (1841–1923) was one of the most prominent Baptist clergymen of that era. C. W. McClure was an Atlanta business owner and member of the Progressive National Committee.

Discussing his visit to the South, Mr. Roosevelt said:

"You, my fellow citizens, my fellow Americans, of my mother's state, which I claim as much my own as New York itself, I would not on any account have missed coming here to appear before you and tell the reasons for the faith that is in me. And it was with peculiar pleasure that I was introduced by my old friend of the last quarter of a century, Dr. MacArthur.

"And now, my friends, I have come to Georgia and the south in the great contest for right, because I feel it borne in upon me to testify to the truth of our cause and to ask you of Georgia and the south to do your share in giving your just proportion of leadership to the movement."

"My mission in the south is two-fold. First and most important I fight for the principle that it is your duty to vote for your own convictions. If you are in sympathy with the progressive platform, then I hold that it is your duty to yourself, your duty to your states, and your duty to the nation, not merely to support the platform, but to give your share of the leadership of the new party which has brought forth that platform."

"If you feel that we are right, then I challenge the right to your assistance and I want you to come with us now, that is unless you are so much an "original package" by inheritance for one political party, generation to generation, that you cannot speak your own mind and vote your convictions."

"The nation has a reservoir of national strength in the manhood and womanhood of the south. We want it drawn up in this struggle for fair play in the political, social and economic world. We need all the wisdom that this country can give, and it is not fair for the south to be robbed of its fair share of the leadership. You cannot accomplish anything in either of the old parties—they have such an inherited way of looking at things! Do not follow—lead! Stand in the forefront of the battle."

Let me illustrate what I mean by the name of Judge Ben Lindsey. Judge Lindsey was born in Tennessee; his father was a Confederate under Forrest, he was a life-long democrat, and to his efforts it was largely owing that Bryan carried Colorado in 1908.[20] But Judge Lindsey has always stood, not merely in name, but in deed, for the great principles of justice and decency, not only in politics, but in business—and no man in this country has done more to put government on an ethical basis, no man has waged a more telling and vigorous fight against the banded forces of political and business corruption."

The difference between the republican and democratic parties on these

20. Nathan Bedford Forrest (1821–1877) was a Confederate general and founder of the Ku Klux Klan. William Jennings Bryan (1860–1925) had run for the presidency as a Democrat in 1896, 1900, and 1908.

issues, he said, was one of "sound and fury in declamation," that there was no difference in their acts and hardly any in their proposed acts.

"Both of them express much platonic sympathy for those who suffer and much hollow wrath against those who do wrong. But they are a unit in opposing every practical measure by which the suffering will be averted or the wrong punished. The difference between them in these points is merely that Mr. Taft is content to see his party fixed permanently on the sodden level to which it has sunk, whereas Mr. Wilson is uneasily conscious that the state of affairs in his own party is not satisfactory, and is now and then betrayed into admitting the fact."

He showed this in his speech of acceptance, when he said that the democratic platform was not a program, and that he did not expect to see it adopted by the people—in which case he had no business to stand on it, for of course if it was not a program, it was a false promise, meant to deceive. Again, the other night, he said "there is only one condition upon which the democrats can gain the confidence of the people. That condition is that the party shall commit itself through and through to progressive policies."[21] This is of course an admission that the democratic party is not now progressive. That party has made its platform and nominated its candidates, and if, nearly three months after the nomination, the candidate is still utterly in doubt as to whether the party is progressive or not, and does not know which way it is going—and therefore which way he is going—it is idle to expect effective leadership from either him or it in grappling with the great problems of the day.

It is doubtless because Mr. Wilson has no clear-cut convictions on these great problems that he is so utterly vague in his propositions for remedying the evils which he admits to exist."

Referring to Mr. Wilson's charge that he had said it was "inevitable" that the trusts should "build up an irresistible power" and that he had suggested that the trusts be made "good, pitiful, kind and just," Mr. Roosevelt said Mr. Wilson affected to quote him, but deliberately attributed to him things he had never said.[22]

"Every one of those statements is simply not true," he declared, and denied each of them in toto. He called on Mr. Wilson to state where he had

21. I have not been able to find this quotation but Wilson said something like it in a speech in New Jersey on 21 September 1912. See "A Speech in Hoboken, New Jersey, Supporting William Hughes for Senator," in Arthur S. Link, et al., eds., *The Papers of Woodrow Wilson, 1912, Volume 25* (Princeton, N.J.: Princeton University Press, 1978), p. 215.

22. Wilson made these comments in a speech at Boston on 27 September. Davidson, *A Crossroads of Power*, p. 294.

ever said any of those things. He said Mr. Wilson had a right to attack his real position, or even to indulge in personalities if he thought it is good taste, but he had no right to attribute to him things he had never said.

"The trouble with Mr. Wilson is fundamental," he said. "He does not understand our active needs today. He does not know the present-day life of this nation. He has no understanding of the deep gulf that separates the needs of the living man of today from the needs of the man of whom he has read in books about the past.

"The other day he stated definitely that 'the history of liberty was the history of the limitation of governmental power,' and he used this as an argument against the progressive proposals for the extension of the governmental power so as to control the trusts and to secure for labor the legislation needed by labor, such as a minimum wage for women and the like.

Mr. Wilson's statement is true as regards medieval Europe, but it is utterly untrue as regards the present day. The 'liberty' which he would preserve by limiting the governmental power is the 'liberty' of the great trust magnates to do wrong; the 'liberty' of the great conscienceless industrial chiefs to grind down the wage-workers and create a condition which make necessary for honest rivals to follow their evil example or go out of business. The control we propose to exercise over industrial corporations is the control the interstate commerce commission is now exercising over the railroads. During my administration as president the law was for the first time seriously and efficiently enforced."

Saying the only remedy Mr. Wilson had offered for the trusts was a reduction of the tariff, he said that could not possibly remedy the evils complained of, the conditions of industrial workers and the like, but might make things worse.

"We progressives had a practical remedy to propose," he continued. "We have committed ourselves to the declaration that by law there shall be established in continuous industries, like that of the steel corporation, an eight-hour day and a six-day week but this can only be done by the extension of government power. And naturally Mr. Wilson not only does not indorse the principle, but in his plea for the limitation of governmental power shows that if consistent he must be against it. Of course, he must be against it unless he abandons his whole theory that the limitation of governmental powers means the growth of liberty, unless he understands definitely that the liberty of those oppressed in the industrial world can only be secured by the extension of governmental powers, and that the limitation of governmental powers such as he advocates leads only to make secure the liberty of the oppressor to oppress.

What the American people fear is the mass of evils, for the most part secret, that will assuredly control our civilization unless we openly and firmly control and restrain them instead. We intend to assert the supremacy of our people, a supremacy of democracy in real and efficient fashion, and the great industrial and social transformations which we intend to secure are to be obtained in such shape as to mean the moral, no less than the material development of the nation. Every observer who saw the progressive convention at Chicago was struck by the religious sincerity of conviction. We are fighting for economic and political betterment, and we are doing so by striving to make our politics and economics the handmaidens of a loft and disinterested morality; and we are strong in the faith for we know in the end we shall succeed."

Atlanta Constitution, 29 September 1912.

A Brief Address from His Railroad Car at Columbus, Georgia, 28 September 1912

My Friends: It is a peculiar pleasure for me to come here to this state on behalf of the progressive party and myself, and I am glad to be here, for I am half Georgian myself. And friends, I now come down to get before you people of Georgia the reasons why Georgia should support the progressive movement, and I feel that we have a right to ask you to look to our proposals on their merits, and what I have come here to ask you to do is to judge for yourselves as to the worth of what we propose and not merely to act as somebody who thinks your grandfather would like you to act if they were alive—if they were right here today. I have no regard for the man who does it. Try to live up to what your father and grandfather did. You can live up to their lives only by meeting your problems of your day as they met theirs of their day. And what I strive—what I wish—what I want you to do is this. I say to you people of the south, as I have said already to those in the east, to those in the north and those in the west, is asking you to join a new party to sunder your connections with the two parties of the past—the democratic and the republican—you must naturally sunder yourselves from a party to which your ancestors belonged. Remember, friends, that in their day they had to take the same kind of action in almost every generation certainly in every second generation. Since our country has been founded it has been necessary to have a realignment of the parties. It is no reflection on the men who in the past, when the parties were alive—it is no reflection upon them to say that the conditions have so changed that the old party names (?) no longer mean anything. I make that statement now because it is a fact.

I ask you to read for yourselves the progressive platform: read what we say about labor; read what we say about farming; read what we say about business; about all the solutions of this country; and you can then compare it with the platforms of the old parties. See that we face the new issues and that they have busied themselves with the issues of a dead and settled past.

And now, friends, I wasn't willing in this contest not to come here and make my appeal to you men of the south to take your part in the leadership of the new party.

I feel that there is in the manhood and womanhood of the south a reservoir of strength for the nation upon which the nation ought to be able to draw, and I want to say now that the chance has come to show that you need not only fall in but you can lead in the new movement.

When I was president nothing struck me more than the artificiality of the political lines that kept me separated from so many senators and congressmen of the south. It was an incongruous thing. Gentlemen, again and again I had to put through some measures of interest to the south in spite of the opposition of democratic senators and congressmen who voted against the interest of their own section rather then support an action that I advocated.

I saw that in the Panama Canal. When I was engaged in securing the Panama Canal for the country I was carrying out a policy dear to the hearts of all southern statesmen in the fourth and fifth decades of the last century. It was the southern people who took the lead for the Panama canal. The south was more vitally interested in it than the north. There was only one other section where the interest was as vital, and yet, friends, over half of the southern senators voted against the treaty, and they voted against it because they were afraid of seeming to favor anything I did, even if it was for the interest of the south.

Now, what I want to see done is the breaking up of that feeling. Those of you who on conviction are opposed to the progressive party—that is all right. I have nothing to say to that; if you are against the principles for which we stand, then you ought to vote against us. My plea is addressed to those who are naturally for the principles we champion, and who are withheld by an allegiance to what is dead from coming with us. We broke up—we progressives have definitely put an end to the republican party. That is dead.

(Loud laughter and applause)

But you democrats need not cheer for we are going to bury the democratic party next.

Voices in audience:

"Never, never, never, not this year."

Col. Roosevelt:

"Sure, sure. I tell you, my friends, my plea is this. That if you are against us on principle, then you stand against us. But if you think our principles are right, then you stand with us. For instance, we declare for a workmen's compensation law; we declare for a continuous industry; for a three shift eight hour day; we are for the limitation of the labor of women in industry to eight hours a day. Now, if you believe in those things, come with us. If you are against them, stay with a dead party.

(Applause)

I ask that you in the south join with those like you in the north."

As the train started out, Col. Roosevelt stated as follows, "I would like to stay here longer, but I can't."

Columbus *Ledger-Enquirer,* 29 September 1912.

After visiting his mother's former house in Atlanta on 30 September, Roosevelt spent the next two days speaking in Tennessee and North Carolina. He arrived home on 2 October for conferences, testimony before the Clapp Committee on 4 October, and then more conferences with his Progressive allies. On 7 October he embarked on what was expected to be his second major campaign swing of the presidential election. His itinerary took him first to Michigan, then to Minnesota, Wisconsin, and Illinois. He was scheduled to be in Milwaukee for a speech on 14 October. The first tour had not shaken Wilson's lead in the election. So Roosevelt faced a difficult struggle as he continued his effort to make the Progressive Party a viable organization.

6

The Second Western Tour

During Roosevelt's first national tour, he had not been able to focus on Woodrow Wilson and his statements with the precision he would have liked. By the time he departed for the Middle West on 7 October, however, his campaign staff on the train was prepared to track what Wilson said so the Progressive candidate could respond promptly. Though this phase of his effort lasted only seven days, Roosevelt sharpened his attacks on his Democratic rival. Whether he was making any headway against Wilson was another matter. If the purpose was to goad Wilson into a gaffe, that goal had not been achieved. By mid-October, Roosevelt had not seriously dented Wilson's lead in the election.

Roosevelt began his trip in Michigan, where he made a significant address at Houghton. Two reports of that speech complement each other, and thus Roosevelt's remarks from both stories are provided here.

Remarks about Woodrow Wilson and Labor at Houghton, Michigan, 9 October 1912

The Progressive Party has deliberately embodied in its platform as its most essential plan, "the supreme duty of the Nation" to secure social and industrial justice. The platform distinctly states that in order to carry out its purpose to establish minimum safety and health standards for wage workers, especially women and children, it will invoke the Federal control over interstate commerce and the taxing power of both Nation and State.

Mr. Wilson has no less emphatically put himself on record for Stateism as opposed to Nationalism. In his book on constitutional government he bitterly denounces as "the alchemy of decay" the proposal to use the power to regulate commerce between the States in the very manner in which the Progressive platform proposes to use it.

He denounces specifically the attempt to "stretch" the power to regulate commerce so as "to include the regulation of labor in mills and factories."[1]

Turn to my messages to Congress. Most of what I advocated then is now embodied as a demand in the social and industrial plank of the Progressive platform.

I declared against convict contract labor. I declared in favor of the eight hour [day]. I demanded among other things that women and children be protected from excessive hours of labor, from night work and from work under unsanitary conditions. I demanded a workmen's compensation law. I urged radical and thorough-going inquiry into labor conditions in factories and mines throughout this country.

At that time I had no party united behind me. The rank and file was with me, but most of the leaders in Congress were at first lukewarm and gradually openly hostile to measures I advocated for legislation of this kind. Yet, I secured some of the things I urged, notably an employer's liability act, a safety appliance act, and a law limiting the hours of labor on railways. At the present time, if again elected President, I shall have the great Progressive Party behind, and all I formerly attempted for labor and for more will I this time secure.

During those years I again and again indorsed labor unions. Now, during those very years, Mr. Wilson was also speaking of labor from time to time. In an address at the People's Forum at New Rochelle as given in the *New York Tribune* of February 27, 1905, he says: "The objection I have to labor unions is that they drag the highest man to the level of the lowest."[2]

In an address before the South Carolina Society as given in the *New York Tribune* of March 19, 1907, he says as follows: "We speak too exclusively of the capitalistic class. There is another, as formidable an enemy to equality and freedom as it is, and that is the class formed by labor organizations and leaders of the country—the class representing only a small minority of the laboring men of the country, quite as monopolistic in spirit as the capitalist and quite as apt to corrupt and ruin our industries by their monopoly."[3]

1. Woodrow Wilson, *Constitutional Government in the United States* (New York: Columbia University Press, 1908), pp. 179 (on interstate commerce), 196 ("alchemy of decay").

2. The *New York Times* also carried a story on 27 February 1905 quoting that sentence from Wilson's speech.

3. "South Carolinians Dine At The Waldorf," *New York Times*, 19 March 1907, also carried Wilson's quoted words.

At the commencement exercises of Princeton University as given in the *New York World*, June 14, 1909, he says, as follows:

You know what the usual standard of the employe is in our day. It is to give as little as he may for his wages. The trades unions make the standard to which to conform. No employe is suffered to do more than the average workman can do. Our economic supremacy may be lost because the country grows more full of unprofitable servants."[4]

These are the sentiments he continued to express up to the time, two years ago, when he became a candidate for public office. He then changed. I am not questioning the sincerity of Mr. Wilson's change, but I wish to call attention to the fact that the extreme lateness of conversion and its very imperfect nature do not warrant him in making any comment whatever on the Progressive platform in this matter.

Philadelphia Inquirer, 10 October 1912.

A Campaign Address at Houghton, Michigan, 9 October 1912

The Progressive Party has deliberately embodied in its platform as the most essential plank the supreme duty of the Nation to obtain social and industrial justice, and in accordance with this policy it declares explicitly that it favors the organization of working men and women and governmental action for their welfare.

As Mr. Wilson has seen fit to attack the Progressive platform about labor, and especially about organized labor, I ask you to compare what I urged on Congress and what I succeeded in getting Congress to do, during the time I was President with Mr. Wilson's utterances throughout the course of those very years.

Turn to my messages to Congress. Most of what I advocated then is now embodied as a demand in the social and industrial justice plank of the Progressive platform.

4. "Woodrow Wilson Hits Labor Unions," *New York Times*, 14 June 1909, also quotes Wilson. Roosevelt compressed Wilson's paragraph. The first two sentences of the quotation are as Roosevelt gave them. Then Wilson said: "Labor is standardized by the trades unions, and this is the standard to which it is made to conform. No one is suffered to do more than the average worker can do." The final sentence from Wilson about the loss of economic supremacy came after several paragraphs on the union issue.

At that time I had no party behind me. The rank and file was with me, but most of the leaders in Congress were at first lukewarm and then gradually openly hostile to measures I advocated for legislation of this kind. Yet I secured some of the things I urged, notably an Employers' Liability act, a Safety Appliance act, and a law limiting the hours of labor on railways. At the present time, if again elected President, I shall have the great Progressive party behind me, and all I formerly attempted for labor and far more will I this time secure.

Mr. Wilson has spoken of labor from time to time. At the commencement exercises of Princeton University three years ago he said:

"You know what the usual standard of an employe is in our day. It is to give as little as he may for his wages. The trades unions make the standard to which to conform. No employe is suffered to do more than the average workman can do. Our economic supremacy may be lost if the country grows more full of unprofitable servants."

Now, if those were sentiments expressed by Mr. Wilson twenty-five or thirty years ago when he was fresh from college, I should attach no importance to them. But I call your attention to the fact that they are the sentiments he has expressed in the last six or eight years, and as recently as three years ago. They are the sentiments he continued to express up to the time, two years ago, when he became a candidate for public office. He then changed. I am not questioning the sincerity of Mr. Wilson's change, but I wish to call attention to the fact that the extreme lateness of his conversion and its very imperfect nature do not warrant him in making any comment on the Progressive platform in this matter.

Mr. Wilson, by a sudden and violent retracing of his steps, and in zigzag fashion, has nearly, but not entirely, reached as advanced a position as I took eleven years ago in my first message to Congress. I congratulate him upon having gotten so far, but this fact does not entitle him to leadership, and in many respects he has still a long way to go.

New York Times, 10 October 1912.

A Speech at Superior, Wisconsin, 10 October 1912

"I probably shouldn't make the reference to Mr. Wilson that I am going to make," said Colonel Roosevelt here today, "if he hadn't attacked me. But when anybody attacks me he might as well understand that I won't take it lying down. I'm a man of peaceful disposition, but I think I am able to defend myself."

Colonel Roosevelt stopped for an hour in Superior this morning on his way to Minnesota. His managers had planned a comparatively easy day for him after two days of rapid fire speech making in Michigan. He was to spend most of the day in Duluth and no speeches elsewhere were scheduled save the one at Superior.

Colonel Roosevelt called attention in his speech to what he said were inconsistencies in Governor Wilson's position.

"Mr. Wilson," said he, "has attacked the proposed federal legislation to prohibit child labor in very strong language, which is to be found in the *North American Review,* volume 187. He here denounces as mischievous the effort for the regulation of labor in mills and factories by the federal government.[5]

"The Democratic platform in one plank takes the same position, saying 'We denounce as usurpation the efforts to enlarge and magnify by indirection the powers of the federal government, this referring to the regulation of interstate commerce.' But in dealing with the trusts the Democratic platform states that it favors denying the trusts permission to engage in interstate trade at all."[6]

"It seems preposterous to discuss two such conflicting positions, and the mere fact that they can be put in the same platform shows the utter worthlessness of expecting serious social reform work from a party capable of taking such action in its declaration of principles."

"But Mr. Wilson's own statement as to the interstate commerce law and child labor, as quoted above, is absolutely incompatible with his position in standing upon the Democratic platform with its plank, given above, about interstate commerce. Either Mr. Wilson and the Democratic platform do not mean what they say, or else it is Mr. Wilson's duty to repudiate either the plank quoted above in the Democratic platform or his own statement about interstate commerce and child labor."

Kansas City Star, 10 October 1912.

5. Woodrow Wilson, "The States and the Federal Government," *North American Review,* 187 (May 1908): 684–702. The comment appears on page 688.

6. For these planks of the Democratic platform, see Democratic National Committee, *The Democratic Text-Book 1912* (New York: Isaac Goldman Printers, 1912), pp. 6, 10. On states' rights, the Democratic platform said: "We denounce as usurpation the efforts of our opponents to deprive the states of any of the rights reserved to them, and to enlarge and magnify by indirection the powers of the federal government," p. 10. The plank on the trusts favored "the declaration by law of the conditions upon which corporations shall be permitted to engage in interstate trade," p. 6.

A Campaign Address at Duluth, Minnesota, 10 October 1912

The other day Mr. Wilson at Gary, Ind., announced that the United States Steel corporation was supporting the Bull Moose ticket, saying: "It is the interest of these gentlemen that monopoly be maintained and they are supporting the Bull Moose party because the Bull Moose party expects to maintain monopoly."[7] At Pueblo, Colorado, three days later, he repeated substantially the same statement, substituting, however, the word "program" for the word "party" and asserting that corroborative evidence of this was to be had every day.[8] I at once challenged the statement, stating that as far as I know the only big man connected with either the Steel corporation or the Harvester company who was supporting me was Mr. Perkins. I stated that Mr. Wilson had no business to make such a statement unless he had the proof and if he had the proof I demanded that he make it public or immediately retract his statement as the only honorable or manly thing to do.

Mr. Wilson had no proof; he had not a particle of evidence, corroborative or otherwise. He could not make his statements good and he would not manfully retract them; so he made public an explanation in which he said in reference to the United States Steel corporation: "What I meant was they are supporting him with their thought." With their thought. Mr. Wilson is not a mind-reader.[9]

I have not the slightest interest in his belief as to what the thought of a trust magnate is. It is mere nonsense to treat such a statement as that Mr. Wilson made at Gary as being meant merely to imply that the Steel corporation was supporting me with its "thought." No human being who read that statement would have dreamed for a moment that Wilson was referring only to the "thought" of the steel trust. But I have an interesting com-

7. "Wilson Pillories Steel Trust In Gary," *New York Times,* 5 October 1912, carries the sentence about U.S. Steel: "Therefore they are in favor of the maintenance of monopoly, and they are supporting the Bull Moose Party because that party expects to maintain monopoly." This speech does not appear in either the Davidson volume of Wilson's speeches or the relevant volume of *The Papers of Woodrow Wilson.*

8. "Address at Pueblo, Colorado, 7 October, 1912," in John Wells Davidson, ed., *A Crossroads of Freedom: The 1912 Campaign Speeches of Woodrow Wilson* (New Haven, Conn.: Yale University Press, 1956), p. 361.

9. "A Campaign Address in Topeka, Kansas," 8 October 1912, in Arthur S. Link, et al., eds., *The Papers of Woodrow Wilson, Volume 25, 1912* (Princeton, N.J.: Princeton University Press, 1978), p. 381, has Wilson's comment: "What I meant was, they are supporting him with their thought, and their thought is not our thought."

Throughout 1912, Roosevelt attracted huge crowds that packed in around his car, as in this picture. No security guarded him from the public who wanted to hear him speak. (Theodore Roosevelt Collection, Harvard College Library)

ment on the accuracy of Mr. Wilson's own thought in the shape of a statement from the Wall Street organ on this very subject.

The day after Mr. Wilson made his Pueblo speech, Messrs. Dow, Jones & Co., publishers of the *Wall Street Journal,* sent over the stock exchange wires to various brokers the following telegram:

"According to a director of the United States Steel Corporation, if Roosevelt gets three votes from the directors of the Steel Corporation he will be lucky. There are now 33 United States Steel directors and according to this Steel corporation representative, Wilson will get more than Taft. Roosevelt will run a bad third among these 33 directors."

Dow, Jones & Company

This is an authoritative statement of the matter; although if I get three votes it will be exactly three times as many as I expect. Mr. Wilson's statement that the steel trust men are supporting me, even in their "thought," is simply not in accordance with the facts, and, moreover, it was not what he had said and it was not what any reasonable man could have interpreted his speech as meaning. Mr. Wilson would have done far better frankly to have admitted that he had made a statement which he could not substantiate, instead of attempting to justify it by assigning a meaning which it did not and could not possess. Mr. Wilson should learn that it is more manly to attack openly and in straightforward fashion rather than by innuendo or indirection; he should also learn that when he has made a statement which he cannot substantiate it is more manly to withdraw it in a straightforward fashion than to try to explain it in the manner he has defiantly adopted.

This is by no means the only instance where Mr. Wilson, when challenged as to some statement he has made, has neither justified it nor retracted it but has attempted to explain it away by asserting that it has a meaning utterly different from the obvious and plain meaning which every intelligent citizen would accept of it as bearing on its face.

I call your attention to what Mr. Wilson has said compared with what he now says on the question of immigration, and especially the immigration from eastern and southern Europe. In the *Atlantic Monthly* November 1889, in his article on Character of Democracy in the United States, he says:

"The union of strength with bigness depends upon the maintenance of character, and it is just the character of the nation which is being most deeply altered and modified by the excessive immigration which, year after year, pours into the country from Europe. Our own temperate blood, schooled to self-possession, is receiving a constant infusion and yearly experiencing a partial corruption of foreign blood. Our own equable habits have been crossed with the feverish habits of the restless [Old] World. We are unquestionably facing an ever-increasing difficulty of self-command with ever-deteriorating materials, possibly with degenerating fibre."[10]

In volume 5 of his History on pages 212–214, he writes as follows:

"There came multitudes of men of the lowest classes from the south of Italy and men of the meaner sort out of Hungary and Poland, men out of the ranks, where there was neither skill nor energy, nor any initiative of quick intelligence, and they came in numbers, which increased from year to year, as if the countries of Europe were disburdening themselves of the more sordid and hapless elements of their population. The Chinese were more to be desired as workingmen, if not as citizens, than most of the coarse crew that came crowding in every year at the Eastern ports. The un-

10. Woodrow Wilson, "Character of Democracy in the United States," *Atlantic Monthly* 64 (November 1899): 577–578; the quoted passage appears on page 585. The newspaper quotation has one word missing, which I have included in brackets.

likely fellows that came in at the eastern ports were considered because they occupied no place but the very lowest on the scale of labor."[11]

When asked to explain this in March last, Mr. Wilson wrote to Mr. Di Silvestro in part as follows: "I was in the passage alluded to only deploring the coming to this country of certain lawless elements which I of course supposed that all thoughtful Italians themselves deplored. I was thinking only of the men who have once and again threatened to give to that whole, fine body of Italians, who have enriched American life, a reputation which they did not deserve."[12] In another letter, published in the *New York Tribune* of March 12, 1912, Mr. Wilson says: "I referred to the class of lawbreakers which was brought under pauper labor contracts."[13]

I think it would have been more frank and more manly for Mr. Wilson either to have announced that he still held the views which he had promulgated in his history or else to have stated that he had come to the conclusion that these views were offensive and that he had abandoned them.

I am reluctantly obliged to say that it is quite impossible to reconcile the two explanations Mr. Wilson gives as I have above quoted them with the facts. Neither in his *Atlantic Magazine* article nor in his history did he make an allusion to pauper contract labor. Nor did he make an allusion to the lawless element. He was contrasting immigrants generally with natives and the immigrants of certain European countries. He was speaking of all the multitudes of men that came from the south of Italy, from Hungary, and Poland and contrasting them disadvantageously with the Chinese. I fail to see how any man can believe that in the passage quoted Mr. Wilson was making any referencc whatever merely to "lawless elements" or "pauper labor." And I regret for Mr. Wilson's own sake that he should have permitted himself to make such a defense.

I ask you people in this economic center what our appeal is. It is the

11. This passage from *A History of the American People* (New York: Harper & Brothers, 1902), 5:212–214, had been brought to light in the presidential campaign by William Randolph Hearst and by other critics of Wilson's views on immigration early in 1912. Roosevelt took parts of the three paragraphs that compose this material in Wilson's book and stitched them together for his speech. The words used, however, are all from Wilson's book.

12. Wilson to Joseph A. Di Silvestro, 4 February 1912, in Arthur S. Link, et al., eds., *The Papers of Woodrow Wilson, Volume 24, 1912* (Princeton, N.J.: Princeton University Press, 1977), p. 134, has some minor changes from what Roosevelt quoted.

13. Woodrow Wilson to John Arthur Aylward, 7 March 1912, in Link, et al., eds., *The Papers of Woodrow Wilson, Volume 24, 1912*, p. 226, has the letter from which Roosevelt quoted. He omitted the last section of the sentence, which reads in full: "I refer to the class of laborers which was brought here under pauper labor contracts by some of the great protected industries."

making of economic betterment and that better life that must be built up with economic betterment a substructure.

For 50 years no such doctrine has been before the people. Not since the time of Abraham Lincoln have the real and live issues of the day been faced as we face them. For 10 years and more there has been a gradually growing recognition that our public representatives too often misrepresent us. Further, it is evident that the legislation that has been shaped and the economic questions that have been met have not been such that our law givers should make if they had been possessed of a sincere desire to do right.

The platforms of the two old parties differ from that of the Progressive party. They deal with the dead issues of the past. We declare ourselves definitely on the issues of the present day.

If you cannot agree with us, you know with what you are disagreeing. We stand for the organization of labor, federal as well as state laws for the abolition of child labor, to limit the hours of women workers to eight, to provide in continuous industries one rest day a week with three shifts of eight hours each, the provision of a minimum wage for women, the protection of that considerable element at the bottom of the industrial world and to provide legislation that will secure to the people the real and not the nominal control over their representatives. It is on these and a dozen similar programs that we stand.

It is said by my opponents that I am trying to do away with responsible government. Nonsense. I am trying to do away with irresponsible government and to change things so that the public and not the bosses or the special interests will rule, and that real justice will prevail.

It is said by my opponents that I preach discontent and class hatred. I preach discontent with what is wrong. I never preach hatred of any class except the class of crooks. Big crooks and little crooks, it is all the same. I never attacked a man because he was big, but because he was a crooked big man.

The lesson that is being shown now is the lesson that it is not the crook who fails that is dangerous but it is the crook who succeeds. The crook who fails is sent to jail but the crook who succeeds goes on and becomes a United States senator, a big financial magnate or a boss.

He debauches the average voter for he teaches the young men that the crooked path is the one to adopt. The path to success does not lie along the lines of crookedness.

I am not opposed to the big man. I have the greatest respect for the big man in either business or politics who has attained his position through serving his fellow man. No matter how big he may be, I am pleased. In fact, the bigger his success, the greater my admiration. It is the big man who has reached his position through swindling whom I oppose. The line I draw is not one of size; it is a line of conduct.

If you analyze the attacks made upon me, you will find that they complain of the way the big men have been treated. The complaint is not that I treat the big man and the little man differently but because I treat them alike. I defy my opponents to prove that I ever let up on a criminal because he was a small man, and when I don't let up on a small man I have no right to let up on a big man. What we stand for is the recognition of the rights of every man. What are his rights? Politically to cast one vote, and what our platform stands for is to see that this one vote is protected and to have it counted and to see that it is not cast for any United States senator who is controlled or for an executive or for any judge, who is corrupt.

Any man can search my record and see where I have always acted in accordance to the principles I have laid down tonight.

Duluth News Tribune, 11 October 1912. I have omitted several paragraphs in which Roosevelt went over the delegate battle at the Republican convention and the role of Jacob Schiff in the campaign, as he had done in the past.

Remarks on the Tariff at Oshkosh, Wisconsin, 11 October 1912

When I became President business had just passed through two terrible earthquakes, there having been two complete and sweeping changes in the tariff in the preceding eight years. It would have been mere folly immediately to have prepared for another change. The time for such another change did not ripen until the very end of my Administration.[14]

The immediate and pressing demand for important legislation was for legislation of a wholly different kind. During the time that I was President there was no complaint at all that I was not doing enough. The complaint of all my enemies was that I was doing too much. The chief demand that the tariff should be taken up came from the great railway and trust mag-

14. Roosevelt is referring to the Wilson-Gorman Tariff of 1894 and the Dingley Tariff of 1897. The higher tariff rates in the Wilson-Gorman Tariff of 1894 did not fulfill the 1892 campaign pledges of the Democrats to lower the tariff. As a result, it contributed to the party's defeat in the 1894 congressional elections. The Dingley Tariff of 1897 implemented Republican protectionism and raised tariff duties.

Woodrow Wilson has the public's attention while Roosevelt endeavors to interrupt to make his campaign pitch. McKee Barclay cartoon. (Library of Congress)

nates who have always been anxious to use the tariff as a red herring to be dragged across the trail whenever action which they dislike is threatened, and Mr. Wilson is obligingly trying to play their game at this moment.[15]

Mr. Wilson, on the tariff, as on almost every other issue, either takes no definite position, or takes so many conflicting positions that it is difficult to know what he means to do. Probably Mr. Wilson has no clear idea of what he does intend to do.

In an interview in *Munsey's Magazine* for October, 1911, he complains bitterly of the methods of tariff making, saying that clauses have been inserted in our tariff laws as "a matter of private arrangement between the representatives of certain great business interests and the members of the

15. There was more to the tariff revision sentiment among Republicans during Roosevelt's presidency than he allows in this speech. Understanding the dimensions of the tariff was never Roosevelt's strongest point.

Ways and Means Committee of the House and the Finance Committee of the Senate."[16]

This is entirely true, and it is to meet this very objection that the Progressives have advocated a scientific, non-partisan business commission which should secure all information about the tariff and give the framework for tariff legislation to Congress. Yet Mr. Wilson comes out against such a commission.

Mr. Wilson keeps asserting that the abolition of the protective tariff will help us grapple with our social and industrial evils, and notably with the high cost of living. Mr. Wilson, if fit to be President, cannot be ignorant of the way the tariff has worked in foreign countries, and unless he is ignorant he must know that his statement is without warrant in fact.

Let him compare the course of economic history in England and Germany for the last forty years. England has been under a free trade system during that time. The cost of living has gone steadily up and the conditions of labor have become so bad as to necessitate the most sweeping effort at reform.

But the experience of Germany is even more impressive. During these same forty years the economic conditions in Germany and especially the economic conditions among the German wage-workers have improved by leaps and bounds as compared to what has obtained in free-trade England during the same time. No small part of the German success has been due to the fact that she has adopted the commission system—the very system which Mr. Wilson ignorantly denounces.

New York Times, 12 October 1912.

A Speech at the Chicago Coliseum on the Trusts, 12 October 1912

The other day Mr. Wilson stated that during my administration I had done nothing against the trusts. Mr. Wilson has criticized the Progressive plank on the trust question before. In the national field he has himself

16. Isaac Marcosson, "Woodrow Wilson, Presidential Possibility," *Munsey's Magazine* 46 (October 1911): 8.

17. At Denver on 7 October, Wilson said of Roosevelt and monopoly that "he simply sat by helpless while it grew up." Link, *Papers of Woodrow Wilson, 1912, Volume 25*, p. 372.

proposed nothing definite. Mr. Wilson never proposed anything definite and concrete on any subject.[17]

So far as his statements can be said to contain any commitment whatever to any policy, they commit him to a continuation of Mr. Taft's policy as regards dealing with the trusts by the national government, and they especially insist upon the duty of the states to deal with trusts.

As he now attacks my own record, and as he has thus definitely committed himself in the duty of the states to deal with the trusts, I shall ask you to compare not only our proposals with his proposals and the proposals contained in the Democratic platform, but also to compare my record as president with his record as governor of New Jersey.

This is perfectly fair to him, for he insists that it is the states who must deal with the trusts, and of all the states in the union it is New Jersey which has had the most to do with the trusts and in which the trust evil has been most rampant.

Mr. Wilson says I did nothing with the trusts when I was president. The answer is that I did everything. Until I became president there had been no effort to deal with the trust evil at all in serious fashion, and one of the amusing features of the criticism of me lies in the fact that it was I, myself, who by my actions and by what I accomplished, created the conditions which in their turn have created the public opinion which demands efficient action in the matter.

These criticisms represent a purpose to apply to the utterly different conditions of ten years ago the standard of today which I myself largely helped to create, because I stopped the old conditions when I was president.

I found the anti-trust law practically a dead letter and the interstate commerce law almost wholly ineffective as regards the prime evil of rebates. There was no precedent for the real enforcement of either law. The railroads were acting with practically entire disregard of the interstate commerce commission, and the Supreme Court of the United States in the Knight case had declared that the anti-trust law did not affect great industrial concerns engaged in manufacturing—a decision which in effect rendered the anti-trust law of little or no use.[18]

The first need was to put these laws on an established basis of working efficiency and to make not only the public, but the biggest magnates in the land understand that the government was even bigger than they were.

18. Roosevelt referred to *United States v. E. C. Knight Co.* (1895), in which the Supreme Court ruled that the Sherman Antitrust Act did not apply to firms that had a monopoly of manufacturing. The decision favored the Sugar Trust and weakened the ability of the federal government to bring antitrust prosecutions against large corporations.

I struck straight at the very biggest railroad magnates and trust magnates in the country and I made them understand that the government was supreme over them.[19]

The Knight sugar case had been decided adversely to the people under the administration of the last Democratic president of the United States, the chief justice of the court at the time being also a Democrat. It was rendered in strict accordance with the states' rights doctrine now zealously proclaimed by Mr. Wilson and the Democratic platform, and it completely emasculated the anti-trust law.[20]

My business was to obtain the recall of that particular decision and I accomplished that purpose. Our first proceeding was to bring the Northern Securities suit, which dealt with railroads and not industrial concerns, and therefore offered a larger chance for the court to reverse in principle a foolish and iniquitous decision while technically refraining from doing so. We won the suit by the margin of one vote, the decision being 5 to 4 in our favor.

I was able by the hardest kind of fighting to get from congress amendments immensely increasing the efficiency of the interstate commerce law and also an important law establishing the bureau of corporations.[21]

I could not get from congress the legislation needed to enable us to deal as efficiently with the big industrial trusts as we had been able to deal with the railroads, but I made so much impression by my repeated messages and addresses that the Republican platform in 1908 did definitely promise action along the lines I had indicated—although the promise was broken by those in charge of the Republican Party as soon as I left the presidency.[22]

In short, at that time, for the first time in our economic history, the anti-trust law and the interstate commerce law were made living and vital. I obtained a good solution of the railroad problem. I made the biggest men in the land yield obedience to the anti-trust law, and I put the whole matter in train for satisfactory solution; and I did all this at the same time when we were accomplishing a literally incredible quantity of work in other directions.

If [?] it would not have been possible for any human being to have ob-

19. The Northern Securities case established the authority of the federal government over large corporations. In effect, the Supreme Court overruled its decision in the Knight case.

20. The case occurred during Grover Cleveland's presidency. Melville Weston Fuller (1833–1910) was the chief justice.

21. Roosevelt obtained these measures from Congress in early 1903.

22. For these events, see Lewis L. Gould, *The Presidency of Theodore Roosevelt* (Lawrence: University Press of Kansas, 1991), pp. 279–281.

tained more or to have made a more satisfactory showing than my administration obtained.

So much for what was actually accomplished during my term as president—and remember, please, that it was accomplished at the expense of the biggest financial magnates in our land, the biggest railroads and the biggest trusts—railroads such as the New York Central, the Southern Pacific, the Northern Pacific, and the Great Northern; industrial trusts such as the sugar trust, the tobacco trust, and the Standard Oil trust.

Now, compare this record with Mr. Wilson's record as governor of New Jersey on the trust question. The comparison is easy—Mr. Wilson's record on this matter is a blank. He did precisely and exactly nothing. It is as simple to describe what Mr. Wilson, as Governor of New Jersey, has accomplished against the trusts as it is to write a volume on the natural history of the snakes in Ireland. There are no snakes in Ireland; and Mr. Wilson during his term as Governor of New Jersey, has not done one least little thing of any shape, sort or description toward dealing with the trust problem.

Yet the opportunity has been ample. And if his own doctrines as to the duty of the States to deal with the trusts are correct, then his failure to act is inexcusable. The same trusts against which I actually did act were incorporated under the laws of New Jersey, and it was perfectly simple for him to act against them, but he never followed my example.

He never even disturbed them; he never took action of any kind against them, and yet he solemnly proclaims that they can be reached only by state action—only by the kind of action which he could have taken and which he did not take.

Mr. Wilson has announced himself as an ardent advocate of the new stateism as against the new nationalism. In a recent interview with Henry Beach Needham he says that of necessity the states are the battlegrounds of economic reform.[23]

"It is the states which incorporate the great business undertakings that threaten to bulk larger than the states themselves in the power which they exercise. The big corporations owe their license to the inadequacy of state laws and their non-enforcement."[24]

23. Henry Beach Needham, "Woodrow Wilson's Views," *Outlook* 48 (26 August 1911): 939–951. Wilson called the states "the chief battle-ground of economic reform" on page 947.

24. These sentences are taken from two pages in the Needham article. The first comes from page 947, and the second comes from page 948, reading as follows with Wilson being quoted first: "The big corporations owe their existence to the laws of the States," and then Needham asks, "And their license?" to which Wilson responds, "To the inadequacy of State laws or their non-enforcement."

The Democratic platform on which Mr. Wilson is standing denounces the effort to deprive the states of any of their rights in connection with dealing with the trusts, insisting that no federal action shall be substituted for state remedies for the prevention of private monopoly—that is, of the trusts.

Therefore it appears that Mr. Wilson explicitly recognizes the theory that it is the prime duty of the state government, rather than of the national government, to deal with trusts, and the Democratic platform no less explicitly recognizes the power and the duty of the States in this matter.

Well, for the most part, the modern American trusts have been incorporated in the state of New Jersey and are subject to its laws. They depend upon the state government for their powers and their very life, both of which may at any time be cut off if the State Government sees fit to take such action.

For nearly two years Mr. Wilson has been the head of this State Government. If the Standard Oil company or tobacco trust has, in Mr. Wilson's opinion, been guilty of gross frauds or attempts to monopolize or of working unwholesome mergers or stock issues their State charters can be readily amended, altered, or repealed.

Section 4 of the New Jersey corporation law provides that "the charter of every corporation or any supplement thereto or amendment thereof, shall be subject to alteration, suspension, and repeal, in the discretion of the legislature, and the legislature may at pleasure dissolve any corporation."[25]

It is, of course, the duty of the Governor to recommend such action whenever it becomes necessary. Moreover, there is a criminal statute in New Jersey applying to corporations, which affords a simple remedy of the kind which Mr. Wilson and his supporters have repeatedly stated would be the most effective to meet the evils of the present situation. Chapter 257 of the laws of 1905 provides as follows:

"Any person or persons who shall organize or incorporate, or procure to be established or incorporated, any corporation or body corporate under the laws of this state with intent thereby to further promote or conduct any fraudulent or unlawful object, shall be guilty of a misdemeanor. Any

25. John Scott Parker, *The Law of New Jersey Corporations: their organization and management with the text of statutes relating to all stock companies, except banks, building and loan associations, canal, insurance, plank road, provident loan, safe deposit, surety, trust and turnpike companies with forms and precedents* (Chicago: Callaghan, 1911), 1:462.

person or persons who, being officers, directors, managers or employes of any corporation or body corporate under the laws of this state, shall willfully use, operate, or control said corporation or body corporate for the furtherance or promotion of any fraudulent or unlawful object, shall be guilty of a misdemeanor."[26]

Yet, nevertheless, although his power is ample, under these provisions of the laws, Mr. Wilson, while Governor of New Jersey, has not urged or attempted to secure the amendment, alteration, or repeal of a single corporation of New Jersey. Nor has he attempted to secure the indictment of any officer, Director, or employe of such a corporation under the act of 1907.

Where Mr. Wilson thus utterly fails as governor of New Jersey to come to what he himself says a governor ought to do it is not to be wondered that his criticisms of the progressive proposals for dealing with the trusts should be futile in their utter unsoundness.

He says that our proposal is to legalize trusts. It is but the attitude of Mr. Taft in the Standard Oil and tobacco trust cases, which is substantially what Mr. Wilson's attitude has meant in his practice as governor of New Jersey—not merely to legalize trusts, but to shelter them for he failed to exercise a single one of the great powers granted to the New Jersey governor for the punishment of the great trusts declared by the Supreme Court of the nation to have been guilty of improper and wicked practices.[27]

We are advocating cooperation in business. We propose to do away with all conditions and practices which produce monopoly in so far as this can be done by legislation. We propose to see that competition remains free wherever possible by prohibiting in effective fashion all unfair practices.

In my address or confession of faith at the Progressive national convention I spoke as follows: "Wherever it is practicable we propose to preserve competition, but where, under modern conditions, competition has been eliminated and cannot be successfully restored, then the government must step in and itself supply the needed control on behalf of the people as a whole."[28]

Mr. Wilson's proposal for the national control of the trusts is merely to

26. J. B. R. Smith, *New Jersey Corporation Law,* 2nd ed. (Newark, N.J.: Soney & Sage, 1923), p. 495, has the provisions of the two statutes that Roosevelt ran together as one law.

27. There is a misprint in the *Chicago Tribune* at this point and the remainder of the text is in the next column.

28. "A Confession of Faith," *The Works of Theodore Roosevelt: Social Justice and Popular Rule* (New York: Charles Scribner's Sons, 1926), 17:282.

continue the ineffective do-nothing policy of Mr. Taft, is merely to continue the effort to regulate the trusts by lawsuits. The Progressive proposal on the contrary is to handle the trusts by a commission as interstate commerce is handled, and to assume over these great industrial concerns powers such as the controller of the currency exercises over national banks.

We propose practical and thorough going action to be taken by the nation. Mr. Wilson proposes the continuation of a do nothing policy by the nation, and while he advocates action by the states he himself as governor of a state has taken not one step of any kind to carry out the policy to which in theory he is committed.

All this throws a curious light on Mr. Wilson's statement, reported in the New York papers as having been made in Denver the other day that there was a "hallelujah chorus of the trusts" in my favor. The quotation is not accurate, I hope, for of course there is not a particle of foundation for such a statement.[29]

The only man to whom Mr. Wilson can refer my supporters as representing any trust is Mr. Perkins, indeed, unless he includes Mr. Munsey. These two men, Mr. Perkins and Mr. Munsey are men of means, precisely as Cleveland H. Dodge and Mr. McAdoo and Mr. Crane, Mr. Wilson's intimate associates, are men of means.[30]

I know Mr. Dodge personally. He is a fine fellow, an upright, honorable, and public spirited man, just as Mr. Perkins is an upright, honorable, and public spirited man. It was on his yacht that Mr. Wilson wrote his letter of acceptance.

Mr. Dodge is a member of big corporations, precisely as Mr. Perkins is a member of certain big corporations. I should strongly denounce any man who tried to incite prejudice against Mr. Wilson because Mr. Dodge is supporting him, and in just the same fashion, any honorable man will denounce as base and dishonorable the effort to prejudice me by the statement that Mr. Perkins is supporting me. The actions of Mr. McAdoo and Mr. Crane come in the same category.

As for the trusts, there is not a single trust supporting me, and Mr. Wil-

29. John Wells Davidson, *A Crossroads of Freedom: The 1912 Campaign Speeches of Woodrow Wilson* (New Haven, Conn.: Yale University Press, 1956), pp. 362–363.

30. Frank Andrew Munsey (1854–1925) was the wealthy magazine publisher who was supporting Roosevelt and the Progressives. Cleveland Hoadley Dodge (1859–1926) was a close friend and financial backer of Wilson. His fortune came from railroads. William Gibbs McAdoo (1863–1941) was another wealthy Democrat who made his money in New York subways and railroads. He was managing the Wilson campaign and would become secretary of the treasury under Wilson. Charles Richard Crane (1858–1939) was a wealthy Chicagoan who had supported La Follette and in the fall backed Wilson.

son knows this well. Mr. Perkins is in the Harvester Company and in the Steel Corporation; he is the one man in either of these corporations that is supporting me. So far as I know, of his associates in these corporations one or two are supporting me, and all the rest are supporting Mr. Taft or Mr. Wilson.[31]

Mr. Wilson and his supporters have asserted that the Progressive proposal is that when monopoly cannot be broken up we propose to control it in the public interest. But whenever possible we propose to break it up. Mr. Wilson fails to understand the distinction between large concentration of industry and monopolies. Monopolies never have been legalized, even under the common law.

So far from advocating the retention of monopoly, we are advocating the only efficient method of breaking up monopoly, of breaking up and destroying monopoly, and are merely preparing to accept, and in accepting to control and regulate [incomplete sentence][32]

Medill McCormick is supporting me. He has no connection, and never has had any connection, with the harvester trust; and he stated the other day in a public speech that his two kinfolk of the same name who are connected with the harvester trust are both supporting Mr. Wilson.[33]

The *Herald's* poll of the stock exchange in New York, taken the other day, showed that 307 Wall Street men were supporting Mr. Wilson or Mr. Taft and only twenty-six were supporting me. That's the ratio in Wall street, say 12 to 1 against me, and so far as I know among the great trust magnates the proportion in Mr. Wilson's favor is very much greater.

The reason is not difficult to find. Mr. Wilson's record as governor has given every trust magnate a feeling of restful security about Mr. Wilson. If we are to judge Mr. Wilson's future by his past performances, this security is more than justified.

If Mr. Wilson were elected president, and if in the presidency he paralleled his record as governor, the trusts would find him a most delightful and harmless companion.

Mayor Gaynor, in address before the National Democratic club on Feb.

31. Except for the first line, this paragraph was dropped from the *Chicago Tribune* text at this point and reappeared some paragraphs later. I have inserted the words from "Roosevelt Attacks Deneen and Wilson," *New York Times*, 13 October 1912.

32. The paragraph ends in an incomplete sentence. The last two lines appear in a previous column as a fragment.

33. Joseph Medill McCormick (1877–1925) was a member of the family that founded International Harvester, an agricultural manufacturer. He was married to Ruth Hanna McCormick, the daughter of Marcus A. Hanna (1837–1904), and would later become a U.S. senator.

9 last, said: "Four-fifths of the trusts of this country are organized and exist under this New Jersey statute. If the people want the trusts broken up or prevented they need only elect governors and legislators who will carry out their will and stay at home to do it."[34]

Mr. Wilson certainly has done nothing while governor of New Jersey about the trusts. The only excuse that can be advanced for him must be that "the states can do nothing against the trusts" which would be to make a plea the direct reverse of the one he has actually made. In dealing with the problem nationally he confines himself purely to criticism and has not a single constructive suggestion to make.

He attacks the Progressive proposal for a commission, saying in an interview with Mr. Needham in 1911: "The great body of public opinion is opposed to regulation of big corporations by a commission," and previously, on Nov. 13, 1907, he also strongly opposed governmental supervision as a remedy for the trusts.[35]

Nevertheless, no man could have spoken more strongly in favor of regulation of all big corporations than he spoke in his inaugural message of Jan. 17, 1911. He explicitly put public utility corporations in the same class as regards remedy-making, saying, after discussing corporations in general, "the matter is most obvious when we turn to what we have come to designate public service or public utilities corporations." He then continues to say that such "commission should have complete regulative powers, the power to regulate rates, the power to learn and make public everything that would furnish a basis for the public judgment with regard to the soundness and efficiency and economy of the business, the power, in brief, to adjust such service at every point and in every respect, whether of equipment or charges or methods of financing or means of service to the general communities affected." It would have been impossible to state more clearly the general lines of policy in which the Progressive party has now committed itself and to which Mr. Wilson makes objection.[36]

34. "Presidential Boom For Gaynor Staged," *New York Times*, 9 February 1912, quotes New York mayor W. J. Gaynor on Wilson's record on the trusts in New Jersey.

35. The statement was made during a speech in Nashville, Tennessee, on 12 November 1907. See Arthur S. Link, et al., eds., *The Papers of Woodrow Wilson, Volume 17, 1907–1908* (Princeton, N.J.: Princeton University Press, 1974), p. 494. Wilson did not say it during a speech on 16 November in Cleveland, ibid., pp. 497–506.

36. "An Inaugural Address," 17 January 1911, in Arthur S. Link, et al., eds., *The Papers of Woodrow Wilson, Volume 22, 1910–1911* (Princeton, N.J.: Princeton University Press, 1976), pp. 348–349. Roosevelt did not quote Wilson precisely. The last lines in Wilson's address read "means of service, to the general interest of the communities affected."

With the change of a few words this quotation from Mr. Wilson himself could be accepted as a brief epitome of the Progressive proposal as regards trusts.

We intend to secure competition wherever possible, whereas, in the case of certain patents or as regards certain monopolies or for other reasons where monopoly does in effect exist and cannot be prevented, we propose stringently to control and regulate it in the public interest.

Moreover, even where there is no monopoly, where the corporation is big, we propose that the government shall exercise thorough going control over it, in the interest not only of the consumer and the general public, but of the employes of the corporation.

Our policy is feasible and practical. We propose something definite and efficient. Mr. Wilson's proposal is to continue in national matters the do-nothing policy of Mr. Taft, and his practice in his own state of New Jersey has been to put this do-nothing policy into actual effect.

The Progressive platform I consider the greatest document put forth for the benefit of humanity in this or any other country, since the death of Abraham Lincoln. Our opponents have been forced to drop their own platform, and to speak ill of me, and they are having difficulty in guessing at the principles for which they stand. If the Democratic platform is not a program, what is it?

It is either a program or a false promise. We promise nothing we cannot carry out, and we don't say from the stump anything we can't make good.

Mr. Archbold does not think I did nothing to the trusts. Before the senate committee at Washington Mr. Archbold and his intimate friend and companion, Senator Penrose, testified, not against me, but against a man who is dead. For seven years they had not opened their mouths.

Then Cornelius Bliss was dead and these two valiant creatures came forward to testify. They said I had administered the Abyssinian treatment of the trusts. That is true, but I wouldn't like to commit myself as to the truthfulness of the rest of Archbold's testimony.

Nor do I care to criticize the careless business methods of the Standard Oil company whereby the receipt for the $100,000 was destroyed.

My answer to them is that every Archbold in the country is now against the Progressive party.

The Standard Oil, tobacco, Northern Securities, and sugar trusts are all incorporated in New Jersey. Likewise, the beef trust and thirty others. We administered the Abyssinian treatment in the sugar trust, and made it pay $4,000,000 into the national treasury. Mr. Wilson is governor of New Jersey, and his present platform, I may say without undue hyperbole that he stands upon occasionally, offers nothing in the way of constructive policy for control of the trusts.

Our opponents say that Wall Street is with us. The statement is inaccurate and I am cultivating the habit of using guarded moderation in my utterances.

The prayer of Wall Street is "O, Providence, give us another dissolution such as the Standard Oil dissolution." After that dissolution those stocks went up 102 per cent but wages did not go up. I don't care whether Morgan owns one-third and Rockefeller owns another third and Guggenheim or somebody else owns another third, but I am interested in getting the hands of the government on all of them.

I am for three shifts of eight hours each for the men who work for them. I am for one day of rest each week, made mandatory by law, and I am for government inspectors in shops to see that there are no occupational diseases and that there is adequate protection for life and limb.

We are interested in getting actual results to benefit conditions for men and women. We are for state's [*sic*] rights when the states can and will take the proper and necessary steps to bring justice. When the states cannot do that then we are for the nation exercising its power.

No man has put a question to me in this campaign that I cannot answer, and I will refer you to the senate committee for the commentary upon this statement.

Chicago Tribune, 13 October 1912.

Although the Chicago Tribune *said it had printed the complete text of Roosevelt's speech, he added other portions of it when he wrote a letter to William Jennings Bryan after the attempt on his life to clarify remarks he had made in the address.*

Excerpts from the Chicago Speech, 12 October 1912

Now, friends, our proposal is to do away with all those conditions that artificially make for monopoly. Our proposal is to establish an administrative body which shall take absolute control over these big industrial concerns, just as the Interstate Commerce Commission does with the railroads or the Banking Department with banks—and a control such as will enable us to go in and inspect every big concern, inspect every practice, put a stop to rebates, put a stop to any issue of watered stock, put a stop to every practice which is not in accordance with the rules of decency and honesty, and then not to stop even there but to exercise such supervision over the big industrial concerns as will insure justice not only to the rival and the stockholders and the general public but to the wageworkers as well. The Democratic platform approves what the Stanley Committee has recommended as a panacea, that we shall divide into at least three the ownership of any industrial organization. Very good. I had a chance to test that the other day. I was in Pueblo, where they have the plant of the Colorado Fuel and Iron Company. It is a competitor of the Steel trust and it is owned by those struggling independent operators, Messrs. Rockefeller and Guggenheim. And they would work their men twelve hours a day and seven days a week and the *Survey* has declared that this is one of the worst plants in the country from the standpoint of taking care of the lives and health and living conditions of the workers. What will the country gain if instead of having the present conditions in the steel industry you had a little less in the power of Mr. Morgan and a little more in the power of Mr. Rockefeller and Mr. Guggenheim? There would not be the change of the weight of your finger. Not one thing would be accomplished by dividing the steel industry in one third between Mr. Morgan, Mr. Rockefeller and Mr. Guggenheim. Is that not so? You would not gain anything by it at all. I do not care a rap what proportion those three men own of the industry. What I am interested in is getting the hand of the Government put on all of them—that is what I want. I want to have the hand of the Government put on the Steel Corporation and I want to have it put on the Colorado Fuel and Iron Company.

Roosevelt to William Jennings Bryan, 22 October 1912, in Elting E. Morison et al., eds., *The Letters of Theodore Roosevelt* (Cambridge, Mass.: Harvard University Press, 1954), 7: 631.

Roosevelt's next scheduled campaign stop was Milwaukee, Wisconsin. When he reached the city, he prepared to get into a car that would take him to his speech. As he waved to the crowd, an assassin, John Schrank, shot him in the chest. The bullet broke a rib but his folded speech, glasses case, and clothing stopped it from penetrating farther into his body. He was in intense pain but insisted that he be allowed to deliver his prepared address. Roosevelt himself then described what had happened to him.

A Speech at Milwaukee, Wisconsin, 14 October 1912

Friends, I shall have to ask you to be as quiet as possible. I do not know whether you fully understand that I have been shot, but it takes more than that to kill a Bull Moose. But, fortunately, I had my manuscript, so, you see, I was going to make a long speech. And, friends, there is a bullet—there is where the bullet went through, and it probably saved the bullet from going into my heart. The bullet is in me now, so that I cannot make a very long speech. But I will try my best.

And now, friends, I want to take advantage of this incident and say a solemn word of warning to my fellow countrymen. First of all, I want to say this about myself: I have altogether too important things to think of to feel any concern over my own death; and now I cannot speak to you insincerely within five minutes of being shot. I am telling you the literal truth when I say that my concern is for many other things. It is not in the least for my own life. I want you to understand that I am ahead of the game, anyway. No man has had a happier life than I have led; a happier life in every way. I have been able to do certain things that I greatly wished to do, and I am interested in doing other things. I can tell you with absolute truthfulness that I am very much uninterested in whether I am shot or not. It was just as when I was colonel of my regiment. I always felt that a private was to be excused for feeling at times some pangs of anxiety about his personal safety, but I cannot understand a man fit to be a colonel who can pay any heed to his personal safety when he is occupied as he ought to be occupied with the absorbing desire to do his duty.

I am in this cause with my whole heart and soul. I believe that the Progressive movement is for making life a little easier for all our people; a movement to try to take the burdens off the men and especially the women and children of this country. I am absorbed in the success of that movement.

Friends, I ask you now this evening to accept what I am saying as absolutely true, when I tell you I am not thinking of my own success. I am not thinking of my life or of anything connected with me personally. I am thinking of the movement, I say this by way of introduction, because I want to say something very serious to our people and especially to the

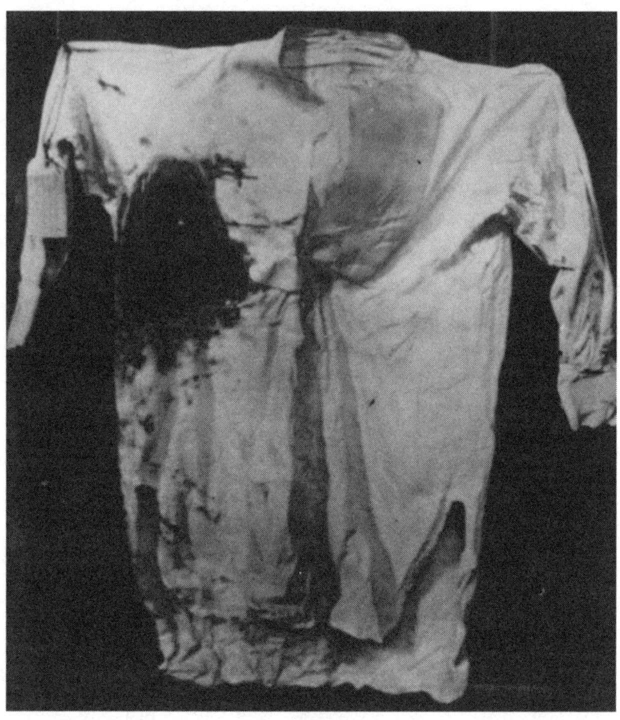

The attempt on Roosevelt's life at Milwaukee left dramatic bloodstains on the candidate's shirt. (Theodore Roosevelt Collection, Harvard College Library)

newspapers. I don't know anything about who the man was who shot me to-night. He was seized at once by one of the stenographers in my party, Mr. Martin, and I suppose is now in the hands of the police. He shot to kill. He shot—the shot, the bullet went in here—I will show you.[37]

I am going to ask you to be as quiet as possible for I am not able to give the challenge of the bull moose quite as loudly. Now, I do not know who he was or what party he represented. He was a coward. He stood in the darkness in the crowd around the automobile and when they cheered me, and I got up to bow, he stepped forward and shot me in the darkness.

Now, friends, of course, I do not know, as I say, anything about him; but it is a very natural thing that weak and vicious minds should be inflamed to acts of violence by the kind of awful mendacity and abuse that have been

37. Albert H. Martin was one of Roosevelt's secretaries during his western tour. "Martin Tells Of His Leap," *New York Times,* 15 October 1912. Oscar King Davis, *Released For Publication: Some Inside Political History of Theodore Roosevelt and His Times 1898–1918* (Boston: Houghton Mifflin, 1925), p. 357, gives Martin's first name as Elbert and describes his role at Milwaukee on pp. 375–376.

"We Are Against His Politics But We Like His Grit." A William A. Rodgers cartoon shows Roosevelt giving his speech in Milwaukee with his wound (on the wrong side) still bleeding. Published in the New York Herald, *16 October 1912. (Library of Congress)*

heaped upon me for the last three months by the papers of not only Mr. Debs but of Mr. Wilson and Mr. Taft.[38]

Friend, I will disown and repudiate any man of my party who attacks with such foul slander and abuse any opponent of any other party; and now I wish to say seriously to all the daily newspapers, to the Republican, the Democratic, and the Socialist parties, that they cannot, month in and month out and year in and year out, make the kind of untruthful, of bitter assault that they have made and not expect that brutal, violent natures, or brutal and violent characters, especially when the brutality is accompanied by a not very strong mind; they cannot expect that such natures will be unaffected by it.[39]

38. Eugene V. Debs (1855–1926) was the presidential candidate of the Socialist Party.

39. In its account of the speech, the *New York Times* said Roosevelt referred to "slanderous, bitter, and malevolent assaults." "Speech Roosevelt Made While Wounded," *New York Times,* 15 October 1912.

Now, friends, I am not speaking for myself at all. I give you my word, I do not care a rap about being shot; not a rap.

I have had a good many experiences in my time and this is one of them. What I care for is my country. I wish I were able to impress upon my people—our people, the duty to feel strongly but to speak the truth of their opponents. I say now, I have never said one word against any opponent that I cannot—on the stump—that I cannot defend. I have said nothing that I could not substantiate and nothing that I ought not to have said—nothing that I—nothing that, looking back at, I would not say again.[40]

Now, friends, it ought not to be too much to ask that our opponents—I am not sick at all. I am all right.[41] I cannot tell you of what infinitesimal importance I regard this incident as compared with the great issues at stake in this campaign, and I ask it not for my sake, not the least in the world, but for the sake of our common country, that they make up their minds to speak only the truth, and not to use the kind of slander and mendacity which if taken seriously must incite the weak and violent natures to crimes of violence. Don't you make any mistake. Don't you pity me. I am all right. I am all right and you cannot escape listening to this speech either.

And now, friends, this incident that has just occurred—this effort to assassinate me—emphasizes to a peculiar degree the need of this Progressive movement. Friends, every good citizen ought to do everything in his or her power to prevent the coming of the day when we shall see in this country two recognized creeds fighting one another, when we shall see the creed of the "Havenots" arraigned against the creed of the "Haves." When that day comes then such incidents as this to-night will be commonplace in our history. When you make poor men—when you permit the conditions to grow such that the poor man as such will be swayed by his sense of injury against the men who try to hold what they improperly have won, when that day comes, the most awful passions will be let loose, and it will be an ill day for our country.

Now, friends, what we who are in this movement are endeavoring to do is to forestall any such movement by making this a movement for justice now—a movement in which we ask all just men of generous hearts to join with the men who feel in their souls that lift upward which bids them refuse to be satisfied themselves while their countrymen and countrywomen suffer from avoidable misery. Now, friends, what we Progressives are trying

40. Most newspapers that reported the speech carried Roosevelt's remarks to this point. See, for example, *Dallas Morning News*, 15 October 1912.

41. At this point Roosevelt was talking with someone who was on the stage with him.

to do is to enroll rich or poor, whatever their social or industrial position, to stand together for the most elementary rights of good citizenship, those elementary rights which are the foundation of good citizenship in this great Republic of ours.[42]

My friends are a little more nervous than I am. Don't you waste any sympathy on me. I have had an A-1 time in life and I am having it now.

I never in my life was in any movement in which I was able to serve with such whole-hearted devotion as in this; in which I was able to feel as I do in this that common weal. I have fought for the good of our common country.

And now, friends, I shall have to cut short much of the speech that I meant to give you, but I want to touch on just two or three of the points.

In the first place, speaking to you here in Milwaukee, I wish to say that the Progressive party is making its appeal to all our fellow citizens without any regard to their creed or to their birthplace. We do not regard as essential the way in which a man worships his God or as being affected by where he was born. We regard it as a matter of spirit and purpose. In New York, while I was police commissioner, the two men from whom I got the most assistance were Jacob Riis, who was born in Denmark, and Oliver [Arthur] Van [von] Briesen, who was born in Germany—both of them as fine examples of the best and highest American citizenship as you could find in any part of this country.[43]

I have just been introduced by one of your own men here—Henry Cochems.[44] His grandfather, his father, and that father's seven brothers, all served in the United States army, and they entered it four years after they had come to this country from Germany. Two of them left their lives, spent their lives on the field of battle. I am all right—I am a little sore. Any body has a right to be sore with a bullet in him. You would find that if I was in battle now I would be leading my men just the same. Just the same way I am going to make this speech.

At one time I promoted five men for gallantry on the field of battle. Afterward in making some inquiries about them I found it happened that two of them were Protestants, two Catholics, and one a Jew. One Protestant came from Germany and on was born in Ireland. I did not promote

42. According to the account of the speech, Roosevelt's friends tried at this point to persuade him to wind up his remarks.

43. Arthur von Briesen (1843–1920), a New York lawyer, was president of the Legal Aid Society of New York from 1889 to 1916.

44. Henry Frederick Cochems (1875–1921), a Milwaukee attorney, had supported La Follette before turning to Roosevelt and the Progressive cause.

them because of their religion. It just happened that way. If all five of them had been Jews I would have promoted them; if they had been Catholics. In that regiment I had a man born in Italy who distinguished himself by gallantry; there was a young fellow, a son of Polish parents, and another who came here when he was a child from Bohemia, who likewise distinguished themselves; and friends, I assure you, that I was incapable of considering any question whatever, but the worth of each individual as a fighting man. If he was a good fighting man, then I saw that Uncle Sam got the benefit from it. That is all.

I make the same appeal in our citizenship. I ask in our civic life that we in the same way pay heed only to the man's quality of citizenship, to repudiate as the worst enemy that we can have whoever tries to get us to discriminate for or against any man because of his creed or his birthplace.

Now, friends, in the same way I want our people to stand by one another without regard to differences or class or occupation, I have always stood by the labor-unions. I am going to make one omission to-night. I have prepared my speech because Mr. Wilson had seen fit to attack me by showing up his record in comparison with mine. But I am not going to do that to-night. I am going to simply speak of what I myself have done and of what I think ought to be done in this country of ours.

It is essential that there should be organizations of labor. This is an era of organization. Capital organizes and therefore labor must organize.

My appeal for organized labor is two-fold; to the outsider and the capitalist I make my appeal to treat the laborer fairly, to recognize that he must organize, that there must be such organization, that the laboring man must organize for his own protection, and that it is the duty of the rest of us to help him and not hinder him in organizing. That is one-half of the appeal that I make.

Now, the other half is to the labor man himself. My appeal to him is to remember that as he wants justice, so he must do justice. I want every labor man, every labor leader, every organized union man, to take the lead in denouncing crime or violence. I want them to take the lead in denouncing disorder and in denouncing the inciting of riot; that in this country we shall proceed under the protection of our laws and with all respect to the laws, and I want the labor man to feel in their turn that exactly as justice must be done them so they must do justice. That they must bear their duty as citizens, their duty to this great country of ours, and that they must not rest content unless they do that duty to the fullest degree.

I know these doctors when they get hold of me they will never let me go back, and there are just a few things more that I want to say to you.

And here I have got to make one comparison between Mr. Wilson and myself, simply because he has invited it and I cannot shrink from it.

Mr. Wilson has seen fit to attack me, to say that I did not do much against the trusts when I was President. I have got two answers to make to that. In the first place what I did, and then I want to compare what I did while I was President with what Mr. Wilson did not do while he was Governor.

When I took office the Anti-Trust Law was practically a dead letter and the Inter-State Commerce Law in as poor condition. I had to revive both laws. I did. I enforced both. It will be easy enough to do now what I did then, but the reason that it is easy now is because I did it when it was hard.

Nobody was doing anything. I found speedily that the Inter-State Commerce Law by being made more perfect could be made a most useful instrument for helping solve some of our industrial problems. So with the Anti-Trust Law. I speedily found that almost the only positive good achieved by such a successful lawsuit as the Northern Securities suit, for instance, was in establishing the principle that the Government was supreme over the big corporation, but that by itself the law did not accomplish any of the things that we ought to have accomplished; and so I began to fight for the amendment of the law along the lines of the Inter-State Commerce Law, and now we propose, we Progressives, to establish an inter-State commission having the same power over industrial concerns that the Inter-State Commerce Commission has over railroads, so that whenever there is in the future a decision rendered in such important matters as the recent suits against the Standard Oil, the sugar—no, not that—tobacco—Tobacco-Trust—we will have a commission which will see that the decree of the court is really made effective; that it is not made a merely nominal decree.

Our opponents have said that we intend to legalize monopoly. Nonsense. They have legalized monopoly. At this moment the Standard Oil and Tobacco Trust monopolies are legalized; they are being carried on under the decree of the Supreme Court.

Our proposal is really to break up monopoly. Our proposal is to put in the law—to lay down certain requirements, and then require the commerce commission—the industrial commission—to see that the trusts live up to those requirements. Our opponents have spoken as if we were going to let the commission declare what the requirements should be. Not at all. We are going to put the requirements in the law and then see that the commission requires them to obey that law.

And now, friends, as Mr. Wilson has invited the comparison, I only want to say this: Mr. Wilson has said that the States are the proper authorities to deal with the trusts. Well, about eighty per cent. of the trusts are organized in New Jersey. The Standard Oil, the tobacco, the sugar, the beef, all those trusts are organized in New Jersey and Mr. Wilson—and the laws of New Jersey say that their charters can at any time be amended or repealed if they misbehave themselves and it gives the Government—the laws give the Government ample power to act about these laws, and Mr. Wilson has been Governor a year and nine months and he has not opened his lips. The chapter describing what Mr. Wilson has done about the trusts in New Jersey would read precisely like a chapter describing the snakes in Ireland, which ran: "There are no snakes in Ireland." Mr. Wilson has done precisely and exactly nothing about the trusts.

I tell you, and I told you at the beginning, I do not say anything on the stump that I do not believe. I do not say anything I do not know. Let any of Mr. Wilson's friends on Tuesday point out one thing or let Mr. Wilson point out one thing he has done about the trusts as Governor of New Jersey.

And now, friends, there is one thing I want to say especially to you people here in Wisconsin. All that I have said so far I would say in any part of this Union. I have a peculiar right to ask that in this great contest you men and women of Wisconsin shall stand with us. You have taken the lead in progressive movements here in Wisconsin. You have taught the rest of us to look to you for inspiration and leadership. Now, friends, you have made that movement here locally. You will be doing a dreadful injustice to the rest of us throughout this Union, if you fail to stand with us now that we are making this National movement, and what I am about to say now I want you to understand if I speak of Mr. Wilson I speak with no mind of bitterness. I merely want to discuss the difference of policy between the Progressive and the Democratic Party and to ask you to think for yourselves which party you will follow. I will say that friends, because the Republican Party is beaten. Nobody need have any idea that anything can be done with the Republican Party.

When the Republican Party—not the Republican Party—when the bosses in control of the Republican Party, the Barneses and the Penroses, last June stole the nomination and wrecked the Republican Party for good and all; I want to point out to you nominally they stole the nomination from me, but really it was from you. They did not like me, and the longer they live the less cause they will have to like me. But while they do not like me, they dread you. You are the people that they dread. They dread the people themselves, and those bosses and the big special interests behind them made up their mind that they would rather see the Republican Party wrecked than see it come under the control of the people themselves. So I am not dealing with the Republican Party. There are only two ways you can vote this year. You can be progressive or reactionary. Whether you vote Republican or Democratic it does not make any difference, you are voting reactionary.

Now, the Democratic Party in its platform and through the utterances of Mr. Wilson has distinctly committed itself to the old flintlock, muzzle-loaded doctrine of States' rights, and I have said distinctly that we are for the people's rights. We are for the rights of the people. If they can be obtained best through the National Government, then we are for National rights. We are for the people's rights however it is necessary to secure them.

Mr. Wilson has made a long essay against Senator Beveridge's bill to abolish child labor. It is the same kind of argument that would be made against our bill to prohibit women from working more than eight hours a day in industry. It is the same kind of argument that would have to be made; if it is true, it would apply equally against our proposal to insist that in continuous industries there shall be by law one day's rest in seven and a three-shift eight-hour day. You have labor laws here in Wisconsin, and any Chamber of Commerce will tell you that because of that fact there are industries that will not come into Wisconsin. They prefer to stay outside where they can work children of tender years, where they can work women fourteen and sixteen hours a day, where, if it is a continuous industry, they can work men twelve hours a day and seven days a week.

Now, friends, I know that you of Wisconsin would never repeal those laws even if they are to your commercial hurt, just as I am trying to get New York to adopt such laws even though it will be to New York's commercial hurt. But if possible I want to arrange it so that we can have justice without commercial hurt, and you can only get that if you have justice enforced Nationally. You won't be burdened in Wisconsin with industries not coming to the State if the same good laws are extended all over the other States. Do you see what I mean? The States all compete in a common market; and it is not justice to the employers of a State that has enforced just and proper laws to have them exposed to the competition of another State where no such laws are enforced. Now, the Democratic platform, and their speakers, declare that we shall not have such laws. Mr. Wilson has distinctly declared that you shall not have a National law to prohibit the labor of children, to prohibit child labor. He has distinctly declared that we shall not have a law to establish a minimum wage for women.

I ask you to look at our declaration and hear and read our platform about social and industrial justice and then, friends, vote for the Progressive ticket without regard to me without regard to my personality, for only by voting for that platform can you be true to the cause of progress throughout this Union.

Elmer H. Youngman, ed., *Progressive Principles* (New York: Progressive National Service, 1913), pp. 102–114.

According to the account in the Kansas City Star, *Roosevelt ended his speech with these words: "I appeal to you to join with us, to work, to fight, but with charity, with kindness, and with generosity, to bring about social and industrial justice."*[45]

45. "Inspired in Slander," *Kansas City Star,* 15 October 1912. The arrangement of paragraphs in the *Star's* account of the address differs from Youngman's account of the speech.

7

The End of the Campaign

After Roosevelt completed his speech at Milwaukee, he was taken first to a hospital in that city and then the following day to a hospital in Chicago. Woodrow Wilson announced that he would cease campaigning as long as Roosevelt was laid up. William Jennings Bryan took a different position and said that the campaign should go on. Roosevelt realized that freezing the campaigning at that point with Wilson ahead would not work to his advantage.

A Statement from the Hospital, 17 October 1912

I wish to express my cordial agreement with the manly and proper statement of Mr. Bryan when, in arguing for a continuance of the discussion of the issues at stake in this contest, he said:

"The issues of this campaign should not be determined by the act of an assassin. Neither Colonel Roosevelt nor his friends could ask that the discussion should be turned away from the principles that are involved. If he is elected President, it should be because of what he has done in the past, and what he proposes to do hereafter."

I wish to point out, however, that neither I nor my friends have asked that the discussion be turned away from the principles that are involved; on the contrary, we emphatically demand that the discussion be carried on precisely as if I had not been shot. I shall be sorry if Mr. Wilson does not keep on the stump, and I feel that he owes it to himself and the American people to continue on the stump.

I wish to make one more comment on Mr. Bryan's statement. It is, of course, perfectly true that in voting for me or against me consideration must be paid to what I have done in the past and to what I propose to do. But it seems to me far more important that consideration should be paid to what the Progressive party proposes to do.

I cannot too strongly emphasize the fact, upon which Progressives insist, that the welfare of any one man in this fight is wholly immaterial compared to the great and fundamental issues involved in the triumph of the principles for which our cause stands. If I had been killed the fight would have gone on exactly the same. Governor Johnson, Senator Beveridge, Mr. Straus, Senator Bristow, Miss Jane Addams, Gifford Pinchot, Judge Ben Lindsey, Raymond Robbins, Mr. Prendergast, and hundreds of other men now on the stump are preaching the doctrines that I have been preaching and stand for and represent just the same cause.[1] They would have continued the fight in exactly the same way if I had been killed, and they are continuing it in just the same way now that I am for the moment laid up.

So far as my opponents are concerned, whatever could with truth and propriety have been said against me and my cause before I was shot can with equal truth and equal propriety be said against me, and it now should be so said; and the things that cannot be said now are merely the things that ought not to have been said before. This is not a contest about any man; it is a contest concerning principles.

If my broken rib heals fast enough to relieve my breathing I shall hope to be able to make one or two speeches in the campaign. In any event, if I am not able to make them, the men I have mentioned and the hundreds like them will be stating our case right to the end of the campaign, and I trust our opponents will be stating their case also.

Social Justice and Popular Rule 17, pp. 332–333.

Roosevelt left the Chicago hospital on 21 October and returned home to Oyster Bay to convalesce. He felt strong enough to appear at a rally on 30 October at Madison Square Garden. Still experiencing the effects of his wound, he was not at his best before the enthusiastic crowd. His remarks were general and lacked bite against his presidential opponents. He could not lift his right arm, and newspapermen spoke of "weariness and weakness" in his delivery.[2]

1. In addition to those previously identified, Gifford Pinchot (1865–1946) had been Roosevelt's close adviser on conservation issues during his presidency and was now a major figure in the Progressive campaign. William A. Prendergast (1867–1954) was the comptroller of New York City who had left the Republicans to join the Progressives. He returned to the Grand Old Party in 1913.

2. "Roosevelt Lets Cheers Go On," *New York Times*, 2 November 1912.

An Address at Madison Square Garden, 30 October 1912

Friends, perhaps once in a generation, perhaps not so often, there comes a chance for the people of a country to play their part wisely and fearlessly in some great battle of the age-long warfare for human rights. To our fathers the chance came in the mighty days of Abraham Lincoln, of the man who thought and toiled and suffered for the people with a sad, patient, and kindly endeavor. To our forefathers the chance came in the troubled years that stretched from the time when the First Continental Congress gathered to the time when Washington was inaugurated as first President of the Republic. To us in our turn the chance has now come to stand for liberty and righteousness as in their day these dead men stood for liberty and righteousness. Our task is not as great as theirs. Yet it is well-nigh as important. Our task is to profit by the lessons of the past, and to check in time the evils that grow around us, lest our failure to do so may cause dreadful disaster to the people. We must not sit supine and helpless. We must not permit the brutal selfishness of arrogance and the brutal selfishness of envy, each to run unchecked its evil course. If we do so, then some day smouldering hatred will suddenly kindle into a consuming flame, and either we or our children will be called on to face a crisis as grim as any which this Republic has ever seen.

It is our business to show that nine-tenths of wisdom consists in being wise in time. Woe to our nation if we let matters drift, if in our industrial and political life we let an unchecked and utterly selfish individualistic materialism riot to its appointed end! That end would be wide-spread disaster, for it would mean that our people would be sundered by those dreadful lines of division which are drawn when the selfish greed of the *haves* is set over against the selfish greed of the *have-nots.* There is but one way to prevent such a division, and that is to forestall it by the kind of movement in which we are now engaged.

Our movement is one of absolute insistence upon the rights and full acknowledgment of the duties of every man and every woman within this great land of ours. We war against the forces of evil, and the weapons we use are the weapons of right. We do not set greed against greed or hatred against hatred. Our creed is one that bids us to be just to all, to feel sympathy for all, and to strive for an understanding of the needs of all. Our purpose is to smite down wrong. But toward those who have done the wrong we feel only the kindliest charity that is compatible with causing the wrong to cease. We preach hatred to no man, and the spirit in which we work is as far removed from vindictiveness as from weakness. We are resolute to do away with the evil, and we intend to proceed with such wise and cautious sanity as will cause the very minimum of disturbance that is compatible with achieving our purpose.

Do not forget, friends, that we are not proposing to substitute law for character. We are merely proposing to buttress character by law. We fully recognize that, as has been true in the past, so it is true now, and ever will be true, the prime factor in each man or woman's success must normally be that man's or that woman's own character—character, the sum of many qualities, but above all of the qualities of honesty, of courage, and of common sense. Nothing will avail a nation if there is not the right type of character among the average men and women, the plain people, the hard-working, decent-living, right-thinking people, who make up the great bulk of our citizenship. I know my countrymen; I know that they are of this type. But it is in civil life as it is in war. In war it is the man behind the gun that counts most and yet he cannot do his work unless he has the right kind of gun. In civil life, in the every-day life of our nation, it is individual character which counts most; and yet the individual character cannot avail unless in addition thereto lie ready to hand the social weapons which can be forged only by law and by public opinion operating through and operated upon by law.

Again, friends, do not forget that we are proposing no new principles. The doctrines we preach reach back to the Golden Rule and the Sermon on the Mount. They reach back to the commandments delivered at Sinai. All that we are doing is to apply those doctrines in the shape necessary to make them available for meeting the living issues of our own day. We decline to be bound by the empty, little cut-and-dried formulas of bygone philosophies, useful once, perhaps, but useless now. Our purpose is to shackle greedy cunning as we shackle brutal force, and we are not to be diverted from this purpose by the appeal to the dead dogmas of a vanished past. We propose to lift the burdens from the lowly and the weary, from the poor and oppressed. We propose to stand for the sacred rights of childhood and womanhood. Nay, more, we propose to see that manhood is not crushed out of the men who toil, by excessive hours of labor, by underpayment, by injustice and oppression. When this purpose can only be secured by the collective action of our people through their governmental agencies, we propose to so secure it.

We brush aside the arguments of those who seek to bar action by the repetition of some formula about "States' rights" or about "the history of liberty" being "the history of the limitation of governmental power," or about the duty of the courts finally to determine the meaning of the Constitution. We are for human rights and we intend to work for them in efficient fashion. Where they can best be obtained by the application of the doctrine of States' rights, then we are for States' rights. Where, in order to obtain them, it is necessary to invoke the power of the nation, then we shall invoke to its uttermost limits that mighty power. We are for liberty. But we are for the liberty of the oppressed, and not for the liberty of the oppressor to oppress the weak and to bind burdens on the shoulders of the heavy-laden. It is idle to ask us not to exercise the power of the government when only by the power of the government can we curb the greed that sits in high places, when only by the exercise of the government can we exalt the lowly and give heart to the humble and the down-trodden.

We care for facts and not for formulas. We care for deeds and not for words. We recognize no sacred right of oppression. We recognize no divine right to work injustice. We stand for the Constitution. We recognize that one of its most useful functions is the protection of property. But we will not consent to make of the Constitution a fetich for the protection of fossilized wrong. We call the attention of those who thus interpret it to the fact that, in that great instrument of justice, life and liberty are put on a full level with property, indeed, are enumerated ahead of it in the order of their importance. We stand for an upright judiciary. But where the judges claim the right to make laws by finally interpreting them, by finally deciding whether or not we have the power to make them, we claim the right ourselves to exercise that power. We forbid any men, no matter what their official position may be, to usurp the right which is ours, the right which is the people's. We recognize in neither court nor Congress nor President, any divine right to override the will of the people expressed with due deliberation in orderly fashion and through the forms of law.

We Progressives hold that the words of the Declaration of Independence, as given effect by Washington and as construed and applied by Abraham Lincoln, are to be accepted as real, and not as empty phrases. We believe that in very truth this is a government by the people themselves, that the Constitution is theirs, that the courts are theirs, that all the governmental agents and agencies are theirs. We believe that all true leaders of the people must fearlessly stand for righteousness and honesty, must fearlessly tell the people what justice and honor demand. But we no less strongly insist that it is for the people themselves finally to decide all questions of public policy and to have their decision made effective.

In the platform formulated by the Progressive party we have set forth clearly and specifically our faith on every vital point at issue before this people. We have declared our position on the trusts and on the tariff, on the machinery for securing genuine popular government, on the method of meeting the needs of the farmer, of the business man, and of the man who toils with his hands, in the mine or on the railroad, in the factory or in the shop. There is not a promise we have made which cannot be kept. There is not a promise we have made that will not be kept. Our platform is a covenant with the people of the United States, and if we are given the power we will live up to the covenant in letter and in spirit.

We know that there are in life injustices which we are powerless to remedy. But we know also that there is much injustice which can be remedied, and this injustice we intend to remedy. We know that the long path leading upward toward the light cannot be traversed at once, or in a day, or in a year. But there are certain steps that can be taken at once. These we intend to take. Then, having taken these first steps, we shall see more clearly how to walk still further with a bolder stride. We do not intend to attempt the impossible. But there is much, very much, that is possible in the way of righting wrong and remedying injustice, and all that is possible we intend to do. We intend to strike down privilege, to equalize opportunity, to wrest justice from the hands that do injustice, to hearten and strengthen men and women for the hard battle of life. We stand shoulder to shoulder in a spirit of real brotherhood. We recognize no differences of class, creed, or birthplace. We recognize no sectionalism. Our appeal is made to the Easterner no less than to the Westerner. Our appeal is made to the Southerner no less than to the Northerner. We appeal to the men who wore the gray just as we appeal to the men who wore the blue. We appeal to the sons of the men who followed Lee no less than to the sons of the men who followed Grant; for the memory of the great deeds of both is now part of the common heritage of honor which belongs to all our people, wherever they dwell.

We firmly believe that the American people feel hostility to no man who has honestly won success. We firmly believe that the American people ask only justice, justice each for himself and justice each for all others. They are against wickedness in rich man and poor man alike. They are against lawless and murderous violence exactly as they are against the sordid materialism which seeks wealth by trickery and cheating, whether on a large or a small scale. They wish to deal honestly and in good faith with all men. They recognize that the prime national need is for honesty, honesty in public life and in private life, honesty in business and in politics, honesty in the broadest and deepest significance of the word. We Progressives are trying to represent what we know to be the highest ideals and the deepest and most intimate convictions of the plain men and women, of the good men and women, who work for the home and within the home.

Our people work hard and faithfully. They do not wish to shirk their work. They must feel pride in the work for the work's sake. But there must be bread for the work. There must be a time for play when the men and women are young. When they grow old there must be the certainty of rest under conditions free from the haunting terror of utter poverty. We believe that no life is worth anything unless it is a life of labor and effort and endeavor. We believe in the joy that comes with work, for he who labors best is really happiest. We must shape conditions so that no one can own the spirit of the man who loves his task and gives the best there is in him to that task, and it matters not whether this man reaps and sows and wrests his livelihood from the rugged reluctance of the soil or whether with hand or brain he plays his part in the tremendous industrial activities of our great cities. We are striving to meet the needs of all these men, and to meet them in such fashion that all like shall feel bound together in the bond of a common brotherhood where each works hard for himself and for those dearest to him, and yet feel that he must also think of his brother's rights because he is in very truth that brother's keeper.

Seven months ago in this city, almost at the beginning of the present campaign, I spoke as follows:

"The leader for the time being, whoever he may be, is but an instrument, to be used until broken, and then to be cast aside; and if he is worth his salt he will care no more when he is broken than a soldier cares where he is sent where his life is forfeit in order that the victory may be won. In the long fight for righteousness the watchword for all of us is spend and be spent. It is of little matter whether any one man fails or succeeds; but the cause shall not fail, for it is the cause of mankind. We here in America, hold in our hands the hope of the world, the fate of the coming years, and shame and disgrace will be ours if in our eyes the light of high resolve is dimmed, if we trail in the dust the golden hopes of men."[3]

Friends, what I said then I say now. Surely there never was a greater opportunity than this. Surely there never was a fight better worth making than this. I believe we shall win, but win or lose I am glad beyond measure

3. "The Right of the People to Rule," Address at Carnegie Hall, 20 March 1912, in *The Works of Theodore Roosevelt: Social Justice and Popular Rule* (New York: Charles Scribner's Sons, 1926), 17:170.

that I am one of the many who in this fight have stood ready to spend and be spent, pledged to fight while life lasts the great fight of righteousness and for brotherhood and for the welfare of mankind.

Social Justice and Popular Rule 17, pp. 334–340.

Following Roosevelt's appearance at Madison Square Garden, Wilson held his own rally there on 31 October. The leaders of Tammany Hall outdid themselves to surpass the demonstration that had greeted Roosevelt. They succeeded in doing so in a manner that so rattled Wilson that the Democratic candidate forgot his prepared text and improvised his remarks. Nonetheless, the Democratic event was a success. Roosevelt decided, against the advice of his doctors, to attend the rally on 1 November, again at the Garden, to speak for the New York Progressive slate. A newspaper report concluded that "he was in much better form physically than he had been at his last appearance in the Garden two nights before."[4]

A Speech to New York Progressives, 1 November 1912

Watch and vote the way you shout. My friends, I have come here this evening especially to speak to you men and women, not merely of the city, but of the State of New York, on behalf of our State and local tickets. Friends, I wish you to remember always that this is no ephemeral or temporary movement. We have gone into this movement making our appeal to all good citizens, without regard to their party affiliations, and with the resolute intention to make this a permanent movement, and a movement which shall deal not merely with National, but with State and local affairs. For, mind you friends, the evils that affect our people are evils which cannot be dealt with by any one branch of the Government alone. We can grapple with them only when the National and State and municipal Governments alike are in the hands of men whose honesty is above proof, and who know and understand and sympathize with the needs of the plain people of the country, of the men and women who make up the bulk of our citizenship.

And friends, at the outset, there are two things I wish to say. In the first place, I wish to ask all our citizens of the State of New York, and particularly those of Brooklyn, to bear with me, because I have not been able to

4. "Roosevelt Lets Cheers Go On," *New York Times,* 2 November 1912.

see them in person, to speak in person in Brooklyn, in Buffalo, and elsewhere throughout the State. I had intended to make this last week one of passing through this, my native State, to appeal to the State, to appeal to the citizens in every part of it. But it has been impossible for me to do so, and so I ask my fellow-citizens of all the State to take the will for the deed, and to treat my appeal for the State and local tickets this evening as an appeal made to all our citizens for the Progressive Party throughout this State.

And the next thing, friends, that I have to say is that I wish to send a message of sympathy, in the name of all of us, which I know you will be glad to have sent. Within the last forty-eight hours a man holding the second highest position in the land has been stricken by death, and I am sure I express the feeling not only of all of you here but of our people everywhere when I say that we were all affected with sorrow and concern for the death of the Vice President, and in your name I shall ask the Chairman of this meeting to send our most respectful sympathy to the stricken woman, the wife of the late Vice President, Mrs. Sherman.[5]

And, friends, I have come here to speak for the Progressive cause in this State, and for the Progressive ticket from top to bottom, and our cause will not have triumphed completely until we have made it triumph in the Nation, in the State, and then here in this City of New York. And I ask that the people of this country and of this State judge us not only by the platform of principles, National and State, but by the character of the men we have nominated to stand on our platforms.

It is naturally a peculiar pleasure to me to speak for my old and intimate and valued friend Oscar Straus, and I have known Mr. Straus intimately. I have watched his work close up for many years. We have never had a better diplomatic representative abroad than Mr. Straus was, and he filled a position of peculiar difficulty at Constantinople, and he filled it admirably.

I do not think we have had—I will change the form of that sentence—I know we never had any man at Constantinople who looked better after the interests not only of Americans and American citizens but of civilization. And I have been told again and again by the missionaries in Turkey that they never had such efficient aid and support as Mr. Straus rendered them—often under peculiarly difficult circumstances.

And then at home, in my Cabinet, he occupied a peculiarly responsible and difficult position, a position which he filled to perfection, for he showed what was a prime necessity in that position—that is the power of

5. Vice President James S. Sherman had died of heart disease on 30 October.

broad sympathy with all our people, the determination to do justice to big men and small men alike; and then, not merely the determination to do justice, but the sympathy that enabled him to do justice.

He never flinched from accepting any responsibility. He never feared to undertake any duty, however disagreeable, and yet he showed the broadest human charity, the utmost generosity of soul in dealing with the many difficult problems that of necessity came to him. And now, friends, we of New York ought to make it a matter of pride to have our representatives in the State Government men of the kind to whom we can point with pride wherever we travel in this Union. And that is just what will be the case if we elect Mr. Straus as Governor. During the last six weeks I have been across the continent from the Great Lakes to the Gulf, from the Atlantic to the Pacific—and everywhere I spoke I found the name of Oscar Straus a name with which to conjure, and it helped the Progressive cause in California and in New Mexico and in Illinois and Kansas that we here in New York had named such a man as our candidate for Governor.

In the same way, friends, we have nominated for Lieutenant Governor a man who has been tried in the furnace at Albany and has come out scathless [*sic*]. Mr. Davenport has served in Albany under peculiarly trying conditions, and he rang true metal on every occasion. We are not asking you to trust untried men. We are asking you to trust men who have sworn that every promise that they make in the campaign will be made good quickly after the campaign.[6]

And, friends, this evening I wish to call your especial attention to our judiciary, and to what it means for the people of this State and the people of the Union to have running for positions as Judges of the Court of Appeals, and here in our own city of the Supreme Court, the men we have named standing on the platform upon which they stand: to speak of Dean Kirchwey of Columbia,[7] of Mr. Alden, of Mr. Fitzgerald, of Mr. Hitchings,[8] and to ask that you consider the plank in our State platform wherein we deal with the courts and the people. And, friends, I wish that I had it in me to impress upon you the vital importance of the judiciary issue in this campaign; I wish that I were able to bring home to your minds the need that we should now begin the reconstruction of our New York State courts for

6. Frederick Morgan Davenport (1866–1956) was a member of the political science faculty at Hamilton College. He had been active in Republican politics before joining the Progressives.

7. George Washington Kirchwey (1855–1942) was dean of the Columbia Law School at this time.

8. Carlos C. Alden (1866–1955) was teaching at the Buffalo Law School. Hector Morrison Hitchings (1855–1926) was a New York attorney. James J. Fitzgerald had been a Democratic member of the New York legislature and affiliated with Tammany Hall before he joined Roosevelt and the Progressives.

the sake of ourselves, for the sake of you here to-night, and, above all, for the sakes of those of our people who are least fortunate in life.

It has been a melancholy thing to every believer in social reform for the last twenty-five years that New York State has lagged behind most other sections of the country in getting those industrial changes for the common betterment which it is imperative that our country should have, and the prime reason for New York's lagging behind has been the fact that while we have had upright and honorable Judges we have not had a judiciary which, as a whole, has possessed the intelligent understanding of and sympathy with the needs of the plain people, the average man and woman, which it is essential, under our form of government, that the judiciary should possess.

And I wish to read to you the plank of the State platform in which we deal with this subject; and, friends, I wish you would read the Progressive State platform in its entirety, you men and women here, and compare it with the platforms of the old parties, and you would appreciate the difference between a platform made by earnest men and women who have thought deeply and mean every word they say, and platforms composed merely by politicians, with the hope to attract votes. Just let me put in one word here in parenthesis. You notice I say platform made by earnest men and women. Remember that I am making my appeal to men and women.

I hope speedily to see the day when here in New York we shall recognize the fact that while there cannot be identity of function between man and woman, there must be an equality of right and that the home keeper, the woman, should have the same right to participate in the Government that the home maker, the man, has.

The section, the plank of the platform to which I allude, runs as follows:

"The selection of Judges by amicable understanding between the bosses of both political parties and lawyers of easy partisanship but ardent devotion to corporate interests we denounce as a fraud and travesty upon the principles of non-partisanship in the choice of judicial officers. To secure real non-partisanship, the nomination and election of Judges should be wholly apart from party columns or party designations on the ballot."

When the question of the nomination of Judges came up in this State, I stated that as regards the Judges I did not care in the least how they stood in reference to the candidates of the Progressive Party, if they stood straight for the principles of the Progressive Party. I am obliged to say that some at least of our candidates for Judges are my personal friends. But I am supporting them not in the least because of their attitude toward me or toward Mr. Straus or any one else. I am supporting them because of their attitude toward the great fundamental questions with which as Judges they will have to deal; and if they were every man of them against me personally, but in good faith and heartily for the principles for which we Progressives stand in the Judicial planks of the platform I would support them just as heartily.

And as illustrating the need of the kind of judicial nominations we have made, and of the kind of judicial platform we have promulgated in State and Nation, I wish to call your attention to the appeal made by some very worthy citizens on behalf of the Republican nominees for the Court of Appeals.

This is a call issued by a number of prominent citizens, excellent men, Mr. Choate, Mr. Root, Mr. Pierpont Morgan, Mr. Jacob Schiff, and a number of other very prominent business men, prominent lawyers, college Presidents, and others, good men, according to their lights, men the great majority of whom are, I am sure, entirely conscientious in the position they take, but men who are fundamentally ignorant of the needs and interests of nineteen-twentieths of their fellow-citizens of this State, in this Republic.[9] These worthy citizens, some of them Republicans and some of them Democrats, announce that they wish precisely the kind of bipartisan bench which the Progressive platform emphatically condemns. Personally, the kind of non-partisanship I wish to see on the bench is that non-partisanship which is keenly alive to the needs and convictions and intimate, high desires of the average plain man and plain woman of this country.

And above all, friends, I wish to see judges put upon the bench who, while inflexible in their independence, and not to be swayed by any pressure of any kind from the course which they deem right, will, nevertheless, frankly realize that it is for us, for the people of this State, to say what is the kind of social justice which they wish to see embodied in the law.

Now, friends, it is always much easier to show what you mean by concrete cases than by mere abstract generalities, and I wish to recite to you three or four decisions of the Court of Appeals rendered during my lifetime in politics, so as to show you why I became convinced that it was necessary for us to have a change in our system of judicial decisions on constitutional questions in this State.

Thirty-two years ago when I left college and began my education, I accepted, without protest, the conventional view, still held by the worthy

9. Joseph Hodges Choate (1833–1917) was a famous New York attorney. He had served as the American ambassador in London from 1899 to 1905. Elihu Root (1845–1937) had been Roosevelt's secretary of state and a close friend until the break with Taft in 1912. Root had chaired the Republican National Convention that denied Roosevelt the nomination.

gentlemen who have signed the call which I just alluded to. And the first thing that opened my eyes was an experience I had in the New York Legislature thirty years ago when I served in that by-no-means arcadian body, and a bill was presented to put a stop to the manufacture of cigars in tenement houses.

I was appointed one of a committee of three to go into the tenement house district and investigate the conditions. It was supposed by those who put us on the committee, and it was supposed by me, that I would be against the bill. I thought I would be against the bill, too. I was at that time brimming over with laissez faire doctrines and political economy, and was prepared in the most conscientious and Spartan mood to take any outward reactionary position. And I went down and investigated the conditions there, and suffered a complete change of heart; and made up my mind that I would have to deal with those conditions not on the basis of what I had read in the study, but on a basis of what I saw happening in the lives of the men, women, and children who were my fellow citizens.

For instance, I remember perfectly in one place, one room we went into, a room about sixteen feet square, in which there lived two families, one with a boarder, and men and women and children in each, all of them engaged in the manufacture of cigars from leaf tobacco, the tobacco in sheets under the foul bedding, or mixed with the scraps of food in the dirty corners of the room. And those two families, men, women, and children, working, sleeping, and living day and night in that room.

Well, we put the law through. I remember that I appeared and argued for it before the then Governor, and there was trouble with it, and a subsequent law was passed; but the net result was that the Court of Appeals declared it unconstitutional. And there was in that opinion this gem that the court said that the Legislature must not interfere with the sanctity of the home. The sanctity of a home of but one room sixteen feet square in which two families, one with a boarder lived.[10]

Now, friends, do not misunderstand me. I am not attacking the Judges who rendered that decision. They were upright, well-meaning men who did as they conscientiously believed they ought to do. They were unfortunately the devotees of an outworn system of political philosophy, and still more unfortunate in that they had been trained in a school which taught them that they and not the people of New York were to decide what kind of law should be passed in the interests of social justice.

10. Roosevelt discussed these events as well in his autobiography, first published in 1913 and most readily available in *The Works of Theodore Roosevelt: Theodore Roosevelt, An Autobiography* (New York: Charles Scribner's Sons, 1926), 20:82–85.

One or two more examples I want to give you. There was a law passed by the Legislature providing that factories must safeguard dangerous machinery. And if not, they would be responsible for the loss of life or limb. And the factory owners at once put a clause into their papers of employment of any man or woman making the man or woman surrender any right of action under that law; and a girl lost her arm, a working girl lost her arm, thanks to a wheel being unprotected. She sued, recovered for it in the lower court, and the Court of Appeals threw out the case and declared the law unconstitutional on this ground: that the Legislature could not interfere with the liberty of that girl in losing her arm. Now, of course, friends, here again I have no doubt those Judges decided with the absolute purpose to do justice as they saw justice. The trouble was that they knew law but didn't know right, and still more, as I have stated, they had arrogated to themselves the right that the people should have—the right to decide what the common sense and justice of the people demand.[11]

Again we passed a law in this State. We found by investigation that in certain factories and sweatshops women were working twelve, and fourteen, and fifteen hours a day, and up until after midnight. We passed a law much milder than I would like to have seen it, limiting the hours of women in industry to ten hours a day, and decided that they should not work after 9 at night. Now, I want to call your attention to the fact that much more stringent laws—an eight-hour law, for instance, had been passed in Massachusetts right over the border. Similar laws had been passed in Western States, but the Court of Appeals in New York decided that we could not pass that type of law, and there was another gem in their decision. They used this language—substantially this language—they said that the time had come for the court "fearlessly to put a barrier to legislation of that kind." I love that word "fearlessly."

Now, friends, let me again say I have no doubt that those worthy Judges were entirely conscientious in the decision they rendered. They were upright and honorable men, but they did not know the conditions of life among the bulk of the men and women who make up the citizenship of this State, and above all they were men who needed to be taught the lesson which brothers Choate, Root, Pierpont Morgan, and the rest of them still need to be taught, that it is for the people themselves to say what the standards of social and industrial justice in the State shall be.

Perhaps, friends, the most striking example of the kind of decision

11. Roosevelt wrote more about this case after the election in "Sarah Knisley's Arm," *Collier's* 50 (25 January 1913): 8–9, 23.

against which we are in revolt was rendered in connection with the Workmen's Compensation act, when we passed a law for workmen's compensation practically identical with, in principle, the Federal law that had been declared constitutional by the Supreme Court of the United States, and which had been declared constitutional by the State courts of Iowa, Oregon, Washington, and other States, and yet on the same language in the Constitution the Court of Appeals declared that the Supreme Court of the Nation was in error, and that the 10,000,000 people in the State of New York had not the power to say that when a brakeman or a switchman was crippled for life, or killed in the discharge of his duty, he should receive compensation for the crippling, or his widow and children should be compensated for his death, if he was killed.

Now, friends, I have spoken of decisions, each one of which affected one obscure man or woman; each one of which affected a single individual with no powerful friends, no means to hire great lawyers, no means to influence great newspapers, no means of appealing to public opinion: I have spoken of cases which, when decided, created hardly a ripple in the circles of society that are most influential, but each one of them served as a precedent for oppressing, for doing injustice to scores of thousands—I do not think I overstate when I say hundreds of thousands—of other men and women, no one of them of influence individually, but all taken together representing a majority of our citizenship.

Now, I wish to make my appeal primarily to the sense of justice of our people, and secondarily, I would make it to those admirable well-meaning people who have been responsible in the past for putting on the bench the kind of Judge who has rendered such decisions, and I would like to tell them that while they may gain temporarily by such decisions that in the long run those decisions do damage greater than can be done by the ravings of the Anarchist orator in the country in the cause of justice and order and good government.

And now, friends, you will see what I mean when I say I do not care a rap about the technical non-partisanship in rendering such decisions as those of which I have spoken, or do not care whether they are rendered by a court half Republican and half Democratic, or all Republican or all Democratic. I am against the court, however, which renders such decisions as these, and that is why I say we wish to put on the bench as Judges men who, being absolutely fearless in the discharge of their judicial functions, will also take the view of the Constitution which will enable them wholeheartedly to recognize the right of the people themselves to set the standard in every such matter of social and industrial justice.

And I appeal to our citizens throughout this State; I appeal to our citizens in this city in supporting our entire State ticket, to pay especial heed to see [two lines garbled at this point]. And now, friends, I have come here only to say these few words of greeting to you. I have spoken a little longer than I intended already, and I make my appeal to you in the name of genuine non-partisanship, in the name of genuine good citizenship. I ask you to stand with the Progressive Party in this contest in this State no less than in the Nation, because we are recognizing in practical fashion the truth that in the long run this country won't be a good place for any one to live in unless we make it a pretty good place for everybody to live in. And I ask you to stand with us because we stand for honesty in business, in our political and our industrial life alike, because we stand for the two National principles of American good citizenship—the right of the people to rule themselves, and their duty so to rule, as to bring nearer the day when social and industrial justice shall be done to every man and every woman within this great land of ours.

New York Times, 2 November 1912.

A Statement on Wilson and the Trusts, 2 November 1912

In view of Mr. Wilson's insistence upon the importance of the trust problem in his speech at Madison Square Garden, I desire to call attention to Mr. Wilson's record on the trust question as Governor of New Jersey, and to his present attitude.[12]

Mr. Wilson explicitly states that the problem of the trust is primarily a problem for the States. On July 6 last, for instance, he said "It is the Government of the States, and not the Federal Government, which must determine the ultimate basis and character of government."[13] And in his interview with Mr. Needham in *The Outlook:* "It is with the States which

12. In his address at Madison Square Garden on 31 October 1912, Wilson had once again attacked Roosevelt's plans to control the trusts. "I do not believe it is safe," he said, "to put the disciplining of business in the hands of any officer of government whatever." See "A Campaign Address at Madison Square Garden," in Arthur S. Link, et al., eds., *The Papers of Woodrow Wilson, Volume 25, 1912* (Princeton, N.J.: Princeton University Press, 1978), p. 496.

13. Roosevelt's comments were based on a news story that appeared in the *New York Times* on 6 July 1912. The account in turn was derived from interviews Wilson had given in December 1911 to the newspaper. Wilson's statement was: "For example, nobody doubts, I suppose, that it is the Government of the States, not the Federal Government, that must determine the ultimate character and basis of government among us."

incorporate the great business undertakings that threaten to bulk larger than the States themselves. The big corporations owe their license to the inadequacy of State laws and their non-enforcement."[14]

Now, this statement is not accurate as regards most of the States, but it is substantially accurate as regards New Jersey, for almost all the big trusts against which there is complaint are organized and now hold their charters in New Jersey. This is true of the Standard Oil Trust, the Tobacco Trust, the Steel Trust, the Beef Trust, and practically every other trust of importance. When running for Governor Mr. Wilson recognized this fact. In a speech on Oct. 7, 1910, he said: "The rest of the country is going forward while New Jersey has stood still. Do you scrutinize any of the corporations which you create in such numbers? Not at all. Corporations authorized to exist by the State of New Jersey are, because of the authority of New Jersey, selling stocks and bonds which are of no value and are robbing the people."[15]

In his first message to the Legislature, Jan. 17, 1911, Gov. Wilson renewed with emphasis his promise to deal with the New Jersey trusts. He described them as having "slipped out of control of the very law that gave them leave to be and can make and unmake them at pleasure," and declared: "We have now set ourselves to control them soberly but effectively and to bring them within the regulation of the law. There is a great obligation as well as a great opportunity, an imperative obligation, from which we cannot escape if we would. No man who wishes to enjoy the public confidence dares hold back, and if he is wise he will not resort to subterfuge."[16]

14. Roosevelt did not quote Wilson with precision in discussing the Needham interview. In the magazine article, Wilson said, "It is the States which incorporate the great business undertakings that threaten to bulk larger than the States themselves in the power which they exercise." On the next page Wilson said to Needham, "The big corporations owe their existence to the laws of the states" and then in response to a question from the interviewer said that corporations owed their "license" "to the inadequacy of State laws and their non-enforcement." See Henry Beach Needham, "Woodrow Wilson's Views," *Outlook* 26 (August 1912): 947, 948.

15. These words do not appear in "A News Report of a Campaign Address in Burlington, New Jersey," 7 October 1910, in Arthur S. Link, et al., eds., *The Papers of Woodrow Wilson, Volume 21, 1910* (Princeton, N.J.: Princeton University Press, 1976), pp. 269–274.

16. "An Inaugural Address," 17 January 1911, in Arthur S. Link, et al., eds., *The Papers of Woodrow Wilson, Volume 22, 1910–1911* (Princeton, N.J.: Princeton University Press, 1976), p. 346. Roosevelt's quotation of Wilson was not precise. Wilson said that corporations have "slipped out of the control of the very law that gave them leave to be and that can make or unmake them at pleasure. We have now set ourselves to control them, soberly but effectively and to bring them thoroughly within the regulation of the law. There is a great opportunity here; for wise regulation, wise adjustment, will mean the removal of half the difficulties that now beset us in our search for justice and equality and fair chances of fortunes for the individuals who make up our modern society. And there is a great obligation as well as a great opportunity, an imperative obligation from which we cannot escape if we would." Four sentences later Wilson added, "No man who wishes to enjoy the public confidence dare hold back, and if he is wise, he will not resort to subterfuge."

There was ample opportunity for Gov. Wilson to act, either by securing legislative action or by proceeding against the trusts without the intervention of the Legislature. Section 4 of the New Jersey Corporation act provides: "The charter of every corporation or any supplement thereto or any amendment thereof shall be subject to alteration, suspension, or repeal in the discretion of the Legislature, and the Legislature may at pleasure dissolve any corporation." Chapter 275 of the Law of 1905 provides: "Any person or persons who, being officers, Directors, managers, or employes of any corporation incorporated under the laws of this State, shall willfully use, operate, or control said corporation for the furtherance or promotion any fraudulent and unlawful object shall be guilty of a misdemeanor."

The Supreme Court of the United States has solemnly declared that the Standard Oil and Tobacco Trusts have been guilty of fraudulent and unlawful conduct which this New Jersey statute declares to be a misdemeanor. Mr. Wilson has been Governor for twenty-two months. He now says that he wishes to proceed against the Directors and managers of these trusts individually. He has, and for twenty-two months has had, as Governor of New Jersey, ample opportunity and every possible means for proceeding against them, and for over a year has had the decision of the Supreme Court as warranty for such procedure, but he has never lifted his finger to take it.

He has had the amplest opportunity, and he has himself declared that it was his desire to proceed against these trusts by legislative act. The Legislature of 1911 stood, one house Republican and one house Democratic. That of 1912 was Republican, but Mr. Wilson in speeches at Trenton on May 5 last, and in Camden on May 18 last, explicitly stated that the Legislature was "docile" and that the Legislature moved forward with zest, "that various reform acts which he advocated passed the Legislature with refreshing ease, though one house was Democratic and the other Republican."[17]

Yet, from these "docile" legislative bodies, which moved forward with zest and which he praises for moving with such refreshing and surprising ease, he never, by so much as a word, endeavored to get the legislation about the trusts which he stated was necessary. Yet members of both parties, when Mr. Wilson failed to give them a lead, themselves endeavored to secure the necessary trust legislation. The Republican Senator, Mr. Colgate, introduced a bill, No. 165, to investigate the New Jersey trust laws; the Democratic assemblyman, Mr. Donnelly, introduced several bills, among

17. Arthur S. Link, et al., eds., *The Papers of Woodrow Wilson, Volume 24, 1912* (Princeton, N.J.: Princeton University Press, 1977), pp. 384–385, do not disclose a speech at Trenton on May 5, and his remarks at Camden on 19 May 1912, ibid., pp. 407–408, do not contain the quoted words.

them one, No. 153, entitled "The New Jersey Anti-Trust Bill."[18] Mr. Wilson had declined to give the Legislature a lead in this matter, and when these members of the Legislature gave him a lead he still declined to lift a finger in their aid. And naturally, in view of this attitude of passive opposition on his part, the Legislature failed to act.

Through Senator Beveridge and on the suggestion of one of the private citizens of the country, Mr. Healy, a headwaiter in one of our hotels, I asked Mr. Wilson certain questions as follows:

1. Is it not a fact that the laws of the State, under which a corporation is organized, prescribe its power?

2. Are not all the powers of Standard Oil and similar monopolies conferred by the laws of New Jersey?

3. Could not these powers have been curtailed by amendments to the New Jersey laws?

4. Why has not Mr. Wilson, as Governor of New Jersey, recommended such amendments?

In my Chicago speech I had already pointed out the statutes under which he could act personally. In response to these questions Mr. Wilson telegraphed to one of his supporters as follows:

"I authorize you to say that the Republican majority in the legislature made a revision of the corporation laws impossible, and no New Jersey official could prosecute or propose a dissolution for breach of Federal statutes."[19]

This is no answer at all. I have shown above that Mr. Wilson himself stated that the legislature did with surprising ease what he asked, and that Republican and Democratic members actually introduced bills such as were demanded by Mr. Wilson's explicit promises.

The New Jersey Legislature of 1911 stood: House, 42 Democrats and 18 Republicans; Senate, 11 Republicans and 10 Democrats. There was thus only one Republican majority against him the Senate, and I have shown that one Republican Senator, Mr. Colgate, actually introduced an anti-trust bill. So that even if he had not been followed by another Republican, Mr. Wilson had a clear majority in both houses if he had chosen to act.

18. Austin Colgate was a Republican state senator from Essex County, New Jersey. Thomas Marcus Donnelly was a Democratic member of the New Jersey Assembly from Hudson County who had been elected in 1910.

19. Woodrow Wilson to James O' Gorman, circa 18 October 1912, cited in John Wells Davidson, ed., *A Crossroads of Freedom: The 1912 Campaign Speeches of Woodrow Wilson* (New Haven, Conn.: Yale University Press, 1956), p. 481. The wording in Davidson differs slightly from what Roosevelt said but the substance is the same.

Moreover, it was his clear duty to try to get action in any event. In the entire Legislature there was no opponent of trust legislation who possessed one one-thousandth part of the influence and control which, while I was President, was exercised by Senator Aldrich in the Senate and Speaker Cannon in the house.[20] But I never made any excuses, and by a succession of the hardest kind of hammering fights, I forced through Congress a mass of vitally important trust and corporate legislation; and yet, under infinitely more favorable conditions and with an infinitely easier task, Mr. Wilson did not even attempt to get any action.

As to the rest of Mr. Wilson's answer, it is no answer at all. I did not ask why he failed to act under the Federal anti-trust law. I asked why he failed to act under the specific provision of the New Jersey anti-trust law, and he did not answer and he cannot answer.

In his speech at the Madison Square Garden, Mr. Wilson says, apropos of the trusts and his treatment of them as Governor, "I have seen the patient lie on the table in New Jersey. I have seen him rise from the table, astonished that he was still alive and rejoiced that he felt better than he ever did in his life."[21] I think this statement is absolutely accurate. I do not in the least wonder that every trust, the Standard Oil Trust, the Tobacco Trust, and the Steel Trust, which is incorporated in New Jersey, should, after twenty-two months' experience of Gov. Wilson, arise with astonishment and delight and declare that he never felt better in his life, and that he no longer had the slightest apprehension as to the conduct of good Mr. Wilson. No wonder that Mr. Wilson was able to mention in his Madison Square Garden speech with modest pride that "the gentlemen in Wall Street are smiling and complacent because of their hope for his election, and that they are betting heavy on him"[22]—although I doubt if any intelligent Wall Street man actually gave the odds which Mr. Wilson's enthusiasm prompts him to believe they gave.

I ask that Mr. Wilson's proposal now be tested by his actions as Governor of New Jersey. We Progressives propose a real, thoroughgoing, and efficient control over the trusts. Mr. Wilson and Mr. Taft nationally proposed the same remedies; that is to put their faith in a continuation of the present

20. Joseph Gurney Cannon (1836–1926) was Speaker of the House from 1903 to 1911.

21. Wilson said, "I have seen the patient lie on the table in New Jersey, astonished that he is still alive, and rejoicing that he felt better than he ever did in his life." "A Campaign Address in Madison Square Garden," 31 October 1912, in Link, et al., eds., *The Papers of Woodrow Wilson, Volume 25, 1912*, p. 500.

22. These words do not appear in the text of Wilson's speech as given in Link, et al., eds., *The Papers of Woodrow Wilson, Volume 25*, pp. 493–501.

policy, which is to allow the eggs to be scrambled, and then, after the damage has been done, to proceed by a lawsuit lasting several years to try partially to unscramble them. Our proposal, on the contrary, is to create a commission like the Inter-State Commerce Commission, and through this commission to supervise the big industrial concerns doing an inter-State business just as the Government now supervises railroads and banks. We will thereby prevent the eggs from being scrambled, and if necessary, unscramble them effectively.

The anti-trust law will remain on the books, and it will be strengthened by prohibiting agreement to divide territory or limit output, by prohibition a refusal to sell to customers who buy from business rivals, by prohibiting the custom of selling below cost in certain areas while maintaining high prices in other areas, by prohibiting the use of the power of transportation to aid or injure special business concerns—in short by prohibiting these and all other unfair trade practices.

The Inter-State Industrial Commission will give us an efficient instrument for seeing that the law is carried out in letter and in spirit, and for effectively punishing every individual who violates the provisions of the law.

The facts given above emphasize the difference between the professions of the Progressive Party and the professions of its opponents, between the practices of the men who are candidates on the Progressive platform as compared with the practices of the two old parties. Under these circumstances it is no wonder that the great majority of the trust magnates are supporting one or the other of the two old parties. Organizations like the Standard Oil, the Sugar Trust, and the Tobacco Trust will support each of the two old parties with which they think the best fight can be made against the Progressive Party, for they know well that is the Progressive Party alone whose platform they have to fear.

The testimony before the Senatorial Committees showed not only the bitter animosity of the Standard Oil Company to the Progressive Party, but showed also that the leading men in the Steel Trust had contributed to and were supporting Mr. Taft, and the President of the Harvester Trust had been similarly supporting Mr. Wilson. As far as I know but one man connected with either trust is supporting the Progressive ticket—which casts a rather comic light on Mr. Wilson's statement which he made some weeks ago, but which he has been compelled to abandon, that these trusts were in their "thought" or in a hallelujah chorus supporting the Progressive ticket.

In short, with the trust as with the tariff, and as with the great question of helping the men who live in the open country, and of securing social and industrial justice for the wage-workers and the small men generally in our great business enterprises, the Progressives have a definite, concrete, and feasible plan of action, and neither of the old parties offers any real plan at all.

As regards the tariff, both the Republicans and the Democrats propose to cling to the old, vicious methods of tariff-making, the Republicans continuing the policy of protection for special privilege and the Democrats proposing in one breath to introduce free trade and in the next asserting that they will work no disturbance of business—which is about like asserting an intention to burn down a house without causing any disturbance of the inmates or the furniture. We propose to reduce all excessive duties while maintaining the principle of protection through the action of a tariff commission like that which in actual practice has worked so admirably in Germany.

The greatest of all issues is honesty—honesty in business and honesty in politics alike. The election of Mr. Wilson would mean the enthronement of Taggartism in Indiana and of Murphyism in New York, just as Mr. Taft's cause is now identified with the causes of the Barneses and the Penroses of the Republican Party. All the men who wish to see perpetuated in American life the reign of crooked politics and of crooked business are banded together against the Progressive Party and will support either of the old parties in the effort to beat it. For this reason we have a right to apply to all the honest men and women in the land to stand with us, for we, and we alone, stand for the real right of the people to rule their own Government, and for the duty of the Government to secure justice and fair play and make this a genuine Democracy, in the world of industry no less than in the world of politics.[23]

New York Times, 3 November 1912.

The day before the election, Elihu Root and three other prominent New York attorneys released a statement attacking Roosevelt's interpretation of the decisions of the New York Court of Appeals in his remarks to the New York Progressives on 1 November. They said that Roosevelt's comments "contain so many inac-

23. Following the election, in response to Roosevelt's criticisms of his position on trusts, Wilson pushed the New Jersey legislature to adopt laws to regulate New Jersey corporations, and those laws became known as the "seven sisters." Their adoption resulted in the movement of corporations to headquarters in Delaware, and the laws were repealed in 1920. See Arthur S. Link, *Wilson: The New Freedom* (Princeton, N.J.: Princeton University Press, 1956), pp. 33–36.

curate statements calculated to mislead voters that it is fit and proper and we deem it our duty to state the true facts in regard to the decisions he assails."[24]

Roosevelt was scheduled to speak to his neighbors at the Oyster Bay Opera House on the evening of 4 November and the news of the Root commentary reached him at his home that afternoon. "His eyes gleamed with joy," wrote the reporter for the New York Times, *"and he promptly heeled himself with a formidable host of documentary evidence and went to the Opera House, determined to heap confusion on the head of Root."*[25]

An Address at the Oyster Bay Opera House, 4 November 1912

I wish to devote a few minutes to certain gentlemen of the other side who answered my Madison Square speech this afternoon, so that, I suppose, they thought I would not have time to make any reply to their answer. I wish to state right at the outset that there is always a presumption against any individuals who wait until the afternoon before the election to traverse the statement of an opponent. The presumption is that they take that course with the hope that it will be too late for him to reply.

The answer to which I refer is that statement of four of the most eminent corporation lawyers of New York, Elihu Root, John G. Milburn, Louis Marshall, and William D. Guthrie, to the statements I made on Friday night discussing the cruel injustices done again and again to workingmen and workingwomen by certain decisions of the Court of Appeals.[26]

I am informed that these four gentlemen attacked the statements as being contrary to both the facts and the law. The first was the case of the tenement cigar manufacturers. That is a case in which Mr. Root and his assistants as their present capacity as counsel against the people say I misstated the law and the facts. Now I will read to you what is said by a woman who knows the conditions of tenement life as few other women and as hardly any man knows them—by Florence Kelley in a book called "Some Ethical Gains Through Legislation," and I cordially commend Mr. Root and his assistants who signed his protest to study that book and to ponder what is meant by the word "ethical" in connection with legislation.

24. "Root and Others Assail Roosevelt," *New York Times,* 5 November 1912.

25. "Colonel's Last Word An Attack on Root," *New York Times,* 5 November 1912.

26. William Dameron Guthrie (1859–1935), Louis Marshall (1856–1929), and John G. Milburn (1851–1930) were prominent corporation attorneys in New York.

Of the Jacobs case to which I referred, Mrs. Kelley says:

"To the decision of the Court of Appeals in case in re Jacobs is directly due the continuance and growth of tenement manufacture and of the sweating system in the United States and its present prevalence in New York."[27]

That is the statement of a woman who as regards knowledge of tenement-house conditions knows so much more than those four great corporation lawyers that her little finger is thicker than their loins when you come to study what they know and what she knows of the subject of which they have ignorantly presumed to speak. Mind you, I am speaking of Mr. Root, of Senator Root. I want you to make no mistake in his identity.

As to the Knisely [*sic*] case to which I next referred, these four great corporation lawyers said to-day that the decision of the Court of Appeals was in accordance with the law and was a proper decision. A decision is reported to-day in the Law Journal, Fits Water [*sic*] vs. Warren, in which the court refers to the Knisely case, and says it has been largely qualified, if not virtually overruled, by a subsequent decision, and then proceeds to render a decision flatly against it. In the course of this decision, Chief Justice Cullen says:

"Speaking of decisions such as that in the Knisely case, there seems at the present day to be an effort by constitutional amendments to render the master liable to his employe for injury received in his employment, although the master has been guilty of no fault whatever, and I feel that such effort is in no small measure due to the tendency evinced at times in the court to relieve the master, although concededly at fault from liability to his employe, on the theory that the latter assumed the risk of master's fault."[28]

The next time Mr. Root rushes to the defense of the Court of Appeals he had better find out where the Court of Appeals stands. The big lawyers who are employed by the very corporations that are at fault come to the front and assail our movement, and say they are defending the course, and that they are defending the law. Defending the law? They are defending a perversion of the law, and they themselves have been responsible for the perversion, and now they are defending the courts for the perversion of justice for which they themselves are responsible, they, the counsel hired

27. Florence Kelley, *Some Ethical Gains Through Legislation* (New York: Macmillan, 1905), p. 253.

28. Edgar M. Cullen (1844–1922) was chief justice of the N.Y. Court of Appeals from 1904 to 1913. The case he was discussing and to which Roosevelt referred was *Jay W. Fitzwater v. Guy S. Warren,* 206 N.Y. 355. See Burdett A. Rich and Henry P. Farnham, eds., *The Lawyers Reports Annotated, New Series, Book 42* (Rochester, N.Y.: Lawyers Co-operative Publishing Co., 1913), p. 1232, for the quoted passage.

by the great corporations, they are the attorneys of the very privilege which we are seeking to cut out of our industrial life; they stand for precisely that perversion of justice, that substitution of legalism for justice against which we protest.

New York Times, 5 November 1912.

A Pre-Election Statement, 4 November 1912

I wish to appeal as strongly as I can to the men and women of this country, to all good citizens throughout the Union, and ask them to support this great Progressive movement for righteousness and for fair dealing. The Progressive movement is in the interest of every honest man and woman in the land, and therefore we have a right to ask that all good citizens, without regard to their past political affiliations, shall stand with us in this fight for clean politics and for the square deal in industry.

Only the Progressive Party has faced the real and vital issues of the day. Not only are both of the old parties boss-ridden and privilege-controlled, but they are wedded to the dead issues of a vanished past, and they show not the slightest conception of the needs of the day or the steps now urgently necessary to take if grave disaster to the Nation in the future is to be avoided.

During the lifetime of the generation which is now in middle life extraordinary social and industrial changes have come over this land. The great forces now at work, social and industrial, are such as were utterly undreamed of half a century ago. Yet the leaders of both of the old parties today are still attempting the futile feat of trying to meet these new conditions by worn-out Governmental expedients and by appeal to little formulas and dogmas which had a certain usefulness before the days of steam and electricity, before the days of concentrated industry and tremendous economic development, but which are now as utterly useless as the flintlocks of the Continental soldiers would be in modern warfare.

The Progressives, and the Progressives alone, have seen that it is utterly useless to hope (and to our minds entirely pernicious to desire) that a great people living under the forms of political democracy and skilled by universal education, will long continue to tolerate in economic matters the reign of an industrial oligarchy, the enthronement of privilege and a permanent and widespread inequality of opportunity. Neither in the platforms of the old parties nor in the utterances of their candidates do we see the slightest sign of any appreciation of this great fundamental issue. The Progressive Party, on the contrary, thoroughly appreciates that this is the issue, and with courage and common sense, and in a spirit of kindliness to all our people, has faced the problems and outlined the necessary first steps toward its solution.

We intend to use the forces of government to secure justice and fair play between man and man, man and woman, not only in the political but in the industrial world. We recognize that it is the duty of all of us so as to shape conditions as to secure favorable economic surroundings for the average man who is honest and industrious. We do not regard economic well-being as the be-all and end-all of life, but we regard it as the indispensable foundation, the foundation which it is necessary to secure for all our people; and then upon it we intend to raise the superstructure of a higher life.

Our opponents, Democratic and Republican alike, have not ventured to particularize as to the action they advocate, whether as regards to the trusts, the tariff, the welfare of the farmer, or the welfare of the wage-worker. Their utterances have been mere generalities, which can mean anything or nothing, accordingly, as men choose to interpret them. We, on the contrary, have set forth specifically and in detail just what we propose to do.

Not since the days of Abraham Lincoln has there been any public document in America comparable with the Progressive platform. I urgently ask every voter in the United States to read that platform this very day and ponder over it, and to-morrow to cast his vote having in mind what is said in that platform. It does not contain a promise which ought not to be made. It does contain every promise which in view of our present conditions ought to be made. Every promise it contains can be kept. If we are given the power every promise which it contains will be kept.

New York Times, 4 November 1912.

On the evening of the election, it was apparent very early that Wilson had won a decisive electoral victory. The Democratic candidate had 435 electoral votes. Roosevelt had carried six states with 88 electoral votes, while Taft had won Utah and Vermont with 8 votes. Roosevelt had come in second in the popular vote. Wilson had 6,293,000 votes, Roosevelt 4,119,000, and Taft 3,485,000. The Socialist candidate garnered just over 901,000 votes. Roosevelt wired Wilson: "The Ameri-

can people, by a great plurality, have conferred upon you the highest honor in their gift. I congratulate you thereon." He greeted the newspapermen in his study at Oyster Bay and issued a postelection statement for their readers.[29]

A Postelection Statement, 5 November 1912

The American people by a great plurality have decided in favor of Mr. Wilson and the Democratic party. Like all other good citizens, I accept the result with entire good humor and contentment. As for the Progressive cause, I can only repeat what I have already so many times declared, the fate of the leader for the time being is of little consequence, but the cause itself must in the end triumph, for its triumph is essential to the well-being of the American people.

New York Times, 6 November 1912.

29. "Roosevelt Meets Defeat Buoyantly," *New York Times,* 6 November 1912.

Index